BISON
BOOKS

STAGES

Series Editors

General Editor: Gerald Prince
University of Pennsylvania

Michael Holquist
Yale University

Warren Motte
University of Colorado at Boulder

Patricia Meyer Spacks
University of Virginia

TOLOGY

Willis Goth Regier

UNIVERSITY OF NEBRASKA PRESS ≈ LINCOLN AND LONDON

Publication of this volume was assisted by
The Virginia Faulkner Fund, established in
memory of Virginia Faulkner, editor in chief
of the University of Nebraska Press.

Library of Congress Cataloging-in-Publication Data
Regier, Willis Goth.
Quotology / Willis Goth Regier.
p.   cm. — (Stages)
Includes bibliographical references and index.
ISBN 978-0-8032-1752-2 (pbk. : alk. paper)
1. Quotation. 2. Quotations — History and
criticism. 3. Quotation in literature. I. Title.
PN171.Q6R44   2010
080.9 — dc22
2010006336

Set in Arno by Bob Reitz.
Designed by Nathan Putens.

For Philip John Regier, who taught me how to say "Sioux"

Why read a book, which you cannot quote?

Dr. Richard Bentley

CONTENTS

ABBREVIATIONS

Full bibliographic information is in the works cited section. Except for Partnow's *The Quotable Woman*, all references are to page and entry number. For *The Quotable Woman*, references are to author and entry numbers.

BBQ   Benham, *Book of Quotations*

BFQ   Bartlett, *Bartlett's Familiar Quotations*, 17th ed.

CDQ   Andrews, *Columbia Dictionary of Quotations*

HBQ   Stevenson, *Home Book of Quotations*

JGDQ   Jeffares and Gray, *Collins Dictionary of Quotations*

NCPQ   Hoyt, *New Cyclopedia of Practical Quotations*

NDQ   Mencken, *New Dictionary of Quotations*

ODQ   Knowles, *Oxford Dictionary of Quotations*, 7th ed.

PDQ   Andrews, *New Penguin Dictionary of Quotations*

QW   Partnow, *The Quotable Woman* (2010 ed.)

WNW   *Webster's New World Dictionary of Quotations*

YBQ   Shapiro, *Yale Book of Quotations*

It is a pleasure to be able to quote
lines to fit any occasion.
Abraham Lincoln

Preface

First chaos, then quotation. Contradiction and cliché came trotting after.

Some say "Well begun is half done" began with Horace: "Dimidium facti qui coepit habet." Another source tracks the phrase back to Aristotle's *Politics*: "ἀρχὴ λέγεται ἥμισυ εἶναι παντός." Another source says it was a common proverb in Athens; Aristotle only quoted it, and Plato quoted it before him.[1]

As quotations go, it's a classic.

It is also a tidy exhibit of quotology's topics: translation, transmission, attribution, pertinence, variation, exactness, and how it happens that a word, phrase, or passage is recognized as quotation.

Quotations assure that "everybody loves a lover," "all is flux," and "life is but a dream."[2] Quotations shout with triumph and joy, sound out Shakespeare, sing like Solomon.

Proverbs turn into quotations, and quotations turn into commonplaces, leaving their creators behind. "God helps them who help themselves" can be traced to Aeschylus and Aesop.[3] "First come, first served" asserts its authority no matter who first served it.[4] What's-his-name said we live between two infinities. We live, someone said, in a shelter of quotations snatched from history's wreck.[5]

Quotology follows the flow of quotations into proverbs and proverbs into quotations. It records the passing of possession from one person to another. Isaac Disraeli is sometimes quoted thus: "The wise make proverbs and fools repeat them." He only repeats a proverb he'd read.[6]

We quote to taste greatness. We quote to peacock and parade. We quote to honor and ridicule, to point, admire, and analyze. We quote to play, prove, provoke, protect, and puncture. We quote to share, celebrate, and inspire. "Sir Henry Lawrence prized above all other compositions Wordsworth's 'Character of the Happy Warrior,' which he endeavoured to embody in his own life. It was ever before him as an exemplar. He thought of it continually, and often quoted it to others."[7]

Quotations' place is everyplace. They are tattooed and graffitied all over the world. Short ones squeeze on buttons and magnets, splay on T-shirts, billboards, and bumper stickers. They're stitched into samplers and welded onto gates. "Ultima ratio regum" — "the final argument of kings" — was engraved on the cannon of Louis XIV.[8] Emerson noticed that "in Europe, every church is a kind of book or bible, so covered is it with inscriptions & pictures."[9] In Arabic letters taller than a man the Koran is quoted on the walls and domes of mosques.

Erasmus loved quotable quotes. He advised readers of the world to get them by heart and copy them everywhere: write them in the front and back of books, inscribe them on rings and cups, paint them on doors and walls, "even on the glass of a window."[10]

Michel de Montaigne inked fifty-seven quotations on the walls and beams of his study. Every day he could look up and read Isaiah: "Vae qui sapientes estis in oculis vestris" (Woe unto them that are wise in their own eyes).[11] For example . . .

A young man sat in an English coach, talking grandly. To impress his companions he quoted a line of Greek.

"Sir," an elderly traveler asked him, "whence comes that quotation?"

"From Sophocles," the youth replied.

"Be so kind to find it for me," the elder asked, pulling a copy of Sophocles from his pocket.

Surprised, the youth corrected himself, saying it was Euripides he meant. From another pocket the elder extracted a copy of Euripides.

Exposed and embarrassed, the youth cried to the driver: "In heaven's name, put me down at once; for there is an old gentleman in here that hath the Bodleian Library in his pocket!"[12]

Poor boy! He had the bad luck of trying to bluff Richard Porson, Regius Professor of Greek of Cambridge University.

What lessons are tucked in this little tale?

1 Some quote to show off.
2 Some quote to fake it.
3 In the world of hard-won learning an imposter is a pest best crushed quickly.
4 Only expertise can expose an imposter.
5 Whoever holds the proof-text holds the field.
6 There is a time to quote, a time to refrain from quoting.

Slightly less obvious are:

7 Quotation is an index of education, and thus
8 an index of class, and thus
9 susceptible to fashion.

What's missing in this quotation tale?

The quotation.

Despite the fine shadings, flair, homophonies, and hardy hybrids of literate languages, quotologists everywhere come up against stiff-necked monolingual parochialism. As he abandons twelve-year-old Shane at a truck stop, Bear the beefy trucker says, "Tempus fugit." Appalled, Shane corrects him angrily, "'Fugit irreparabile tempus,' which means, irretrievable time is flying!"

Bear asks him, "Get beat up much?"[13]

In one of Walter Savage Landor's *Imaginary Conversations* Professor Porson quotes Catullus from memory:

Porrigens teneras manus
Matris e gremio suae
Semihiante labello

Porson quickly adds, "Pardon a quotation: I hate it! I wonder how it escaped me," as if confessing a fault. Isn't that the case these days? If someone quotes Latin, won't it seem pompous? But Landor's Porson quotes Catullus with the speed of a reflex. He may hate quotation less than the habit of it.[14] In Aldous Huxley's *Crome Yellow* Anne Wimbush chides Denis Stone, "You have a bad habit of quoting. As I never know the context or author, I find it humiliating."[15]

Before taking leave of Professor Porson, know him a little better, then reconsider the anecdotes already told. He was a man as notorious for hard drinking as for his scholarship ("he could drink anything"), something of a rake, and celebrated for his wit. A gentleman said to him, "Dr. Porson, my opinion of you is most contemptible."

"Sir," Porson replied, "I never knew any opinion of yours that was not contemptible."[16]

We quote to attack. We quote to counterquote. We quote to rule and rebel.

When tyrants persecute, quotations talk back. Socrates was indicted because he quoted poetry in public. His crime? Quoting Homer quoting Odysseus. Whenever Odysseus heard someone shouting, he scolded him "with loud words, 'Good sir, sit still and hearken to the words of others that are thy betters.'" Socrates displayed how impertinent, unruly, and dangerous it can be to quote Homer.[17]

We quote to silence and speak out.

Quotations praise quotations, and quotations insist silence is true wisdom. Everywhere you look you find quotations saying the same thing: be smart, shut up.

Quotations take a beating in medical journals. In a 1990 study 29 percent of quotations in surgical journals were misquoted. Matters were somewhat better in otolaryngology: errors occurred in 17 percent of the quotations, but 11.9 percent were considered "major errors. This prevalence is similar to the established error rate in medical literature."[18]

Misquotation is quotology's swamp. Amateur quoters mix and mangle Shakespeare and Scripture. Professors gaffe and printers bungle. It's a mess we must wade into.

Downright dismal is plagiarism. One of Oscar Wilde's most quoted quotations is his reaction to a remark from James Whistler. "I wish I'd said that," said Oscar. Whistler replied, "You will, Oscar, you will." Eugene Field borrowed this from James Boswell without saying so: "Milton was accused of plagiarism, and one of his critics [William Lauder] devoted many years to compiling from every quarter passages in ancient works which bore a similarity to the blind poet's verses." Joseph Jacobs thought that "generally speaking Latin literature is but one vast plagiarism from the Greek."[19]

Quotology looks at all kinds of quotations, sacred and profane. Musicologist William Kinderman was delighted when his four-year-old daughter, Marie, walked around the house quoting Disney's *Beauty and the Beast*: "My father isn't crazy. He's a genius!"

Quotology wouldn't be nearly as rewarding if it didn't enjoy jokes, jibes, sublimated spite, and ironies of all kinds. Baseball fans quote Yogi Berra: "I really didn't say everything I said."[20] The yogis of India quote the Vedas, and the Vedas quote themselves.

Quotologists encounter happy surprises, bright books by faded authors, treasures hidden under dust. I was thrilled to discover John Heywood's *Proverbs and Epigrams* (1562) and was tickled by Frederic Swartwout

Cozzens's *Sayings of Dr. Bushwhacker, and Other Learned Men* (1867).
The learned Dr. Bushwhacker, "purple with eloquence and indignation,"
is a comic type, the quotation show-off.[21] We will encounter the type
again.

Under the heading "Parties," the *Columbia Dictionary of Quotations*
quotes Erasmus's *Praise of Folly*. Erasmus impersonates a woman who
says, "Whether a party can have much success without a woman present
I must ask others to decide, but one thing is certain, no party is any fun
unless seasoned with folly."[22]

Is Erasmus right? Observe a woman at a high society party: "When
George the Second was once at a masquerade, he observed Miss
Chudleigh in a habit which very closely bordered upon the naked: 'My
dear lady,' said the good natured monarch, 'suffer me to put my hand
on that soft bosom.' — 'Sire,' said she, 'give me your hand, and I will put
it on a much softer place.' She took his right hand and put it on his own
forehead."[23]

The folly is King George's; she makes fun of it.

Quotations sing. They cry, clash, and accuse. In *Mary Barton* (1848)
Elizabeth Gaskell "quotes radical verse, dialect verse, and women's verse
in abundance." Her characters copy, recite, discuss, and sing in quotations "because she was centrally concerned with finding a new voice in
which to 'give some utterance,' as she put it, to the agony of Manchester
people."[24]

Quotations can be lovely, witty, rhythmic, rhymed, blunt, piercing,
or enigmatic, and the best of them are brief. Common phrases and odd
words become quotations. "Leviathan" leapt from the pages of the Bible
to be the pet of Thomas Hobbes; "nevermore" evermore evokes Poe's
raven; Sinclair Lewis commandeered *Main Street*.

Quotation experts ply many vocations: the wise deacon who quotes
to calm and console; the business mogul who wages Sun Tzu's *Art of
War* in the boardroom; the scholar who brings fables, proverbs, and

parables to life. There are occasions that only quotations can satisfy: sermons, gossip, testimony.

When quotation is important, it can be exceedingly so. At their heights and most highly charged, quotations recite the words of God. Heretics and skeptics were prosecuted with quotations from the Bible and church fathers. In John Foxe's massive *Actes and Monuments of Martyrs* (1563) learned men pester martyrs to death with quotations.

In the everyday world quotations are merchandise. *Reader's Digest* retails Quotable Quotes every month. Since 1976 BBC Radio has broadcast Nigel Rees's popular program *Quote... Unquote*. Calendars, newspapers, and Web sites offer quotes of the day. Today large quotation collections traffic under brand names: Bartlett's *Familiar Quotations*, the *Oxford Book of Quotations*, and the *Yale Book of Quotations* are only the most famous.

Ralph Keyes calls quotation collectors "quotographers," the men and women who gather catchwords, watchwords, war words, winged words, maxims, mottos, sayings, and quips into books of a thousand pages. Through the centuries quotation collectors have saved quotations that would otherwise be lost. Fragments of Protagoras, Sappho, Sophocles, Jesus, and John the Baptist survive solely because someone quoted them.

Quotology owes all its prestige and much of its property to the quotographers who paved and lit the way: Zenobius, Diogenes Laertius, Plutarch, Valerius Maximus, Stobaeus, Abū'l-Wafā al-Mubaššir bin Fātik, Erasmus, Grotius, John Heywood, John Ray, Samuel Johnson, David Evans Macdonnel, Édouard Fournier, John Bartlett, Georg Büchmann, Jehiel Keeler Hoyt, Edward Latham, Kate Louise Roberts, Christopher Morley, Louella Everett, Burton Stevenson, H. L. Mencken, Emily Morison Beck, Elizabeth Knowles, Robert Andrews, Nigel Rees, Elaine Partnow, Justin Kaplan, and Fred Shapiro are the best of the best. From their labor and for their fame this book proceeds.

Quotation is often synecdochic: a part speaks for a whole. Many say "The Bible says" when what was said was said by John or Jeremiah. Quotation

satisfies with a phrase, a fraction. Democritus and Zeno speak in fragments. In *Quotology* "speak" and "say" are also synecdochic, standing
for all kinds of repeated expression. Paintings quote paintings, films
quote films, comics quote comics, music quotes music, architecture
quotes architecture. Rap and hip-hop quote in samplings.[25] Cliques
quote lyrics and film scripts as passwords and inside jokes.

Quotology deals with written and spoken quotations, called up to
speak for themselves, spark against each other, show how sharp and
short and how hard and fast they can be. W. H. Auden wrote, "In general, when reading a scholarly critic, one profits more from his quotations than from his comments."[26] Here quoted, Auden tests his thesis.
Walter Benjamin praised Jules Michelet as "an author who, wherever
he is quoted, makes the reader forget the book in which the quotation
appears."[27] I won't quote Michelet.

"Dimidium facti qui coepit habet" — if you can believe it and have come
this far, pause, take a breath! You're already half done. The rest should
be as easy as returning home.

QUOTOLOGY

I

The noble-minded are principled,
but never dogmatic.
Confucius

Principia

1

I often please myself with the fancy, now that I may have saved from oblivion the only striking passage in a whole volume, and now that I may have attracted notice to a writer undeservedly forgotten.
Samuel T. Coleridge

Elements

Oh, to say something so fine, so memorable, that it carries across time, oceans, and languages! Sweet dreams and high hopes are invested in quotations, high as immortal fame, as if a few sentences, or one alone, could touch hearts, grasp truth, and endure.

Samuel Smiles quoted Benjamin Disraeli in the House of Commons: "There is this consolation remaining to us, when we remember our unequalled and irreparable losses, that those great men are not altogether lost to us — that their words will often be quoted in this House — that their examples will often be referred to and appealed to, and that even their expressions will form part of our discussions and debates."[1]

Alexander Smith wrote, "Fine phrases I value more than bank notes. I have ear for no other harmony than the harmony of words. To be occasionally quoted is the only fame I care for."[2] Today this quotation is all the fame he has.

One writer's dream is another's nightmare. Jacques Barzun worried that despite his thirty-eight books and decades of teaching he would be remembered for one line only: "Whoever wants to know the heart and mind of America had better learn baseball." Bartlett's *Familiar Quota-tions* (hereafter BFQ) has only that.[3]

Quotations adorn memorials and function as memorials themselves. If it is too grand a dream, too vain an ambition to hope to be remembered for a battle, discovery, or building, then perhaps a quotation will do, surviving as small things do, coins, jewels, amulets.

QUOTATION

It seems simple: a quotation is a repetition of a saying. But leading language philosophers — Frege, Tarski, Geach, Quine, Searle — recognized that quotations are trouble.[4] Donald Davidson was taught that quotation is "a somewhat shady device" and an "invitation to sin."

> In quotation not only does language turn on itself, but it does so word by word and expression by expression, and this reflexive twist is inseparable from the convenience and universal applicability of the device. Here we already have enough to draw the interest of the philosopher of language.

Quotation might "appear trivial" yet also be "an easy entrance to the labyrinth" of other heady problems: propositional attitudes, explicit performatives, and picture theories of reference.[5] A labyrinth indeed.

Davidson gave philosophy impetus with a set of questions more or less ignored before him, a quotation, and a quotation within a quotation, that became "famous" within philosophy: "Quine says that quotation '. . . has a certain anomalous feature.'"[6] Davidson took a long look at what goes on between quotation marks.

The notion that a quotation can be verified by reference to a prior, certain, and stable iteration goes only partway. Many quotations are quoted because they make strong truth claims that can be affirmed or contested but elude proof. They express genial principles: "Two heads are better than one," "All is well that ends well."[7] They express grand universals: "The place where optimism most flourishes is the lunatic asylum," "Every man has his theory, most of them ridiculous."[8] They express anxieties: "Human history becomes more and more a race between education and catastrophe," "There is no off switch to the technological."[9] In a sentence or two they give a view of the world.

Prophecies make awesome truth claims. Some prophecies are straightforward enough: Madame de Pompadour's "After us the deluge" (true), Nikita Khrushchev's "We will bury you" (false), and Robert Frost's "Some say the world will end in fire" (to be decided).[10] When quoted, a prophecy's potency depends on its past: failed forecasts of world's end dissuade most of us from believing there's no tomorrow.

Prophecies are notoriously vague. Nostradamus predicted: "The white coal shall be expelled by the black one."[11] Is this ominous or insipid? Rather than make sense, a gnomic prophecy like this sets the conditions by which it can be made sensible; it is a puzzle whose parts limit what can be made out of it. Davidson writes that quotations "shape" meaning; prophecies certainly do. They deserve a chapter all their own; I prophesy they'll get one.

QUOTATION MARKS

In "quotation" is the quotation the word only or the word plus the quotation marks? What do quotation marks add and take away? How important is it that a quotation be marked?[12]

In antiquity quotation was signaled by saying "the Lord said," "Bhīma spoke," "the goddess answered," and the like. It was easier to say when the gods started than when they stopped.

Punctuation entered literature as a means for marking pauses to enable reading aloud. Quotation marks, which mark meaning rather than pauses, are of more recent origin. They first appear as diples — < > — in the margins of the *Libri etymologiarum* of Isidore of Seville (ca. 560–636). "The equivalent of quotation marks or dots in the outer margin next to the quoted passage is the oldest method; it goes back to the patristic book and carries up through the twelfth century, when it is replaced by two other methods: underscoring the quotation in red, and giving the author's name in the margin as an index reference."[13] The etymology of quotation recapitulates:

> *quote* < Middle English *coten*, to mark a book with numbers or marginal references < Old French *coter* < from Medieval Latin *quotāre*, to number chapters < Latin *quotus*, of what number < *quot*, how many.[14]

When printing matured in the sixteenth century, quotations were first signaled by italic fonts, but the use of diples slowly revived and spread.[15] Quotation marks didn't become widely adopted until the eighteenth century and then in different forms. Douglas C. McMurtrie found "quotations indicated one way in England, another way in France, and with yet other and differing methods in Germany, Holland, Sweden, and so forth. There is no element of punctuation of which the same is true, with the limited exception of the inverted exclamation point and question mark placed at the beginning of sentences in Spanish printing. This indicates a varying historical development in each country."[16] Antoine Compagnon sees the different marks as different signals: French guillemets — « » — enclose, *italics* and underlining emphasize.[17] The beloved book designer Richard Eckersley preferred English single quotes — ' ' — to American doublets — " " — simply because they were less intrusive.

Speakers have different means for indicating when a quotation starts and stops: changes in voice, significant pauses. An exchange in *Science* in 1926 led to familiar suggestions — use "quote" and "unquote," or flex fingers in the air as "clothespins," kinetic quotation marks. One scientist proposed signaling a quotation's beginning with "coo" and its ending with "eo" but found no takers.[18]

Quotation marks are sometimes used for no other purpose than to set off "one part of a sentence" from "another," as language philosophers do when discussing quotation. Thus spake Wittgenstein: "What an odd question: 'Can we imagine an endless row of trees?'"[19] Quotation marks also mark the titles of poems and songs. Or they simply draw attention to a word or phrase.

Quotology concentrates on "quotation" as restatement and on its most notable forms of recital. Because there is much to cover I mainly rely on compact examples and tight clusters. John Bartlett told his publisher, "The sensation of fullness is agreeable, that of repletion is painful."[20] It is a fine line, one of several.

QUOTATIONS OF QUOTATIONS

Emerson knew that "most of the classical citations you shall hear or read in the current journals or speeches were not drawn from the originals, but from previous quotations."[21] Generations of scholars got their Aristotle and Plato through Cicero. Much Greek history and literature survives solely in the quotations gathered by Stobaeus and Photius. In the twelfth century a large body of quotations "came at second hand, through the Fathers, the Latin grammars and glossaries, and the various collections of extracts. Chief among such sources was the Latin grammar of Priscian, whose ten thousand lines of quotations from the ancients include a large amount of Cicero, Sallust, and the poets, quotations to which many readers were indebted for whatever acquaintance they possessed with these authors."[22]

Intermediary quotations often abbreviate. "Money is the root of all evil" is a common form for "The love of money is the root of all evil."[23]

In the first volume of his *Dictionary of Quotations* (1896) Philip Dalbiac hoped "to correct many errors which crept in through 'Quotations of Quotations,'" a hope that justifies the regular appearance of revised compendia.[24] Every speaker who pages through BFQ for something spicy and pertinent relies on intermediary quotation.

Many of Montaigne's quotations came from intermediaries. Intermediaries preserved Muhammad's sayings. John Locke warned:

> Passion, interest, inadvertency, mistake of his meaning, and a thousand odd reasons or capriccios men's minds are acted by (impossible to be discovered) may make one man quote another man's words or meaning wrong. He that has but ever so little examined the citations

of writers cannot doubt how little credit the quotations deserve where the originals are wanting, and consequently how much less quotations of quotations can be relied on. This is certain, that what in one age was affirmed upon slight grounds, can never after come to be more valid in future ages by being often repeated. But the further still it is from the original, the less valid it is, and has always less force in the mouth or writing of him that last made use of it than in his from whom he received it.[25]

Locke is right that quotations ought to be traced to their sources but wrong in asserting that repetition reduces force. It is *because of repetition* that a quotation gains force. The words of Jesus in agony, "My God, my God, why hast thou forsaken me?" (Matthew 27:46 and Mark 15:34) quote Psalm 22:1. Quotable quotations are measured by how often they are quoted, over how many years, and by whom. Boswell declared, "I like to recollect all the passages that I heard Johnson repeat: it stamps a value on them."[26]

In theory, the number of intermediaries is limitless. Quotations can pierce multiple contexts and thread them together. Quotations can be quilted; they can be padding ("Quotations have been thus easily and craftily multiplied to swell a volume to a marketable size, and to encrease the price").[27] Quotology knows of quotations embedded in quotations many layers deep. For instance:

> Epicurus, Lucretius, and Petronius, would rather make their gods lazy, and enjoy their immortal nature in an uninterrupted tranquility, than see them active and cruelly employed in ruining ours.
>
> Nay, Epicurus, by doing so, pretended he showed his great respect to the gods; and, from hence proceeded that saying which Bacon so much admires, "*Non Deos vulgi negare profanum, sed vulgi opinionem diis applicare profanum.*"[28]

This passage from the Reverend Charles Caleb Colton's *Lacon* is entirely a quotation from "one of the finest writers of the last century," left unnamed. The unnamed source quotes Bacon's "Of Atheism," which quotes a Latin translation of Diogenes Laertius's *Lives*.[29] Colton's publisher gave a translation of the Latin: "It is not profanity to deny the gods of the vulgar, but it is profanity to measure the gods by the opinions of the vulgar." The Epicurus quotation thus lies seven layers deep: Epicurus → Diogenes Laertius → Latin translator → Bacon → Colton's unnamed source → Colton → this book. The quotation is fortified by the collective approval of Diogenes Laertius, Sir Francis Bacon, "one of the finest writers," Reverend Colton, and yours truly.

Pass it on.

PARTS OF QUOTATIONS

A complete quotation statement has nine parts. All nine are evident here:

> In a letter to Gustave Flaubert, George Sand argued, "*There is only one sex. A man and a woman are so entirely the same thing, that one hardly understands the mass of distinctions and of subtle reasons with which society is nourished concerning this subject.*"[30]

1 I, your devoted author, am the QUOTER, the person, real or pretended, who quotes.
2 "Argued" is the QUOTER'S VERB. Quotations can pivot on verbs of writing, belief, reading, will, thought, fear, making, and so on. The verb can be neutral or loaded, safe or stretched: Sand *wrote*, Sand *insisted*, Sand *supposed*.
3 Sand is the QUOTEE (speaker, author, conveyor) to whom the quotation is attributed.
4 The quotation comes from a SOURCE, in Sand's case, her correspondence, in which the quotation can be verified.
5 The source occurred in the QUOTEE'S CONTEXT, the language, time, and place from which the quotation comes.
6 The QUOTEE'S TARGET is the person or persons in the quotee's context whom the quotee addressed. Sand's target was Flaubert in his midforties, fat, famous, and writing *L'éducation sentimentale*.

7 The quotation is given now in a CURRENT CONTEXT: this chapter, this book, this time of troubles.

8 The QUOTER'S TARGET is you, dear reader.

9 Between quotation marks (or including them) is the QUOTATION.

Quotology would be quickly done if it only labeled parts. Intrigue lies in their interplay.

Quotee and quotation: "There is only one sex" is a line from a woman who wrote in the name of a man and whose fame was fed by her love affairs. Sand knew how to scandalize and repent, incite and conciliate. What does she do here?

Quotee and target: What of ardent Sand and Flaubert the flabby bachelor? What was their affair? Did she really suppose she could persuade him that sex is superficial? Was she serious or teasing?

Quotation and current context: Have words altered meanings? Is the quotation misty or clear, fresh or clichéd?

Quotee and current context: Is the quotee now forgotten or famous?

Source context and current context: How alike are here and there, now and then?

Quotation and counterquotation: La Bruyère wrote, "A woman always looks upon a man as a man, and so a man will look upon a woman as a woman."[31] At first sight, the quotations from Sand and La Bruyère contradict. Can they be reconciled?

Source context, quotee, quoter, and quoter's target: How much can I presume you know? What are my motives in choosing quotations?[32]

Every part of a quotation statement is vulnerable to naive, careless, ignorant, malicious, mischievous, prudent, and inventive change. A quoter might disregard some, even most, parts of the statement. It may be enough to find a wise or witty quotation, not too well known, trimmed and oiled to fit current context.

Whether quoters quote quotations with or without quotees depends on how much the quotee brings to the table. Source context can be evoked strongly, vaguely, or not at all. An otherwise ordinary word or phrase becomes a quotation when uttered by a notable quotee in a memorable context. Julius Caesar's last words "Et tu, Brute?" are often quoted because they set a scene drenched with betrayal and consequence.[33] "I shall return" would be ho-hum if Douglas MacArthur hadn't said it in the midst of world war and if he hadn't returned.

Kings and queens, poets and philosophers, saints and sinners are quoted. Everyday cleverness spreads anonymously or attaches to celebrity. Charles I's single word, "Remember," is remembered in the *Oxford Dictionary of Quotations* (hereafter ODQ) because he uttered it at his execution.[34]

QUOTATION MOTIVES

If a motive can speak, it can quote: quotations inform, confirm, persuade, amuse, confuse, warn, excuse, tickle, surprise, intimidate, flatter, curse, and razzle-dazzle. Traditional quotations carry weight. Quotations never heard before make waves. Commonly, quoters quote to make a point and turn around it. Vanity courts quoters: "Quote me! Quote me!" Benjamin Franklin heard that "nothing gives an Author so great Pleasure, as to find his Works respectfully quoted by other learned Authors."[35]

In the twenty-first century close attention to precise quotation is practiced in colleges, courtrooms, and places of worship. *Don't "quote"* is the motto of the quotation underground, quoters who quote secretly, a nameless unnumbered mob, maybe everybody, for whom the whole purpose of memorizing quotations is to use them as though they came to mind in a moment of brilliance. For rehearsed spontaneity a quotation's success depends on avoiding any hint of quotation. Subtle quoters quote without showing they're quoting, content that anyone clever enough to know they're quoting will smile knowingly and stay mum.

Charles-Maurice de Talleyrand studied *L'improvisateur français* (1804–5), a twenty-one-volume collection of bons mots, from which he filched as if inventing phrases on the spot.[36] Édouard Fournier wrote, "Whenever a clever phrase was wandering about in search of a parent, he adopted it."[37]

QUOTATION SUPPRESSION

"I don't know" is modest and admitted by the wise. Confucius answered again and again, "I don't know," "I don't know."[38] If confessing ignorance is embarrassing, quote Confucius, name and all.

"I will forget" consoles. "I will be forgotten" grieves. "I forgot" gets by because we all forget. Names are slippery. Thomas Fuller compared memory to "a purse — if it be overfull that it cannot shut, all will drop out of it."[39] For memory's ease, a later Thomas Fuller collected *Gnomologia* (1722), 6,496 "remarkable Sentences and Sayings, as are useful in Conversation and Business." Fuller's sayings are sayings without sayers. He recites "A Man without Money, is no Man at all," "All Work and no Play, / Makes *Jack* a dull boy," and "Women's Work is never done" without source or quotee.[40] So easily do quotations become proverbs. Economy cries for it.

Because common wisdom is supposed to be a better counselor than a single individual, authors can soon lose claims to their quotations. John Ray and Thomas Fuller appropriated the best of John Florio and George Herbert.

Compendia now attribute to Fuller proverbs he collected. When conditions are ripe, proverbs reattach.

QUOTATION ATTACHMENT

Robert Andrews's *Concise Columbia Dictionary of Quotations* includes this entry:

> "A woman once made equal with man becomes his superior."
> *Margaret Thatcher (b. 1925)*
> *British prime minister*

Russell Lewis's *Margaret Thatcher* reports that the prime minister said this memorable sentence but as a quotation from Sophocles.[41] But it is not in Sophocles. Innumerable books, articles, and Web sites attribute the quotation to Socrates, and none of them gives a source. The quotation cannot be found in Plato, Xenophon, or Diogenes Laertius or in any other ancient Socratic source, but it can be found attributed to Socrates as early as 1598 in Nicholas Ling's *Politeuphuia*: "A woman once made equal with man becommeth his superior."[42] A provocative quotation like this one requires a distinguished quotee, Thatcher, Sophocles, or Socrates.

Quotations will climb if they can. Alexander Pope rhymed:

> But let a *Lord* once own the *happy Lines*,
> How the *Wit brightens*! How the *Style refines*![43]

QUOTATION MIGRATION

Arthur Koestler plugged this epigraph into his *Ghost in the Machine*:

> Benjamin Franklin's reply to a lady who queried the usefulness of his work on electricity: "Madam, what use is a new-born baby?"[44]

Walter Gratzer's *Eurekas and Euphorias: The Oxford Book of Scientific Anecdotes* includes this:

> When Chancellor of the Exchequer William Gladstone, having witnessed Michael Faraday's demonstration of the newly discovered phenomenon of electromagnetic induction, asked "But what use is it?" . . . his riposte was supposed to have been, "What use is a newborn baby?"[45]

We know that Faraday knew he was quoting Franklin, but readers of *Eurekas and Euphorias* might not. Other sources attribute the quotation to Faraday or Pasteur; when attributed to Franklin, the quotation changes setting and language.[46]

When one famous person quotes another, the quotation circulates with the authority of either or both. "The best is the enemy of the good" began its career in Italian, was promoted by Voltaire, and became a maxim of management in the late twentieth century.[47] "'Tis his at last who says it best," says James Russell Lowell.[48] 'Tis really?

In a frequently quoted sentence Isaac Newton admitted, "If I have seen further it is by standing on the shoulders of giants," an adage that predated him by centuries. Because Newton is more famous than the eldest known source of the quotation he gets the credit for it, empirical proof that different people have different quotational gravity.[49]

Thomas à Kempis counseled, "Seek not to know who said this or that, but take note of what has been said."[50] This bad advice bears repeating solely because it comes from Thomas à Kempis. Gary Saul Morson believed that "the attribution of a speaker is in fact a *part* of the quotation. Some statements simply are better if a certain famous person said them."[51] Though it is obvious, it must be said.

QUOTABILITY

Robert Andrews warranted that "quotability, not niceness or correctness," was the prime criterion for inclusion in *The Columbia Dictionary of Quotations* (hereafter CDQ). For Andrews, quotability requires a quotee because without one "the words are orphaned.... [A] true quotation cannot be divorced from the character who uttered or scribbled it."[52]

"Blood, sweat, and tears" is everyone's Sir Winston Churchill.[53] It is an heirloom Churchill passed along. A century earlier Lord Byron had sneered at shallow patriots:

> Safe in their barns, these Sabine tillers sent
> Their brethren out to battle — why? for rent.
> Year after year they voted cent. per cent.,
> Blood, sweat, and tear-wrung millions — why? for rent![54]

John Donne wrote, "Mollify it with thy tears, or sweat, or blood," and Theodore Roosevelt trumpeted, "Because of the blood and sweat and tears, the labor and the anguish, through which, in the days that have gone, our forefathers moved on to triumph."[55] A note in the centennial edition of BFQ cites Garibaldi and other works of Churchill.[56] But none of these quotations appeared in the compendia before Churchill gave his famous speech, confirming Jorge Luis Borges: "A great writer creates his precursors."[57]

BREVITY

Brevity is the soul of quotation. Rufinus praised the Sentences of Sextus, saying, "A vast meaning is unfolded in each line, with such power that a sentence only a line long would suffice for a whole life's training."[58] Rufinus heartily exaggerated to make his point alluring, promising a writer's dream, "a sentence only a line long" that "would suffice for a whole life's training." If only education were so easy!

Because of brevity, quotations favor adages, anecdotes, aphorisms, apophthegms, epigrams, maxims, proverbs, and witticisms, types that overlap like rustling leaves.[59] Luther is more quotable than Calvin, Nietzsche more quotable than Kant. Noting that quotes from Kipling and Tennyson outnumber those of Jane Austen and Henry James, the editors of the ODQ explained that "quotability is no real criterion of either popularity or merit in a writer."[60]

Maybe so, but writers want to see their words in quotation collections. Nathan Haskell Dole thought BFQ was a haven where quotations knocked "for admittance to its classic hall of fame."[61] With spacious American optimism, Frederic Cozzens dreamt:

> The man who writes a single line,
> And hears it often quoted,
> Will in his life time surely shine,
> And be hereafter noted.[62]

Sorry, no, not necessarily. Few quotees withstand posterity's withering selection to be remembered for a single quoted line. Singleton quotations in BFQ barely preserve the fame of Arthur J. Lamb ("She's a bird in a gilded cage"), Ninon de L'Enclos ("Old age is woman's hell"), Texas Guinan ("Hello, sucker!"), Porfirio Díaz ("Poor Mexico, so far from God and so close to the United States"), and others on the brink of oblivion.[63]

Hundreds of quotees have slipped in and out of BFQ's temporary immortality, many quoted in one edition only. Robert Chambers and Firdousi appeared in the 8th edition only; Francis Osgood only in the

9th; Mary E. Coleridge, W. W. Crapo, Agnes Darmesteter, and fifteen others in BFQ 10th; and Alice Rice, James Rorty, Benjamin Scoville, and so on in BFQ 11th. One hundred forty-one quotees debuted in BFQ 12th and vanished thereafter, including Burton Stevenson, editor of the rival *Home Book of Quotations* (hereafter HBQ).[64] Come and gone are Benedetto Croce, Maria Edgeworth, Zane Grey, John Neihardt, and W. J. Turner.

But lo, the elect are resurrected! Theodor Seuss Geisel (Dr. Seuss) debuted in BFQ 12th, vanished in BFQ 13th, and returned in BFQ 16th. Hesiod, Sophocles, Euripides, Menander, Diodorus Siculus, Valerius Maximus, Sir Thomas More, Johannes Kepler, Charles II, John Marshall, and Rimbaud have been in, out, and in again.

Explaining his selections for BFQ 11th (1937), Christopher Morley wrote that he retained quotations from Axel Gustafsson Oxenstiern and Eligius von Münch-Bellinghausen "for their names alone," a rare caprice.[65] Remarkable names did not preserve places for Will Allen Droomgoole, John Revelstoke Rathom, and Menella Bute Smedley.

QUOTOLOGY

Quotology disdains no quotations whatsoever, a duty it bears stoutly, with bloodshot eyes and sagging shelves. Big and burly as it is, quotology has criteria.

Authority

Identical words mean different things depending on who said them and under what circumstances. "God may pardon you, but I never!" can be cited from the novelist Ouida, but an elder and regal source is Elizabeth I.[66] Borges takes this to the absurd: Pierre Menard immerses himself so deeply in the study of Cervantes and his times that he is able to re-create three parts of *Don Quixote* exactly, word for word, but the re-creation is then "more subtle," "more ambiguous," "almost infinitely richer" than the original novel.[67]

Pedigree
Is the source of the quotation original or intermediary? Can it be trusted? Muslim scholars sought to solve the problem of fake hadith by checking their *isnād*, or line of transmission. "They attached great importance to it, and considered it an indispensable part of every tradition. In order to ascertain the relative value of the various *isnāds* and their different classes, they produced a vast literature on the biographies of their transmitters and developed a system which was almost scientific in its precision and rigour."[68]

Language
Is the quotation in the original language? If not, did translation alter it? When a quoter's target can be expected to understand different languages, choices are possible — nuance, cadence, concision, allusive echoes — that will affect the impact of a quotation. "He himself said it" lacks the impress of "Ipse dixit."[69] "Seize the day" drains dignity from "Carpe diem."[70] "The rockets' red glare, the bombs bursting in air" won't allude in Russian or Chinese.

Variation
Are there two or more variations of the same quotation? Do they corroborate each other or differ significantly? Saint Augustine declared: "The apostles, who themselves have quoted prophetic testimonies from . . . the Hebrew [Old Testament] and the [Greek] Septuagint, have thought that both should be used as authoritative, since both are one, and divine."[71] Confronted by the Hebrew book of Jonah, which says that Nineveh would be overthrown in forty days, and the Septuagint, which says three days, Augustine asserted that in prophetic discourse they together point to Christ's resurrection and to the forty days spent with his disciples thereafter.

Pertinence
Quotations are called upon to do work, and the sooner they do it, the better. Novelty and strangeness have uses, too. A quotation may be odd yet apt if it intrigues, sets a tone, or amuses.

Length

There are famous one-word quotations. In response to critics who thought painting was easy, Zeuxis bid them "Try!" Asked to surrender, Gen. Anthony McAuliffe was defiant and curt: "Nuts!" was all he said. At the other extreme is Chrysippus, who quoted all of Euripides' *Medea* in one of his books.[72] The longest quotation in BFQ 17th is Lincoln's Gettysburg Address, every word of it.[73]

Number

In different works and different ages, more or fewer quotations are approved. Charles Darwin scarcely quoted in *On the Origin of Species* (1859) but quoted heavily in *The Descent of Man* (1871). In the first place he hurried to establish his originality, in the second to genealogize his descent.[74] Sir Thomas Browne sniped that "Pineda quotes more Authors in one work, than are necessary in a whole World."[75] Grotius gathered quotations by the armful. Quotes bloat desperate dissertations.

Genre

Greek and Roman historians thought it their duty to write speeches for the dead. When Coriolanus says, "Let it be your principal care that the cause of your war be just and honest," his words flow from his historian, Dionysius of Halicarnassus.[76] Some decades quote poetry; some prefer prose. Once a dominant genre in English, sermons have rapidly retreated in importance. Quotations from bishops and archbishops were abundant in nineteenth-century quotation collections; few survive.

Community

The beatitudes abide better in a chapel than in a war crimes trial. Local events, divided loyalties, and passing fashions also sway. Quotees respected in one place are wasted in another.

ANTIQUOTATION

Quoters have vices: pedantry and parroting, abstraction and dullness. In *Modern English Usage* (1944) Henry Fowler used most of his "Quotation" entry to warn of its abuses: contemptible pretension, repulsive tedium. Ethel Smyth recorded "a fact, which I think will be found indisputable, namely, that the majority of critical, and plenty of uncritical, readers find quotations a bore."[77]

Improve ethics? Forget it. Quotations can be found to justify almost anything. Timeless truth? Hah! "All men are liars," says the Psalmist, quoting himself (Psalm 116:11).

Appeal to quotation fetters the present to the past. Quotations burden memory at the expense of invention. Quotations calcify into clichés. Dependence upon quotation puts words in the way of the world as it is. Blah blah blah.

In a letter in which he quotes extensively, Thomas Paine bragged, "I scarcely ever quote; the reason is, I always think."[78] Paine means, I suppose, that he does not let quotations do his thinking for him. But by quoting, he shows they can do his writing for him, pummeling an adversary in his own words.

There are quoters and overquoters. Reverend Colton complained of "persons whose erudition so much outweighs their observation, and who have read so much, and reflected so little, that they will not hazard the most familiar truism, or common-place allegation, without bolstering up their rickety judgments in the swaddling bands of antiquity, their doating nurse and preceptress. — Thus, they will not be satisfied to say that content is a blessing, that time is a treasure, or that self-knowledge is to be desired, without quoting Aristotle, Thales, or Cleobulus."[79]

Maria Edgeworth grumbled against vandals who ruined immortal works by quoting the life out of them. "How far our literature may in future suffer from these blighting swarms, will best be conceived by a glance at what they have already withered and blasted of the favourite productions of our most popular poets," Shakespeare, Milton, and Dryden, scissored, patched, and frayed.[80]

Quotations that attack quotations are collected by quotographers who chortle at the irony. The ambitious collect all kinds, most of them wee, harmless, and bright.

Let us go then, you and I, where quotations are spread out like butterflies.

> Every book is a quotation, and every
> house is a quotation out of all forests and
> mines and stone quarries, and every man
> is a quotation from all his ancestors.
>
> *Ralph Waldo Emerson*

2

Types

Quotations come in types that twist, overlap, and mimic.[1] This chapter seeks not to establish an exhaustive catalog (an infinite task) but rather to extend the working lexicon and identify the most significant distinctions. We have already seen four types: migratory, suppressed, intermediary, and antiquotations. Here in plain labels are fifty-five more.

Language philosophy classifies four basic types:

A1   In the troubled reign of Charles I, John Selden said, "The wisest way for men in these times is to say nothing."[2]

A2   John Selden said that in dangerous times wise men should say nothing.

A3   John Selden said that in dangerous times wise men should "say nothing."

A4   The wisest way for men in these times is to say nothing.

A1 is a DIRECT QUOTATION, *oratio recta*, complete with quotee and quotee's context. It is the type that concerns us most and that subsumes most other types.

A2 is a paraphrase. It is an INDIRECT QUOTATION, *oratio obliqua*, and it too gives the quotee. "In direct quotation," says Gottlob Frege, "a sentence designates another sentence, and in indirect quotation a thought."[3]

A3 is a MIXED QUOTATION, mixing A1 and A2.

A4 is an example of what Herman Cappelen and Ernie Lepore call a PURE QUOTATION, since only the quotation appears.[4] A pure quotation is nothing but quotation. A pure quotation is a subspecies of UNATTRIBUTED QUOTATION that lacks source, context, and quotee because it has no use for them.

Montaigne and Emerson often quoted without attribution, but Montaigne's motives weren't pure. He liked luring readers into undisclosed quotations.

Matters quickly get more complicated. Consider:

B1   Shakespeare wrote, "The better part of Valour, is Discretion."

B2   Beaumont and Fletcher wrote, "It shew'd discretion, the best part of valour."

B3   "Cowardice is not synonymous with prudence. It often happens that the better part of discretion is valour."

B4   An insurance executive thought that "the better part of discretion was value."[5]

Here relations between quotations come into view. B1 and B2 raise the question of precedence: Which came first? Which repeats? Shakespeare's version first appeared in 1597; Beaumont and Fletcher's in 1611. The Beaumont and Fletcher quotation is an ALLUSION, a very common thing. Or both B1 and B2 point to a precedent PROVERB, a type that converts pure quotation into common property.

B3 and B4 are two types of QUOTATION TWIST. B3, from William Hazlitt, inverts B1's terms. B3 is a TRANSPOSAL TWIST. A second example: "The best planned lays of mice and men go oft awry."

B4, from Richard Powers, is a PHONIC TWIST. Phonic twists substitute words that sound alike, or nearly. A second example: "To buy or not to buy."

Quotation twists play with a reader's ability to bounce them off the originals, often as puns, quips, and parody.

A sparkling fountain of spite, Dorothy Parker said:

C1 "You can lead a horticulture, but you can't make her think."[6]

C2 "You may lead a whore to culture, but you can't make her think."[7]

C1 and C2 are quotation twists of a proverb. Samuel Johnson told it to Boswell, "One man may lead a horse to water, but twenty cannot make him drink."[8] C1 and C2 are transcribed from Parker's conversation, different versions of what auditors heard. They are VARIANT QUOTA-TIONS, miniature examples of a tremendous problem for quotology. Transcriptions differ and transmitters cut, add, alter, and take off in new directions. There are differing transcriptions of the Lincoln-Douglas debates, different *Mahābhāratas*, variants of Isaiah and Acts of the Apostles, two versions of *King Lear*, three of *Hamlet*, perhaps five of *Macbeth*.[9] It takes care to quote them truly.

Quotations plunge into the dark. Some are so profoundly recondite they almost disappear:

D "Here then was I (call me Mary Beton, Mary Seton, Mary Car-michael or by any name you please — it is not a matter of any importance) sitting on the banks of a river . . . in fine October weather, lost in thought."

D is from Virginia Woolf's *A Room of One's Own*. In its midst is a CRYP-TIC QUOTATION.[10] Patricia Yaeger tracked the phrase "Mary Beton, Mary Seton, Mary Carmichael" to the sixteenth-century "Ballad of Mary Hamilton":

Last night there were four Marys,
Tonight they'll be but three.
There was Mary Beton and Mary Seton,
And Mary Carmichael and me.

Woolf says the names are of no importance, and unless the reader knows sixteenth-century British ballads, the Marys will not be recognized. Few could guess the fourth Mary to whom the three Marys allude: Mary Hamilton, who drowned her baby and was executed for it. An arcane allusion to drowning in a quotation by Virginia Woolf shows in a shimmer how much quotations can hide beneath a shiny surface. At this brink quotations enter the company of passwords and code.

If you know the harrowing ballad, Woolf's quotation is harrowing. If not, it's just cryptic. Marjorie Garber told me the quotation isn't cryptic to the thousands who know Joan Baez's arrangement of the ballad, recorded on *Joan Baez* (Vanguard 1960), and it isn't cryptic very long for readers of Susan Gubar's edition of *A Room of One's Own* (2005), whose notes include Baez's lyrics and five stanzas from *Sharpe's Ballad Book* (1824). Ideally, a cryptic quotation is like this one: buried treasure.

Carl Van Doren was fond of the type. "The writer lets his submerged quotation rise nearly to the surface, and the reader enjoys catching him at it."[11] In his *Praise of Folly*, written for Sir Thomas More, Erasmus mixed cryptic quotations to "create what was virtually a private language" that he and More shared.[12]

Mikhail Bakhtin believed that "one of the more interesting stylistic problems during the Hellenistic period was the problem of quotation. The forms of direct, half-hidden and completely hidden quoting were endlessly varied, as were the forms for framing quotations by a context, forms of intonational quotation marks, varying degrees of alienation or assimilation of another's quoted word. And here the problem frequently arises: is the author quoting with reverence or on the contrary with irony, with a smirk?"[13]

As a group, B2, B3, B4, C1, C2, and D show that allusive quotations have relative depth. In B3, B4, C1, and C2 the reading pleasure lies mainly in the wordplay, regardless of quotee, context, or source. In D the quotation would glide by invisibly unless its source and context are known.

E1 through H2 are for connoisseurs:

E1   "Our sins are mulish, our confessions lies;
       we play to the grandstand with our promises,

we pray for tears to wash our filthiness,
importantly pissing hogwash through our eyes."

E2 "Our sins are stubborn, our contrition lame;
we want our scruples to be worth our while —
how cheerfully we crawl back to the mire:
a few cheap tears will wash our stains away!"[14]

E1 is a TRANSLATION by Richard Howard of a Baudelaire poem, and
E2 is Robert Lowell's IMITATION of the same lines. Both openly call for
comparison with the original. Imitation was popular in the eighteenth
century: Voltaire imitated Seneca; John Dryden, Alexander Pope, and
Jonathan Swift imitated Horace; and Dr. Johnson imitated Juvenal.
Though imitation is less popular nowadays, translation remains an art
that attracts writers who aim high. Great works of literature often make
their first appearances in different languages in bits and pieces quoted
before the complete works are translated. The first English words of
Petrarch are quotations, translated by Chaucer.[15]

Now compare:

F1 "This hand is not the color of yours, but if I pierce it, I shall feel
pain. . . . The blood that will flow from mine will be the same
color as yours."

F2 "Hath not a Jew hands, organs, dimensions, senses, affections,
passions? . . . If you prick us, do we not bleed?"[16]

F1 (Standing Bear) and F2 (Shakespeare's Shylock) present what Dr.
Bushwhacker calls an ACCIDENTAL RESEMBLANCE.[17] As Samuel Johnson warned, "It is indeed certain that whoever attempts any common
topick, will find unexpected coincidences of his thoughts with those of
other writers; nor can the nicest judgment always distinguish accidental
similitude from artful imitation."[18] There is no reason to suppose that
Standing Bear read *The Merchant of Venice*. However, there is reason to
suppose F1 is a GHOST QUOTATION (see example R below).

Now contrast:

G1   "Speak, that I may see thee." — Ben Jonson[19]

G2   "Speech was given to man to disguise his thought." —
          Talleyrand

G1 and G2 are APPROPRIATED QUOTATIONS, a quotation attributed to someone who said or wrote it, though its use was predated by someone else. G1 has a rich history. In *Florida*, a selection of quotations from his own works, Apuleius of Madauros (second century) told an anecdote about Socrates. "Once when he saw a youth of handsome appearance who remained for a long time without uttering a syllable, he said to him, 'Say something, that I may see what you are like.'" Petrarch condensed the anecdote: Socrates "met another youth with a noble expression but a silent demeanor: 'Speak,' he said, 'that I might see thee.'" The quotation reappeared in still richer form in Erasmus's *Apophthegmata* (1531): "A certain rich man sent his son to Socrates in order to judge of his genius. His pedagogue, having introduced the youth, says, 'Socrates, his father sent this young man by me, on purpose that you might see him.' 'Very well,' replied the philosopher, 'Come, young man,' continues he, 'speak up, that I may see thee.'"[20] The quotation frequently reappeared thereafter, in Latin and translations from it, in sermons, travel accounts, and other distinguished places. It recurs in Dryden's *An Evening's Love, or, The Mock-Astrologer* (1671): "'Tis the Sentence of a Philosopher, Loquere ut te videam; speak that I may know thee." The great compendia of our day attribute the quotation to Jonson, forgetting Erasmus, Petrarch, Apuleius, and Socrates, though it is through their combined authorization that the quotation won currency.

Molière wrote, "Speech has been given to man to express his thought." A quotation twist turned this into G2, a quotation usually attributed to Talleyrand.[21] It sounds like Talleyrand, it's slick and slippery like Talleyrand, but Édouard Fournier traced the phrase back to *Le nain jaune*, a journal published by a Monsieur Harel in Paris between December 1814 and July 1815. "When Harel wished to put a joke or witticism into circulation, he was in the habit of connecting it with some celebrated name, on the chance of reclaiming it if it took," and he did reclaim it, but to no avail. It is now Talleyrand's, whether or not it was Harel's in the first place.[22]

G1 and G2 also illustrate COUNTERQUOTATION, an exceedingly important type discussed in greater detail at the end of this chapter.

> H1 "Whoever is acquainted with the history of philosophy, during the two or three last centuries, cannot but admit, that there appears to have existed a sort of secret and tacit compact among the learned, not to pass beyond a certain limit in speculative science." — Coleridge
>
> H2 "Whoever knows the history of philosophy in the last centuries must admit that there appears to have been a kind of secret and silent agreement among the learned not to take science beyond a certain limit." — Felix Schelling

H1 is an outright PLAGIARISM of H2, one of the most notorious in literary history.[23] Plagiarisms have been the subject of study by scholars and attorneys and the pastime of paranoids.[24] They are the bane of writers and the nuisance of professors; hunting them down is an established business.

Art Linkletter asked a child, "What's your definition of 'genius'?" The child replied, "Someone who cheats and doesn't get caught." This bears an accidental resemblance to the statement of the Sanskrit connoisseur Rājashekhara: "There is no poet that is not a thief, no merchant that does not cheat, but he flourishes without reproach who knows how to hide his theft" and to Stravinsky's "A good composer does not imitate, he steals." That formidable quotologist Bergen Evans shrugged, "Authors are magpies, echoing each other's words and seizing avidly on anything that glitters."[25]

The five types B, E, F, G, and H are wavering clines rather than rigid categories, their distinctions more or less disputable depending on whether lawyers are involved.

Another tricky usage comes in several types:

11 "The philosophers' 'proofs' of the soul's immortality, even if they were logically correct, would be irrelevant."[26]

12 "What the 'higher schools' in Germany really achieve is a brutal training, designed to prepare huge numbers of young men . . . to become usable, abusable, in government service."[27]

13 "In the past, many wars were fought for the sake of the 'glory' resulting from victory."[28]

14 "It would be frivolous to think that 'Descartes,' 'Leibniz,' 'Rousseau,' 'Hegel,' etc., are names of authors, of the authors of movements or displacements that we thus designate. The indicative value that I attribute to them is first the name of a problem."[29]

15 "Even though Dostoevsky 'had' epilepsy, it remains unclear what he had or what we have at hand when we think we are discussing the condition so named."[30]

These examples show SCARE QUOTES, a type with several very different species that share one common feature: their quotation marks signify that the word or phrase should not be understood literally. With various degrees of alarm, scare quotes put words under suspicion, holding them up for question or contempt.

Imbedded in 11, 12, and 13 are examples of IRONIC QUOTATION and a subset of it, SNEER QUOTATION. An ironic quotation can wink at a word or despise it. In 11, 12, and 13 contempt punctures "proofs," "higher schools," and "glory."

Detecting when a quotation is ironic is sometimes difficult. Lev Shestov asserted, "In his late works, Dostoevsky used the word 'humanity' in an ironic sense only, and he always wrote it in quotation marks."[31] This is literally not true. Perhaps Shestov was ironic.

14 and 15 are examples of SUSPENSE QUOTATION. In 14 Derrida warns of associating the names of authors with the movements that are presumed to be theirs. Writing on Dostoevsky, Avital Ronell uses scare quotes around "had" in 15 to draw attention to it, hesitate over it, and question what it means "to have" an illness, particularly a mental one. If a possession, what is possessed?

Some quotations are politely borrowed.

J   "Freedom's just another word for nothin' left to lose."

The quotation in J can be correctly attributed to Janis Joplin, who sang it on her album *Pearl* (1971), but the song in which it appears, "Me & Bobby McGee," is by Kris Kristofferson and Fred Foster.[32] It is a PERFORMANCE QUOTATION, usually an appropriated or ghost quotation. The power of performance quotation warms the ambitions of comedians and singers who dream of delivering lines that set them apart: Frank Sinatra's "My Way," Edith Piaf's "Non, je ne regrette rien," and Rodney Dangerfield's "I don't get no respect" are other examples. Not all performance quotations are appropriated: Groucho Marx is the author of "I don't care to belong to any club that will accept me as a member," a quote that bears an accidental (?) resemblance to one by Robert Benchley. Surprised to get a loan from his bank, Benchley withdrew his savings from it, saying, "I don't trust a bank that would lend money to such a poor risk."[33]

K   "I cannot speak well enough to be unintelligible."

K is uttered by Catherine Morland, a character in Jane Austen's *Northanger Abbey*. K is a CHARACTER QUOTATION, a very familiar type: Hamlet's "To be or not to be," Ali Baba's "Open sesame!" Bugs Bunny's "What's up, Doc?" are others. To quote Catherine as the quotee would be unobjectionable, but to attribute the tastes, wishes, attitudes, opinions, or beliefs of a character to an author is to commit the authorial fallacy. Catherine Morland isn't Jane Austen, Jane Eyre isn't Charlotte Brontë, Prospero isn't Shakespeare. Emily Dickinson confided to Thomas Higginson, "When I state myself, as the representative of the verse, it does not mean me, but a supposed person."[34]

But in the absence of other evidence it is an overreaction to assume that an author does *not* believe what her characters say. When an author might, or might not, share a character's ideas and opinions, quotation provides a mask. "Every profound spirit needs a mask," wrote Nietzsche, "even more, around every profound spirit a mask is growing continually."[35]

K is also a PURE IRONIC QUOTATION: the irony lies in the quotation itself, no matter who the quotee is or whether it has one. Henry Tilney replies to Catherine, "Bravo! An excellent satire on modern language."[36]

Speaking of speaking well, now hear this:

> L   "He spoke well who, in answer to the question, 'What have we in common with the gods?' said 'Kindness and truth.'"

In L Longinus relays a CONTESTED QUOTATION, a quotation attributed to two or more different authorities, in this case Pythagoras and Demosthenes. Notice that when Longinus cites it, he names no one. The quotation had become consensual; it no longer mattered to him whether it came from a philosopher or a lawyer. The quotation had graduated into a proverb, that potent type of pure quotation. Proverbs also go the other way and attach to a quotee. Ecclesiastes and the book of Proverbs were attributed to Solomon; Arabic gnomologies attribute several of Solomon's proverbs to Pythagoras.[37]

We now enter quotology's foggy swamp, infested with misquotations.[38] They come big and small, some of them bite, and some are deadly.

> M1   "God said 'Let there be light,' and there was light. 'Let there be earth,' and there was earth."
>
> M2   "Truth makes part of happiness in a Tertullian-like sense, in the sense of *credo quia absurdum*."
>
> M3   "You stand in your own light."
>
> M4   "Corporeal charms may indeed gain admirers, but there must be mental ones to retain them; and Horace had a delicate feeling of this, when he refused to restrict the pleasures of the lover merely to his eyes, but added also those of the ear: —
>
> *Qui sedens identidem, te*
> *Spectat et audit.*"[39]
>
> M5   "Thou shalt commit adultery."
>
> M6   "He saith, *Bellarmin dares not deny, the Oration published under*

the name of Sixtus V. to be none of his; when, in the very place quoted for it, he doth expresly deny it."[40]

Emil Cioran wrote, "A garbled quotation is equivalent to a betrayal, an insult, a prejudice."[41] In different ways M1, M2, M3, M4, M5, and M6 vindicate Ambrose Bierce's definition: "Quotation, n. The act of repeating erroneously the words of another. The words erroneously repeated."[42] The first four types are common, usually benign, and occasionally benevolent. The fifth and sixth approach scandal.

M1 is also from Longinus, living up to his reputation as an erratic quoter.[43] Longinus slightly misquotes Genesis, but the misquote is not malicious or even serious, it is only a QUOTATION FROM MEMORY. Quotations from memory have different status in different disciplines and in different contexts. They can reveal how quotations were interpreted, indicate separate lines of transmission, and indicate how important quotations were to a person and milieu. Edmund Burke's *Philosophical Enquiry in the Origin of Our Ideas of the Sublime and Beautiful* misquotes Job and *Paradise Lost*.[44] Saint Gregory Nazianzen "is rarely accurate and his misquotations are the despair of collectors of classical fragments."[45] Day-to-day conversation would be barren without quotations from memory, which shade into mixed quotations and paraphrase. "Most of our talk is garbled quotation," wrote Robert Frost. Oliver Wendell Holmes considered misquoting a "privilege of talking."[46]

M2, a translation from Miguel de Unamuno's *Del sentimiento trágico de la vida* (The Tragic Sense of Life), ends with a TRADITIONAL QUOTATION, a slight misquote that nonetheless stays close enough to the original to attain currency.[47] Other common examples are the character quotations, "Play it again, Sam," from the movie *Casablanca* and "Elementary, my dear Watson," presumed to have been said somewhere by Sherlock Holmes but nowhere found in Conan Doyle.[48]

M3 is a MODERNIZED QUOTATION as it appears in *The Home Book of Quotations*. The original reads, "Ye stand in your owne light."[49] Editors of Chaucer, Shakespeare, Burton, and many other majestic writers modernize with the best of intentions.

M4 is from Reverend Colton's *Lacon*. At best it is an ADAPTED QUO-
TATION, in which a small change is made to fit the quotation to the
occasion. Colton adapted quotations throughout *Lacon*, changing sin-
gulars to plurals or vice versa, adding, dropping, or substituting words.
Love lyrics for Phyllis, Laura, or Stella can be readdressed to Margot,
Hannah, or Amy. "Found poems" are adapted quotations.[50]

M4 also includes a MISATTRIBUTED QUOTATION coming not from
Horace but from Catullus.

M5 is a TRANSMITTAL ERROR that turns the original upside down.
It comes from the so-called Wicked Bible of 1632, inspiring every lecher
who read it. Aristotle liked "ancient witnesses" because "they cannot
be corrupted."[51] Modern editors have amassed piles of evidence to the
contrary. Quotations from ancient witnesses are in perpetual danger of
corruption due to miscopying, careless typesetting, or technical glitch.
The Murderers' Bible of 1795 was so called because Mark 7:27 read:
"Let the children first be killed" instead of "filled."[52] Because of broken
type, an 1849 edition of Colton's *Lacon* reads, "We moderns must also
become ancients in our urn."[53]

M6 cites a MALICIOUS MISQUOTATION; the misquotation is both
serious and deliberate. Regarding M6 and its like, the pseudonymous
"A.L." declaimed that Jeremy Taylor "sometimes quoted Books that
never were, or that, in the places quoted, have not any least syllable to
the purpose they are quoted for; and frequently quoted them in a Sense
they never dreamt of; yea, and divers times by adding, curtailing, or
otherwise altering them, misquoted the very words themselves."[54]

Schopenhauer protested, "How little honesty there is among authors
is seen in the unscrupulous way in which they interpolate and tamper
with the quotations from the works of others."[55] Natalie Clifford Barney countered that "to mis-quote is the very foundation of original
style. The success of most writers is almost entirely due to continuous
and courageous abuse of familiar misquotation."[56] Hesketh Pearson
famously wrote, "Misquotations are the only quotations that are never
misquoted"; not so famously, three pages later he wrote about Thomas
Heywood, "The misquoter is now misquoted."[57]

Misquotations are abundant and amusing enough to fill books.[58]

N "MISSION ACCOMPLISHED."

N is an ASSOCIATIVE QUOTATION attached to President George W. Bush, a quotation he did not utter but which became his all the same. On May 1, 2003, he stood on the deck of an American aircraft carrier and declared: "In the Battle of Iraq, the United States and our allies have prevailed." He did not say, "Mission accomplished," but a large banner behind him did, in huge capital letters. As American casualties in Iraq mounted through the end of his presidency, "MISSION ACCOMPLISHED" ceased to be a declaration of a happy ending and became instead a sneer quotation ceaselessly repeated.

01 Thomas Hardy said, "Fate stalks us with depressing monotony from womb to tomb, and, when we are least expecting it, deals us a series of crushing blows from behind."

02 "Congressmen who willfully take actions during wartime that damage morale and undermine the military are saboteurs and should be arrested, exiled, or hanged." — President Abraham Lincoln

01 and 02 are specimens of SPURIOUS QUOTATION. 01 is attributed to Hardy in Hesketh Pearson's *The Whispering Gallery*, but the book was a hoax and the quotation invented.[59] After the 2003 Iraq invasion 02 was widely circulated in the American media. It first appeared in an article by J. Michael Waller, was quoted four years later by Frank J. Gaffney, Jr., in the *Washington Times*, was recited the same day by Congressman Don Young (R-AK) in the U.S. House of Representatives, and soon appeared on partisan Web sites, always attributed to Lincoln.[60] In *Quotesmanship* Paul F. Boller, Jr., calculated that "spurious Lincoln quotations are even more common than fake Washington quotes" and gives twelve pages of examples.[61]

P1 "Darkness and silence were before the world was made,

and silence spoke a word and the darkness
became light."[62]

P1 is a paraphrase of Genesis and a PSEUDOQUOTATION attributed to
Philo of Alexandria till scholars recognized the attribution was implau-
sible. The text is real enough, but its author is long forgotten. There
are many pseudoquotations drawn from pseudotexts, among them a
life of Homer attributed to Herodotus, *The Book of Secrets* attributed
to Roger Bacon, thirty dialogues falsely attributed to Plato, and correspondence between Seneca and Saint Paul, assumed for centuries
to be genuine.[63]

This needs to be distinguished from a similar type:

> P2   "Why has government been instituted at all? Because the pas-
> sions of men will not conform to the dictates of reason and
> justice, without constraint." — Publius
>
> P3   "There is a moment of difficulty and danger at which flattery
> and falsehood can no longer deceive, and simplicity itself can
> no longer be misled." — Junius[64]

P2 and P3 are PSEUDONYMOUS QUOTATIONS. They fall into a hazy
zone where, as a kind of pure quotation, they say what needs to be said
against law and power or, alas, spew the slander of rogues. We now
know that the "Publius" of P2 was Alexander Hamilton; "Publius" was
sometimes John Madison or John Jay. Who "Junius" was remains a
mystery.

Hazlitt wrote, "Authors who acquire a high celebrity and conceal
themselves, seem superior to fame. Producing great works *incognito* is
like doing good by stealth. There is an air of magnanimity in it, which
people wonder at. Junius, and the Author of Waverly are striking examples.
Junius, however, is really unknown; while the Author of Waverly enjoys
all the credit of his writings without acknowledging them. Let anyone
else come forward and claim them; and we should see then whether
Sir Walter Scott would stand by."[65]

Prolific authors like Fanny Crosby (almost one hundred different pseudonyms) and Joyce Carol Oates ("Rosamond Smith" and "Lauren Kelly") took on pseudonyms to bypass critics who complained they published too much.

Here I could give what compendia call an ANONYMOUS QUOTATION, but I won't, and for two reasons. First, there are abundant examples elsewhere: the YBQ gives 35 "Anonymous" quotations; the ODQ 134; JGDQ 266; and WNW 332. There's an old yarn about the man amazed to see how much Anonymous wrote. And second, "anonymous quotation" is a catch-all term for other types of quotations that can be more precisely defined (examples Q and s below).

Of all quotes ever quoted, most would be of this type:

Q1   "The Egyptians, they said, were the first men who reckoned by years and made the year to consist of twelve divisions of the seasons."[66]

Q2   "They say that I am bewitched, and that demons have taken control of me. I know nothing about such things, but if it is true, I am the most wretched girl alive."[67]

Q1 and Q2 relate HEARSAY. Q1 is from Herodotus, the father of history, illustrating why he is also the father of folklore. He often gave no better source than "they say," "it is said," and "so the story runs." Suspect in science and scholarship, strictly regulated in courts and audits, hearsay is the milk and bran of gossip and reputation. Q2 highlights why hearsay is tactically invaluable: it introduces an idea or opinion under the guise of a quotation to test its truth or acceptability. A hearsay quotation may not be a quotation at all but a hypothesis masquerading as one.

Nigel Rees cheered up BBC radio with hearsay quotations like these: A man said his mother said she overheard one woman telling another, "'Well,' I says to him, I says to him, I says, says I, 'Well, I says,' I says." An Irish woman remarked on the situation in Ulster, "Ah well, they say it's not as bad as they say it is."[68]

R   "When I look back now from this high hill of my old age, I can still see the butchered women and children lying heaped and scattered all along the crooked gulch as plain as when I saw them with eyes still young. And I can see that something else died there in the bloody mud, and was buried in the blizzard. A people's dream died there. It was a beautiful dream." — Black Elk

R is a GHOST QUOTATION, a quotation that was written by one person and attributed to someone else, who accepted credit for it. In this case, John G. Neihardt puts his words in the mouth of Black Elk.[69] Frowned upon in some circles, the practice thrives in as-told-to memoirs, formal documents, and political speeches. According to Tacitus, Nero was the first ruler to hire a speechwriter.[70]

Though famous persons may not author the speeches they give or the books they autograph, they are held responsible for them. Sir Winston Churchill won the Nobel Prize for Literature chiefly on the basis of his six-volume *Second World War*, books largely ghost-written.[71]

"At a newsman's banquet President Harding appeared as guest speaker and delivered what struck [Heywood] Broun as the epitome of cliché-ridden, *ghost-written* addresses. After a brief moment of respectful applause, Broun rose from his chair and cried, 'Author! Author!'"[72]

S1   "Now for something completely different."

S2   "Guns save life."

S3   "Arbeit macht frei" (Work makes you free).

S1, S2, and S3 are examples of COLLECTIVE QUOTATION, quotations attributable to a group. A collective quotation goes by the name of a group — NATO, OuLiPo, the Grateful Dead — or by the name of a document — the Declaration of Independence, the Magna Carta, the Bible.

S1, from Monty Python's Flying Circus, is also a CATCHPHRASE, a phrase used to identify a performer, troupe, clique, or character. The Three Musketeers say, "All for one, one for all." "Shazam!" calls Captain Marvel.

S2 and S3 are examples of INSTITUTIONAL QUOTATION. S2, from

the Champaign County Rifle Association, is also a SLOGAN, relayed via the association's Web site, newsletter, and rhyming road signs. It is also a MOTTO, expressing a belief that defies denial. It doesn't matter who wrote an institutional quotation: it goes by the name of the club, company, agency, or the like who promotes it. Quotations from *Punch, Pravda*, or the *Wall Street Journal* are institutional quotations.

s3 is the slogan that in wrought iron greeted victims at the gates of Auschwitz, Dachau, and other concentration camps. Gladly doing his all to kill millions, Adolf Eichmann ran trains on slogans like that. In his defense at his murder trial he spoke "of 'winged words' (*geflügelte Worte*, a German colloquialism for famous quotes from the classics) when he means stock phrases, *Redensarten*, or slogans, *Schlagworte*. . . . He was genuinely incapable of uttering a single sentence that was not a cliché."[73]

Eichmann defended himself by claiming to have followed Kant's "categorical imperative," mistakenly supposing that it meant "the duty to obey orders to the best of his ability."[74] Hannah Arendt wrote: "The longer one listened to him, the more obvious it became that his inability to speak was closely connected with an inability to *think*, namely, to think from the standpoint of someone else. No communication was possible with him, not because he lied but because he was surrounded by the most reliable of all safeguards against the words and the presence of others, and hence against reality as such."[75]

Quotations cause all kinds of trouble.

T1   In Balzac's *Old Goriot* we find, "There is a cure for temptation. . . . Yielding to it."

T2   Oscar Wilde wrote, "The only way to get rid of a temptation is to yield to it."

It seems Wilde swiped another aphorism, but no: T1 is a quote from a 1907 translation of *Père Goriot* (1834–35); nothing like it appears in the original French. T1 is a TENDENTIOUS TRANSLATION, made to echo and antedate the famous line from Oscar Wilde's *Picture of Dorian Gray* (1891).[76]

When translated, quotations are clipped, amplified, retuned, and mauled. Since its 15th edition, BFQ has nicely presented Callimachus's epigram — ἔγα βιβλίον μέγα κακόν — as "Big book, big bore." Other compendia translate this "A great book is like a great evil," turning vinegar into piss.[77]

Out of clean air come . . .

> U1   "A theory should be as simple as possible, but not simpler." — Albert Einstein
>
> U2   "Sometimes a cigar is just a cigar." — Sigmund Freud

U1 and U2 are ATTRIBUTED or UNVERIFIED QUOTATIONS. Fred Shapiro tracked a version of U1 down to a 1972 newspaper (Einstein died in 1955) and added, "No source has been traced."[78] U1 is quoted hither and yon, usually with Einstein attached.

U2 owes its currency to Peter Gay, one of Freud's ablest biographers, who expressed doubts about its authenticity. The quotation is one of Freud's most famous, whether or not he said it.[79]

> v   "*Sapere aude*! Have the courage to use your own reason! — that is the motto of enlightenment." — Immanuel Kant[80]

In v *Sapere aude* is an example of a VOUCHED QUOTATION, one of the most important types. Vouched quotations present agreement between quoter and quotation. Vouched quotations are enhanced or eroded by their quoters. *Sapere aude* (Dare to be wise) is a quotation from Horace (*Epistles* 1.2.40) adopted as a motto. Vouched by Immanuel Kant, it gains. When Nazis vouched quotations from Nietzsche, they contaminated them. "Who cannot claim him for their own?" Kurt Tucholsky asked. "Tell me what you need and I will supply you with a Nietzsche citation."[81]

> w   "'I have endeavoured,' says Lord Chesterfield, 'to gain the hearts of twenty women, whose persons I would not have given a fig for.' The libertine who in a gust of passion, takes advantage of unsuspecting tenderness, is a saint when compared with this

cold-hearted rascal; for I like to use significant words." — Mary Wollstonecraft[82]

w, a quotation turned against its quotee, is a WEAPONIZED QUOTA-TION, the antitype of a vouched quotation. The use of weaponized quotations is a favorite tactic in polemics, competitive conversation, and courtroom cross-examination.[83]

Parents and children, students and teachers, pundits and politicians know the sharp sting of hearing their own words thrown back at them as mistake, contradiction, hypocrisy, or lie. Martin Luther warned his enemies, "I will condemn you out of your own mouth," quoting Saint Luke.[84] Samuel Johnson was greatly provoked when someone did "what he could least of all bear, which was quoting something of his own writing, against what he then maintained."[85]

Print made quotations even more potent weapons. Anthony Grafton observed that since its appearance print, "cold, distant and precise, enabled writers to excerpt, anatomize and mutilate their opponents' words, paragraph by paragraph and sentence by sentence, using all the textual violence they could devise."[86] Burke exhorted, "Before our opinions are quoted against ourselves, it is proper, that, from our serious deliberation, they may be worth quoting."[87]

X1 "I hate quotations. Tell me what you know." — Ralph Waldo Emerson

X2 *"Vincit amor patriae:* The noblest motive is the public good." — Richard Steele

X1 and X2 are QUOTATIONS OUT OF CONTEXT, a type hereafter condensed to QUOOX (rhymes with "pokes"), a bonanza to Scrabble players everywhere. Of course, most quotations are quotations out of context: to be precise, a quoox is a quotation that is seriously depleted or distorted when presented as is.

X1 appears in the *CDQ, ODQ, PDQ,* and *YBQ; JGDQ* reduces it further to "I hate quotations"; all five note that it comes from Emerson's *Journals.*[88] The remark is shocking for a quoter like Emerson, but there it is, written to himself, May 1849. How can this be? Emerson admires quoters like Plato, Plutarch, and Montaigne; the great quotation compendia prove he knew how to compose in order to be quoted; his remark occurs in a notebook crammed with quotations. How could Emerson hate quotations?

He didn't. BFQ and PDQ give the quotation with enough flesh still on it to prevent it from losing shape:

> *Immortality.* I notice as soon as writers broach this question they begin to quote. I hate quotation. Tell me what you know.[89]

Emerson is himself again, passionate and sensible. He hates quotations about immortality, about which, by 1849, he had heard quite enough. His hatred is focused and particular. Good for him. There are some topics that no number of quotations can settle or certify.

X2 is taken from a nineteenth-century edition of the *Spectator*. It is all kinds of things: a quoox, a traditional quotation, and a tenacious tendentious translation, modernized, of a line from Virgil: "Vincet amor patriae laudumque inmensa cupido" (Yet shall a patriot's love prevail and unquenched thirst for fame) (*Aeneid* 6.823). What happened between Virgil and Steele?

In *The City of God* Augustine quoted the line but changed the verb from the future to the present tense (*vincet > vincit*).[90] That form became a traditional quotation, often reprinted and reproduced on medals, monuments, and family crests. Macdonnel translates "Vincit amor patriae" as "The love of my country prevails."

And what of "The noblest motive is the public good"? "Vincit amor patriae" appeared at the head of *Spectator* no. 200 (October 19, 1711) without translation.[91] The essays from the *Spectator* were published and republished as books as early as 1713. To assist readers who lacked Latin or Greek, the editors of the 1744 edition provided English translations for its epigraphs; to "Vincit amor patriae" was added "The noblest Motive is the Publick Good."[92] It stuck. The translation was modernized and made its way into innumerable texts and on to public buildings. It is inscribed on the ceiling of the south corridor of the Library of Congress and attributed to Virgil.[93] A mistranslation became a quotation.

Quooxes are opportunistic. Milton Mayer coined the term "contextomy" to describe the creation of TRUNCATED QUOTATIONS, made useful by cutting out unwanted words.[94] Movie blurbs and book ads routinely truncate. A verdict of "a terrific waste of time" is easily trimmed to "terrific."

Book reviewers are notorious for cruel quooxes and contextomies. Leo Tolstoy described a reviewer who "so adroitly selected his quotations that to those who had not read the book (and evidently hardly anyone had read it) it would appear quite clear that the whole book was nothing but a collection of high-sounding words, not even used appropriately (as was indicated by notes of interrogation), and that its author was a totally ignorant man."[95]

Quooxes say whatever you like. Is *Quotology* important? Einstein wrote, "Indeed, it is indispensable."[96]

We're almost done.

Y   Demosthenes told the *ekklēsia*, "If anyone asked you, 'Are you at peace, Athenians?' you would reply, 'Certainly not; we are at war.'"[97]

Demosthenes presumes he can speak for his audience and does so with a PRESUMPTIVE QUOTATION. Here he presumes to speak for "you," which in the original context would have been Athenian citizens, who could accept or deny his presumption on the spot. On radio and TV the role of respondent has been replaced by talk show hosts, who presume for millions.

z   "Some anonymous liberal hag on Air America Radio, which no one knew was still on the air, fell down outside her Park Avenue apartment this week, and her liberal colleagues were claiming it was Kristallnacht."[98]

z is from Ann Coulter's Web site. It is a SCARECROW QUOTATION in paraphrase, attributing a claim to an opponent without citing a source.

Talk shows, quarrels, blogs, and partisan newsletters set up scarecrow quotations to controvert when actual quotations won't do. If you can't find them, invent them, attribute them, and put them to work.

Y and Z are examples of INVENTED QUOTATIONS. They would be spurious quotations except for this: their target audiences are presumed to recognize they're invented.

Every example, A1 through Z, is an EVIDENTIARY QUOTATION, introduced as an exhibit. Most quotations in *Quotology* are of this type.

At the beginning of this chapter and every subsequent chapter is an EPIGRAPH. These quotations are normally expected to arouse interest in what follows.

Though it would be easy to continue, type after type, I have reached the point of diminishing returns. We've enough to establish how a single quotation can be of several types and why typing matters.

Marjorie Garber points to a particularly slippery quotation from Keats's "Ode on a Grecian Urn."

> When old age shall this generation waste,
> Thou shalt remain, in midst of other woe,
> Than ours, a friend to man, to whom thou say'st,
> "Beauty is Truth, truth beauty" — that is all
> Ye know on earth, and all ye need to know.

Garber notes that the "'originals,' or rather the period transcriptions of Keats's 'original,' all lack quotation marks," allowing interpreters to treat the last two lines as all spoken by the urn.[99] We can take the five words or the two lines as a character quotation (like those of the chatty crockery in Aesop and Disney); as a hoax; as a vouched quotation; as a pseudoquotation; or as a translation from a language only poets can hear: what urns teach, what breezes whisper, what the thunder says.

COUNTERQUOTATION

The best retort to a potent quotation is a contrary one, preferably from the same source or a better one. Plato is quoted against Plato, Augustine against Augustine, the Koran against the Koran.

In the West the Bible is a favorite arsenal. Would you rather war or peace? Against the command from Joel 3:10 — "Beat your ploughshares into swords, and your pruning hooks into spears" — can be quoted Isaiah 2:4 — "They shall beat their swords into ploughshares and their spears into pruning hooks."

Attack or defense? When Queen Elisabeth of France was widowed, her imperial parents urged her to remarry. To persuade her they engaged a Jesuit, who quoted "all the most telling passages of Holy Scripture of every sort that might advance his object. But the Queen did straight confound him with other and more appropriate quotations, for since her widowhood she had applied her earnestly to the study of God's Word."[100]

COMPARISONS

Seneca the Younger wrote, "Sapiens inter se omnia conparabit" (The wise will compare all things with one another).[101] Let us be wise and compare.

The 1st edition of BFQ (1855) quotes the last line of Donne's eighth elegy, "The Comparison": "She and comparisons are odious." BFQ 3rd (1860) added a note that cites Robert Burton's *Anatomy of Melancholy* (1621) as another source. BFQ 5th (1868) added George Herbert's *Jacula Prudentum* (1640). BFQ 7th (1875) added John Granger's *Golden Aphroditis* (1577). By BFQ 8th (1882) Bartlett could cite nine different sources for "Comparisons are odious": Cervantes, John Fortescue, John Lyly, Christopher Marlowe, Thomas Heywood, Donne, Burton, Herbert, and Grange ("Granger" had been an error).[102] If we follow Bartlett and treat "Comparisons are odious" as a quotation rather than a proverb, his cited recurrences recapitulate multiple quotation types.

Don Quixote says, "Comparison between wit and wit, valor and valor, beauty and beauty, birth and birth, are odious."[103] To quote "Comparisons are odious" from this source is to give a character quotation and a truncated quotation. The quotation from Marlowe comes from *Love's Dominion*, a seventeenth-century play Marlowe did not write: it is a misattributed quotation.

In another character quotation Heywood's Jenkin says, "O Slime, O Brickbat, do you not know that comparisons are odious?"[104] In another Lyly's Philautus says, "Lest Comparisons seem odious" while comparing one woman to another. Where Burton wrote, "Comparisons are odious," he too, was comparing women, as if it were just this kind of comparison that were hateful.[105] His *Anatomy* is otherwise packed with comparisons. The quotation from Herbert is one in a series of maxims. In Grange it's a proverb tossed into an epilogue.

John Fortescue cites "Comparisons are odious" as a saying of King Henry VI's, to whom his whole text is addressed.[106] It is an appropriated quotation that Fortescue bestows on his king. Attributed by Bartlett to Fortescue, it is a truncated and appropriated quotation, translated for English readers.

Constable Dogberry's fragrant phrase, "Comparisons are odorous," is simultaneously a quotation twist, a character quotation, a mangled quotation from memory, and a malapropism.[107]

In 1888 "Bibota," an astute and pseudonymous quotologist, surpassed Bartlett, citing a second instance of "comparisons are odious" in *Don Quixote* and its appearance in still other works: Robert Greene's *Manilia* (1583), Boiardo's fifteenth-century *Orlando innamorato* ("la comparazione son tutte odiose"), and a French reference book that cited a thirteenth-century manuscript ("Comparaisons sont haineuses").[108]

Swift used "comparisons are odious" in a letter to Pulteney (March 7, 1736). A jealous Mary Wollstonecraft used "comparisons are odious" to rebuke Godwin. Dickens used it in *Barnaby Rudge*. Charlotte Perkins Gilman used it in *Herland*.[109] Hoyt and Roberts cited Carew's *Describing Mt. Edgcumbe*, Lodowick's *Marrow of History*, Harvey's *Archaica*, a sixteenth-century *Pasquine*, and Whitgift's *Defence*. Stevenson's HBQ added Lydgate's *Political Poems* and Swift's "Answer to Sheridan's Simile." Bergan Evans added Hazlitt's *Table-Talk*.[110] If it once was a quotation, it's a proverb now.[111]

Quotations slide. Character quotations, pseudoquotations, hoaxes, quooxes, and tendentious translations fool even the smartest for a year, a few centuries, or forever. What passes as a "true" quotation is often a matter of convention in which ambiguity, longstanding traditions, and wishful thinking play parts.

Classic quotations do more than last: they renew, claiming space for difference in the midst of the same. In a saying collected and passed through the ages Socrates said, "Do not force your children to [follow] your ways, because they have been created for a different age than yours."[112]

Is this a true quotation, pseudoquotation, or proverb? Is it heritage or hoax?

Who's to say?

Listen gladly to every godly argument
And see that no wise proverb escapes you.
Jesus ben Sirach

3

Collections

In phrases as brief as a breath worldly wisdom concentrates. "Who knows the oldest and greatest becomes the oldest and greatest," says the oldest and greatest Upanishad.

"Imperturbable wisdom is worth everything," said Democritus. He lived to be 109. His wisdom survives solely as quotations in other people's books.

"*Wisdom* is a *Fox*," wrote Jonathan Swift, "who, after long hunting, will at last cost you the Pains to dig out." "Dig within," Marcus Aurelius told himself. "There lies the well-spring of good: ever dig, and it will ever flow."[1]

When wisdom is valued, venders sell it. Much of the world wants wisdom in a hurry, and why not? Wisdom wants to be wanted. Greek or Roman, Christian or Chinese, wisdom comes in concise sayings, firm, juicy, and refreshing, easy to carry, easy to keep. They scan, they stick, they rhyme. Throughout his travails the knight Hudibras "Cheer'd up himself with ends of verse / And sayings of philosophers."[2]

Wisdom wears the names of the wise: the *Maxims* of La Rochefoucauld, *Pensées* of Pascal, hadith of Muhammad, sermons of Augustine, *Discourses* of Epictetus, letters of Pliny and Paul, parables of Jesus, Plato's dialogues, Aesop's fables, the dicta of Latin and *doxa* of Greek, the sutras of Buddha, and the proverbs of Solomon, king of Israel. For Solomon, Wisdom is a woman crying at the gates:

> Receive my instruction, and not silver; and knowledge rather than choice gold. For wisdom is better than rubies; and all the things that may be desired are not to be compared to it.

Solomon says: "He that keepeth his mouth keepeth his life: but he that openeth wide his lips shall have destruction." He then says, "A fool's mouth is his destruction, and his lips are the snare of his soul."[3]

SILENCE

Wisdom repeats and rephrases. Ahiqar the Assyrian said, "Keep watch over your mouth, lest it bring you to grief." Pythagoras made his pupils keep silence for five years. Lao Tzu taught, "One who knows does not speak, one who speaks does not know." A Japanese proverb runs, "The silent man is the best to listen to." Saint James bade, "Let every man be swift to hear, slow to speak." Sextus, the bishop of Rome, wrote, "With silence, the wise man honors God." Abba Poemen said, "If you are silent, you will have peace wherever you live." Gracián thought that "cautious silence is the holy of holies of worldly wisdom." Lavater believed, "He knows not how to speak who cannot be silent."[4]

Silence, the pause in the pulse of quotation, proxies the unspeakable. Samuel Beckett effed, "What we know partakes in no small measure of the nature of what has so happily been called the unutterable or ineffable, so that any attempt to utter or eff it is doomed to fail, doomed, doomed to fail."[5]

Amy Tan's mother told her, "Fang pi bu-cho, cho pi bu-fang," "which is commonly uttered by Chinese parents, and which translates approximately to: 'There's more power in silence.' . . . The strict linguist might want to note that the literal translation of that Chinese phrase runs along these noble lines: 'Loud farts don't smell, the really smelly ones are silent.' . . . My mother's saying is a good quotation. You should use it often."[6]

Round the world and down the ages the Wise advise: do not speak, and if you must speak, say little. If that were all the wise advised, you could stop here and now. But no: there is more. Wisdom repeats. Wisdom contradicts.

"Silence speaks volumes" is proverbial. Still, silence says nothing clearly.

SPEAK FOR YOURSELF

Marie de France professed:

> Whoever God has given knowledge
> and eloquence in speaking,
> should not be silent and secretive,
> but should willingly show it.[7]

"The essence of a person is speech," says the Chāndogya Upanishad. Ben Jonson declared, "Speech is the only benefit man hath to express his excellency of mind above other creatures."[8] Indeed, man hath more speech than he can comprehend. He hath need of guides and lists, digests, abstracts, indexes, histories, dictionaries, and translations, thousands of translations.

THE WISDOM OF THE EAST

When England was still west of most of the world, William Caxton printed a book of quotations, the first book printed in English to bear a publication date (November 18, 1477). It was *The Dictes and Sayings of the Philosophers*, a translation of the *Dits moraulx* of Guillaume de Tignonville. The *Dits* were translated from the *Liber philosophorum moralium antiquorum* (late thirteenth century), a Latin translation of the Spanish *Bocados de oro* (early thirteenth century), itself a translation of the Arabic *Muḥtār al-ḥikam wa-moḥāsin al-kalim* (Choicest Maxims and Best Sayings) collected by Abū'l-Wafā al-Mubaššir bin Fātik (ca. 1053). Tignonville abridged the Latin text (numerous books based on his *Dits* made further subtractions), and what remained came into English as *The Dictes and Sayings of the Philosophers*, a translation of a translation of a translation of a translation of an Arabic book relaying sayings of the Greeks.[9]

In the *Dictes* Socrates is said to have said, "There is less profit in him that holds his peace than is in him who speaks well."[10]

REFLECTIONS

"Speech is the mirror of action," said Solon. Dionysius of Halicarnassus approved the "general opinion that a man's words are the images of his mind." "Oratio speculum mentis" (Speech is the mirror of the mind) was a Latin proverb translated into the languages of Europe and with parallels everywhere.

Erasmus wrote, "Qualis vir, talis oratio" (As the man is, so is his talk), quoting Seneca quoting a Greek proverb. "The way a man speaks proclaims his soul," says the *Mahābhārata*. "The expression of a man's thoughts reveals his character," says Ecclesiasticus. Ibn 'Aṭā'illāh taught, "Every utterance that comes forth does so with the vestment of the heart from which it emerged."[11]

YES, BUT . . .

Ibn 'Aṭā'illāh also taught, "Infer the existence of ignorance in anyone whom you see answering all that he is asked or giving expression to all that he witnesses or mentioning all that he knows." Plutarch thought, "Timely silence is a wise thing, and better than any speech." "Good as is discourse," wrote Emerson, "silence is better, and shames it."[12]

Pascal advised, "Do you wish people to believe good of you? Don't speak." Lincoln is said to have said, "Better to remain silent and be thought a fool than to speak out and remove all doubt." George Eliot beatified: "Blessed is the man who, having nothing to say, abstains from giving wordy evidence of the fact."[13]

"God's poet is silence," wrote Joaquin Miller, poet of the Sierras.[14]

What then: silence or saying? Say what you want without saying it yourself: quote. Very useful, this, sometimes lovely, and versatile, too: big thoughts in small pieces, neatly wrapped and bundled in bulk, in different flavors for different tastes.

GNOMOLOGIES

In streets, courts, and temples smart sentences for making a living and staying out of trouble were gathered as precepts for impressionable youth. Hundreds of quotations were drilled into them in expectation that quotations would improve their grammar and guide their lives.

In his *Rhetoric* Aristotle told his readers to teach gnomologies, the sayings of the wise. Here are two of his: "No sensible man should have his children taught to be too clever" and "There is no man who is happy in everything."[15] Gnomologies have been collected, passed down, and pillaged like legacies. A good gnome does double duty: it moralizes and it's easy to remember; gnomologies moralize seriatim. *The Dictes and Sayings of the Philosophers* is a gnomology.

SENTENTIAE

The *Rhetorica ad herennium* (first century BC) defined a sententia as "a saying drawn from life, which shows concisely either what happens or ought to happen in life, for example, 'Every beginning is difficult.'"[16] Quintilian taught that "the oldest type of *sententia*, and that in which the term is most correctly applied, is the aphorism, called *gnóme* by the Greeks." He gives an example from Domitius Afer: "Princeps, qui vult omnia scire, necesse habet multa ignoscere" (The prince who would know all, must ignore much).[17]

Greek and Arabic gnomologies gathered aphorisms for study and emulation. Roman youths were taught to speak, write, and behave by memorizing sententiae. They were expected to quote them in public speaking and legal argument. Porcius Latro memorized a *sententiarum supellectilem* — a "stock" of sententiae — on fortune, cruelty, riches, and so on for use in public.[18]

Worried about his wife's chastity while he was away, Porphyry copied a hundred sayings of Epicurus and Pythagoras to chastise her. For the eternal salvation of noble Avita, Rufinus translated the *Sentences of Sextus*. Because of her we have them now. Sextus wrote, "The greatest wisdom is to know how to endure the stupidity of the ignorant."[19]

In a collection that would be widely used to teach Latin to Europe, Dionysius Cato (fourth century) reduced the sententiae for going along and getting ahead to 154 distichs and 57 monostichs, each a brief *do* or *don't: Mundus esto. Libros lege. Vino tempera.* Keep clean, read books, don't drink too much.[20] Cato wrote:

> Virtutem primam esse puto compescere linguam:
> Proximus ille deo est, qui scit ratione tacere.
> [The primary virtue is: hold your tongue;
> who knows how to keep quiet is close to God.]

That again. Quotations quell quotations: *shanti, siópa, tace,* hush. Simeon, son of Rabban Gamaliel, said, "All my days have I grown up among the Sages and I have found naught better for a man than silence."[21]

That chatter persists will not surprise the Wise, who advise the talkative, too: tell the truth, be clear, be brief, be cheerful, and by all means know what you're talking about. In an Arabic gnomology Socrates is said to have said, "If he who does not know kept silent, discord would cease."[22]

The Wise supply quotations to revive, take heart, buck up, and move on. For anyone unable or unwilling to learn that little, there is nothing left to say.

PROVERB, COUNTERPROVERB

Sir Francis Bacon wrote, "It is generally to be found in the wisdom of the ancients, that as men found out any observation which they thought good for life, they would gather it and express it in some short proverb, parable, or fable."[23] Bergen Evans added, "To every proverb there seems to be an anti-proverb." Stanislaw Lec explained, "Proverbs contradict each other. That is the wisdom of a nation."[24]

In consecutive lines proverbs of Solomon say, "Answer not a fool according to his folly, lest thou also be like unto him" and "Answer a fool according to his folly, lest he be wise in his own conceit." Ecclesiastes, long attributed to Solomon, pairs proverbs, pro and con: "Wisdom is better than strength: nevertheless the poor's man wisdom is despised, and his words are not heard" and "Wisdom is better than weapons of war: but one sinner destroyeth much good."[25] Quoting the Babylonian Talmud — "Solomon, is it not enough for you that your words contradict those of your father? They also contradict themselves" — Maimonides wrote his *Guide of the Perplexed* (late twelfth century) to get as close to God as words would let him.[26]

Aristotle, Clearchus, and Chrysippus gathered proverbs. Redactors plucked Plutarch's proverbial plums. Zenobius, a second-century Sophist, condensed the thirteen books of proverbs collected by Didymus of Alexandria and Lucillus Tarrhaeus into a collection of 552 proverbs. Diogenianus of Heraclea collected 776. They have about 300 proverbs in common. Tradition could choose Zenobius, who names names, or Diogenianus, who doesn't. Tradition chose both. Their collections were copied and recopied through the darkest of dark ages.[27] They relayed the form and much of the matter of Erasmus's *Adages*.

GREATER THAN GOLD

Wisdom says, "I love them that love me; and those that seek me early shall find me. Riches and honour are with me; yea, durable riches and righteousness. My fruit is better than gold, and my revenue than choice silver."[28]

Quotation collections clutch that metaphor: a treasure greater than jewels, silver, or gold. Collections call themselves treasuries, Latin *thesauri* and Sanskrit *ratnakoshās*. Quoting Hafiz, John Watson compared

his *Poetical Quotations* (1847) to "orient pearls at random strung." Sarah
Josepha Hale thought her *Complete Dictionary of Poetical Quotations*
(1849) was "a precious casket, where the most perfect gems of Genius"
were set. Anna Ward advertised her *Dictionary of Quotations in Prose*
(1889) as a "treasury of lofty thoughts."[29] Charles Wallis titled his quotation collection *The Treasure Chest* (1965).

Shining bright or enclosed in caskets, wisdom is as small and durable
as diamonds. Like diamonds, it can be hidden or handed down.

CHRISTIAN COLLECTIONS

Saint Augustine believed the Bible was boundless and eternal, instruct-
ing "everything useful."[30] Boundless and eternal, its contents are made
more accessible by concordances, indexes, and guides. To answer how
the Bible replies to life's hard questions, scholars gathered Bible quotations topically, with gradually greater sophistication.

In his *Sic et non* (Yes and No, ca. 1130), Peter Abelard gathered 158
questions that disturbed Christian churches: Is God the cause of evil?
Is it possible to resist God? Is it ever permissible to lie? Abelard gave
quotations from Scripture and church patriarchs on both sides of each
question.[31] In his prologue Abelard proposed that contradictions were only
apparent, and in gathering them he intended only to make it possible to
study and reconcile them. Even saints could err, he added, even Augustine
published retractions.[32] So too Abelard admitted he might err.

Like every great quotation collection, *Sic et non* includes quooxes.
Marcia L. Colish says, "Examples of passages where Abelard fails to
take into account the theological perspectives informing the views of
authorities he cites, or where he misapplies them, could easily be multiplied."[33] Even so, it is a great book, still read, still admired.

The anonymous *Sententiae divinitatis* (mid-twelfth century), the *De
sacramentis fidei christianae* of Hugh of Saint Victor (1137), the anonymous
Summa sententiarum (mid-twelfth century), the *Sententiae* of Robert
Pullen (1142–44), and the *Sententiae* of Robert of Melun (1150–60)
refined the practice of gathering quotations under theological headings,

with commentaries and reflections. These collections culminated in the *Sententiae* of Peter Lombard (1155–57), the brilliant bishop of Paris.

Lombard organized his collection in four books — God and the Trinity, the Creation and the Fall, the incarnate Christ, and the sacraments and the apocalypse — with unprecedented command of the tradition. His book "is based more thoroughly on his own independent reading of his sources, whom he cites more fully and accurately and whom he considers more thoroughly and analytically than anyone else."[34] His book was internationally influential (Aquinas, Bonaventure, Peter Auriol, Duns Scotus, and William of Ockham wrote commentaries on it) and became a touchstone for later Scholastics whose prestige largely depended upon the accuracy of their quotations and the precision of their citations.

Plagiarism was common.[35]

FLORILEGIA

Florilegia, or "books of flowers," are quotation miscellanies. The *Liber scintillarum* of Defensor of Ligugé (seventh century), the *Communiloquium* of John of Wales (between 1270 and 1285), and the anonymous and various *Proverbia philosophorum* and *Sententie philosophorum* (who knows when) are quotation collections that seeded the field. New forms for organizing quotations emerged.

Quotations in the *Liber scintillarum* (once attributed to the Venerable Bede) are organized by topics, most of them ethical. Quotations within topics follow a rough hierarchy, with the Gospels quoted first, then other New Testament books, then other books of the Bible, then Augustine, Ambrose, Gregory, and other church fathers. Its topics — sins, virtues, silence, and wisdom — suggest it is a book for monasteries.

Two of the most honored florilegia are the *Florilegium* of Stobaeus (fifth century) and the *Bibliotheca* of Photius (ninth century).[36] Stobaeus's *Florilegium* was prepared for the education of his son and became a key source for later scholars; Photius commended it, Scaliger helped publish it, and Hugo Grotius wrote gratefully, "Whenever I have marveled at the various fragments which survive in the work of Stobaeus, I have, in my affection for the art of poetry, always taken a singular delight in the remains of the poets that we possess, preserved by his good work."[37]

Stobaeus organized his quotations in paired antitypes: aletheias (truth) is followed by pseudous (lying); parresias (frankness) by kolakeias (flattery); asotias (waste) by pheidolias (thrift); and so on. His topics include navigation, the fine arts, masters and servants, and voluptuous love.

Photius, the patriarch of Constantinople, compiled his *Bibliotheca* for his brother, gathering "unique excerpts from 280 subsequently lost Greek works."[38] He gathered his quotations under the names of authors, an organizational method used in most gnomologies and adopted by Bartlett a millennium later.

Two florilegia from Clairvaux, the *Flores paradysi* and the *Liber exceptionum*, were developed in the first half of the thirteenth century for monastic use. They were the major sources for an especially popular florilegium, Thomas of Ireland's *Manipulus florum* (Bouquet of Flowers) of 1306, "a key to some of the most quotable words of the orthodox authors."[39] It contains 6,000 extracts arranged under 266 topic headings. Thomas of Ireland took another important step: he arranged his topics in alphabetical order. The selection draws heavily on Lombard's *Sentences* and on Augustine (whose quotations fill half its pages), Aquinas, and Seneca the Younger. Later scholars were dependent on it; some never got past it.

Florilegia bear relics of the lost. Stobaeus's *Florilegium* includes fragments of otherwise unknown works by Aeschylus, Sophocles, Euripides, and Plutarch. Stobaeus saved a quotation from Epictetus otherwise unknown: "Under all circumstances take thought of nothing so much as safety; for it is safer to keep silence than to speak."[40]

CONTRA COLLECTIONS

Collections are not always praised. They are blamed for displacing complete works. A. D. Knox indicted Stobaeus: "It is an odd coincidence that that collection which destroyed the necessity of independent reading, coincided with the total decay of Greek prose. . . . Proverbs, allusions, quotations, tricks of phrase become canonized."[41] Great works were reduced to pieces and patches, scraps and quooxes, and were misunderstood and vulgarized.

The Rouses assumed that "works such as the *Manipulus florum* were responsible for a deterioration in vitality and originality, since they were used as substitutes for the whole works, and since they were usually applied mechanically. It is on these grounds that Petrarch castigated an opponent for making use of the *Manipulus* . . . 'which the frivolous French regard as the equivalent of all books.'"[42]

FLORILEGIA, II

The anonymous author of the *Flores paradysi* "offers grace to readers, as if it were filled with the finest flowers of Paradise . . . which, like the flowers of Paradise, never alter, but rather alter their admirers for the better."[43]

Later florilegia drew on the Bible, church fathers, secular literature, national history, and each other. Richard and Mary Rouse concluded that the customary sources for florilegia "are earlier *florilegia*, and their most frequent literary heirs, subsequent *florilegia*. One also has to consider the possibility of fraud. We have previously examined a large family of *florilegia*, the *Lumen anime* texts, which treated citations of source rather like items of decoration, names to be inserted where they appear to best effect, without regard for reality. . . . No citations of source may ever be accepted at face value, without verification and, especially, without a search for an intermediate source."[44]

For instance, the *Floresta española* of Melchior de Santa Cruz (1574) collects anecdotes and snatches of dialogue to show off the wit and wisdom of the Spanish court and church. The *Floresta* shows that noble Spaniards knew how to quote.[45] It borrowed from Erasmus, Castiglione, Guicciardini, and other quotees, their names eclipsed by those who quoted them. The Spanish queen is said to have said that "el que tenía buen gesto llevaba carta de recomendación" (he who has a kind face carries a letter of recommendation), a sentiment expressed by Aristotle.[46]

The floral metaphor thrives. William S. Walsh recommended his *Prose and Poetical Quotations* (1908) "as a variegated bouquet." H. G. J. Adams offered his *Cyclopedia of Poetical Quotations* (1865) as a "collection of choice flowers, culled from the gardens of poesy," and Henry Southgate's *Many Thoughts of Many Minds* (1858) is a bouquet of "flowers of intellect." The prize for floridity goes to the 1st edition of Charles Douglas's *Forty Thousand Quotations* (1904), titled *Forty Thousand Sublime and Beautiful Thoughts Gathered from the Roses, Clover Blossoms, Geraniums, Violets, Morning-Glories and Pansies of Literature.*[47]

HONEYBEES

Poor is the soul who has few proverbs. Solomon went on for nearly nine hundred verses. Ecclesiastes added two hundred more, including "Be not righteous over much; neither make thyself over wise" and "Let your words be few." Wisdom in Ecclesiasticus is again a woman, who says:

Come to me, all who desire me
And eat your fill of my fruit.
To think of me is sweeter than honey,
To possess me sweeter than the honeycomb.
Whoever feeds on me will hunger for more.

Seneca told Lucilius, "We should follow, men say, the example of the bees, who flit about and cull the flowers that are suitable for producing honey, and then arrange and assort in their cells all that they have brought in."[48] Tryon Edwards defended authors who quote copiously by asking "whether honey is the worse for being gathered from many flowers." The Reverend Stewart Salmond said of the quotations collected in the *Exposition of the Orthodox Faith* of John of Damascus that "he culled on every hand the flower of their opinions, and concocted most sweet honey of soundest doctrine."[49]

Silence is golden, but speech is sweet, and wisdom is best enjoyed with friends, food, and drink.

TABLE TALK

Plutarch recalled that "the early Pythagoreans considered silence a god-like thing, since even the gods reveal their wishes, to those who can understand them, by acts and deeds without speech." He says so in his *Symposiakon biblia*, or, as it comes to us, his "Table Talk."[50] The nine books of the *Symposiakon* are typical of the form: dialogues of friends with cups never empty, at their leisure and free to speak. Their table talk talks about travel, history, literature, philosophy, and the mysteries of God.

Well-lubricated table talk has been a source of memorable quotations since Plato's *Symposium*. The *Symposium* of Xenophon, Plutarch's "Seven Sages," Athenaeus's *Deipnosophists* (wise men at dinner), Lucian's parodic *Symposium*, and Petronius's account of Trimalchio's feast fed centuries.

The *Saturnalia* of Macrobius (early fifth century) is a quotation collection composed as dinner and breakfast conversations of a dozen learned men. In its preface Macrobius tells his son that he created the book as "a literary storehouse," "a repository of much to teach you and to guide you." "Things worth remembering have not been heaped together in confusion, but a variety of subjects of different authorship and divers dates have been arranged to form, so to speak, a body, in such a way that the notes which I had made without any plan or order, as aids to memory, came together like the parts of a coherent whole." Citing Seneca, Macrobius says his book is like honey.[51]

The twelve converse about Virgil and compare him to Homer. Their quotations show how well each speaker knew the poets and how well the poets knew the world. Virgil's quotations illuminate history, Latin, geography, and religion. Macrobius quotes prior Virgil scholars; a guest quotes the *Sententiae* of Publilius Syrus; another quotes the *Problemata* of Aristotle.[52] Quotations praise the food and wine.

Most of book 6 discusses Virgil's debts to earlier poets, his borrowed ideas, phrases, whole lines, metaphors, and single words. Macrobius devoted page after page to examples that test the borders between allusion, imitation, accidental resemblance, common usage, and theft. "I could give you a number of examples to show how widespread has been this practice of mutual pilfering among the authors of our old literature," he says, then promptly forgives Virgil, proposing that Virgil's predecessors owe him thanks, "since by transferring something of theirs to his own immortal work he has ensured that the memory of these old writers — whom, as the tastes of today show, we are already beginning to deride as well as to neglect — should not wholly perish."[53]

The table talk of Macrobius relays fabulous stories and the words of the wise. Novelists and film directors use dinner tables, taverns, and party scenes to oppose ideas and perceptions, amicably in Oliver Wendell Holmes's *Autocrat of the Breakfast-Table* (1858) — "He must be a poor creature who does not repeat himself" — and bibulously in Rabelais — "I love you with all my liver."[54] As the proverb says, "In vino veritas."[55]

Devoted students and close friends transcribed the mealtime conversation of people they admired. More than twenty men collected the comments and opinions Martin Luther expressed over beer and bread, collections eventually gathered as Luther's *Tischreden* (*Colloquia Mensalia*, or *Table Talk*). To Luther's table we trace a remark many times repeated: "For where God built a church, there the Devil would also build a chapel."[56]

Because his *Table Talk* captures Luther at ease and off guard, it is valued as a portrait of the man himself. Because it is entirely composed of transcribed quotations and quotations from memory, and because comments ascribed to Luther strike some as superstitious or lewd (Luther had doubts about parts of the Bible, he farted at the devil to make him go away, he got himself drunk to prepare a sermon on Noah), its authority has been questioned, and its quotations have been culled.[57] For his edition, John Aurifaber (1566) took the quotations he liked and arranged them under topics. William Hazlitt's English translation (1848) took over a bare quarter of Aurifaber's edition but kept a topical order: "Of God's Word," "Of God's Works," "On the Nature of the World," and so on. Bits of Luther obscure Luther.

Samuel Taylor Coleridge called Luther's *Table Talk* his "*Bosom* book," "next to the Scriptures my main book of meditation, deep, seminative, Pauline."[58] Coleridge could read Luther in German and expected others to take his word for it. He adapted a section from it as an aphorism in his *Aids to Reflection*.[59]

Coleridge himself was a legendary talker. "He would talk from morn to dewy Eve," Charles Lamb reported, "nor cease till far midnight: yet who ever would interrupt him."[60] His nephew, John Taylor Coleridge, caught some of his talk in 1811 and 1823 but admitted, "He astonishes you, he electrifies you almost as he goes on, but you cannot remember the train afterward, nor much of the separate members."[61] John's transcriptions of Coleridge's table talk record only four occasions. Another nephew, Henry Nelson Coleridge, was more determined and successful, recording specimens from 1822 to 1834. Here is a sample of Coleridge's talk or, rather, Henry Coleridge's stenography:

> Burke was a great and universal talker — yet now we hear nothing of this except by some chance remarks in Boswell. The fact was, Burke, like all men of Genius who love to talk at all, was very discursive and continuous — hence he is not reported; for he seldom said the sharp short things that Johnson almost always did.[62]

In *The Friend* (1818) Coleridge commended Samuel Johnson's *Dictionary* for its quotations: they made it "popular even as a reading book."[63]

Johnson's *Dictionary* is built upon quotations, mostly Shakespeare. ("Example is always more efficacious than precept," Johnson says in *Rasselas*.) James Boswell caught Johnson's quick wit in his tavern and table talk. Robert Orme, the historian of India, told Boswell, "I do not care on what subject Johnson talks; but I love better to hear him talk than any body. He either gives you new thoughts, or a new colouring." The Reverend Dr. Maxwell lamented, "What pity it is, that so much wit and good sense as he continually exhibited in conversation, should perish unrecorded!" Johnson told Boswell, "The worst thing you can do to an author is to be silent as to his works."[64] So Boswell quoted him as best he could, though at times he "was so wrapt in admiration of his exceptional colloquial talents" that he found it hard "to recollect and record his conversation with its genuine vigour and vivacity."[65] Following Johnson from tavern to club and private dinners, Boswell did what he could. In ODQ 7th, 144 of the 241 Johnson quotations come from Boswell's *Life*; four of the six pages of Johnson in BFQ 17th come from it.

According to Emerson, "the best" of the table talk collections are Saadi's *Gulistan*, Luther's *Table Talk*, Aubrey's *Lives*, Spence's *Anecdotes*, Selden's *Table Talk*, Boswell's *Life of Johnson*, Eckermann's *Conversations with Goethe*, Coleridge's *Table Talk*, and Hazlitt's *Life of Northcote*.[66] Alexander Dyce collected the *Table Talk* (1856) of Samuel Rogers, the banker and art collector who ruled London literary circles for half a century. Ernest Hemingway's *A Moveable Feast* (1964; revised ed., 2009) recalls the banter and fusillades of Ezra Pound, F. Scott Fitzgerald, Gertrude Stein, and others.

In time "table talk" shed its origins, losing any pretense of capturing conversation. The *Table Talk* volumes of Leigh Hunt, William Hazlitt, and A. Bronson Alcott are essay collections. Other collections, like William O. Stoddard's *Table Talk of Abraham Lincoln* (1894) and Alan Ansen's *Table Talk of W. H. Auden* (1990), are ana: anecdotes and scraps of conversation picked up and written down any which way.

COMMONPLACE BOOKS

The *Attic Nights* of Aulus Gellius (second century) is a miscellany of notes on history, grammar, law, literature, and whatever else caught his fancy. As such it is an early example of a commonplace book, a notebook in which people transcribed memorable bits of conversation and copied out favorite passages from their reading. According to Earle Havens, commonplace books constitute "the foundation of the early production of standard works of reference that are taken for granted in the present century."[67] Some are extraordinary.

In the late light of the Roman Empire the *Meditations* of Marcus Aurelius quoted Homer, Hesiod, Euripides, Plato, Epictetus, and others. At the dawn of the Renaissance Petrarch's *Rerum memorandarum libri* (1343–45) recorded his reading. Immediately useful to others, the

Rerum was quickly copied and dispersed throughout western Europe. Printed editions appeared as early as 1496 in Basel and 1501 in Venice. A German translation was published in Augsburg in 1541.

With the *Rerum* a host of quotations from Latin writers (and Latin translations of Greek writers) was made available in condensed and convenient form, endorsed by Petrarch's reputation. For easy use, Petrarch arranged his quotations and commentaries under topical headings: "Leisure and Solitude," "Memory," "Invention and Eloquence," "Providence and Divination," "Oracles."[68]

ADAGES

Like a golden river the writings of Greece and Rome flowed into the works of Desiderius Erasmus (1469?–1536). He read tirelessly, wrote in Latin exhaustively, and devoted his life to the publication of books that would advance education and strengthen faith. Erasmus filled his books with quotations to show how to speak, write, think, interpret,

1. Desiderius Erasmus (ca. 1466–1536), portrait by Hans Holbein, 1523.

and behave. In his *Parabolae* (1514) he published a set of quotations from Aristotle, Pliny the Elder, Plutarch, and Seneca, "many jewels in one small book," he called it.[69] For his *Apophthegmata* (1531) Erasmus drew heavily from Plutarch to gather the wise and witty sayings of great Greeks and Romans. A guide for princes, a diversion for kings, the *Apophthegmata* was Erasmus's array of the very best quotations of the very best quotees. The best of the best came first: Socrates, Aristippus the wit, and Diogenes the cynic.

In 1500 Erasmus published his first collection of *Adages*, "proverbial sayings drawn from Latin authors of antiquity and elucidated for those who aspired to write an elegant Latin style."[70] A sample:

> *Laconismus.* Laconic. A quasi-proverbial epithet for the use of few words, either because the Spartans in Laconia excelled in deeds rather than words or because pithy aphorisms were a Spartan specialty. But the particular appeal of such aphorisms is that they should contain a great quantity of meaning in the fewest possible words.[71]

Erasmus stocked the *Adages* with proverbs, anecdotes, fables, epic exemplars, and learned asides. The *Adages* set several precedents for later compendia:

1. Prior collections are ransacked. Erasmus plucked quotations from the collections of Apostolius, Arsenius, Diogenianus, Plutarch, Pollux, the *Suda*, and Zenobius.
2. Borrowings from those collections are not always acknowledged.
3. Quotations from different centuries are compared.
4. He quotes himself.
5. As edition followed edition, the collection grew. The 1st edition had 818 adages; by the time he died in 1536, Erasmus had 4,151.

Erasmus refrained from citing adages from the Bible. When he did, he was exceedingly careful, as in "Culicem colant" (Straining at a gnat). He gave his reasons:

> It did not seem proper to me to include a large number of these expressions, partly because to people excessively devoted to poetry

anything that smacks of sacred scriptures seems unattractive; partly because I believe they are clear enough to anyone; but mostly because I am afraid that some pious individual might consider that I insult holy scripture if I mingle them in this work where there are not only pagan expressions, but even some not very decent ones.[72]

Erasmus was nothing if not careful.

The *Adages* was a reservoir in which great writers fished: Shakespeare, Bacon, Rabelais, Montaigne, and Burton returned to it often. Though Montaigne reviled authors "who scatter whole passages from ancient writers throughout their own worthless works," he quoted the *Adages* with this excuse: "I only quote others the better to quote myself."[73] Shakespeare, the most quoted quotee in English, helped himself to the *Adages*. Quotations from it appear in *Cymbeline*, *King John*, *Two Gentlemen of Verona*, and *Romeo and Juliet*.[74]

Sir Francis Bacon, the first great quoter in English, quoted the *Adages*, but he could read classics himself and make his own collections. In his *Advancement of Learning* (1605) Bacon recommended the practice of collecting quotations to King James as "of great use and essence in studying."[75]

Mrs. Henry Pott edited and annotated one of Bacon's commonplace books, his *Promus* (Storeroom), written between 1594 and 1596. Mrs. Pott wished to prove that Bacon was the author of Shakespeare's plays, with arguments inventive, industrious, and hopeful. No matter how dubious her motive and conclusions, she performed a valuable service: she tracked down Bacon's sources, noted when his quotations departed from standard texts, and published all 1,655 entries. She made it easy to see how closely Bacon read the *Adages*, Heywood's *Proverbs*, the Bible, and the wisdom literature of Europe.

Intrigued by what the *Promus* tells us about Bacon (you are what you quote), James Spedding examined its fifty handwritten sheets and described them "as an illustration of Bacon's manner of working. There is not much in it of his own. The collection is from books which were then in every scholar's hands. . . . My conjecture is, that most of these selected expressions were connected in his mind by some association, more or less fanciful, with certain trains of thought, and stood as mottoes (so to speak) to little chapters of meditation."[76]

This makes good sense. For example, *Promus* entry 228 quotes Proverbs 12:23: "Prudens celat scientiam, stultus proclamat stultitiam" (The prudent man concealeth knowledge; but the fool proclaimeth his folly). The next forty entries, filling a folio, deal with speech, lies, testimony, and trust, matters the Wise mull always. Entry 1148 reads, "Upon question whether a man should speak or forbear speech"; it is followed by six quotations from the Vulgate that address that very point.[77]

Dedicated readers with broad interests face the problem of how best to copy quotations and how to find them again. In his *De Copia* (1512) Erasmus recommended a system for collecting commonplaces. To teach others his own index scheme, John Locke published *A New Method of Making Common-Place Books* in 1686.

A commonplace book presumably assists its maker to improve both writing and conversation. Lord Chesterfield advised his son, "Keep a useful and short commonplace book of what you read, to help your memory only, and not for pedantic quotations."[78] Jonathan Swift explained:

> A common-place book is what a provident poet cannot subsist without, for this proverbial reason, that "great wits have short memories"; and whereas, on the other hand, poets being liars by profession, ought to have good memories. To reconcile these, a book of this sort is in the nature of a supplemental memory; or a record of what occurs remarkable in every day's reading or conversation. There you enter not only your own original thoughts, (which, a hundred to one, are few and insignificant) but such of other men as you think fit to make your own by entering them there. For take this as a rule, when an author is in your books, you have the same demand upon him for his wit, as a merchant has for your money.[79]

Swift grumbled that he had gathered 738 quotations but after five years had been able to force no more than a dozen into conversation.[80]

LACONICS

Laconics, says Charles Simmons, must be truthful and profound, luminous and pungent, "pearls and diamonds, which will enrapture the world."[81] In 1701 Thomas Brown anonymously published his *Laconics: Or, New Maxims of State and Conversation Relating to the Affairs and Manners of the Present Times*, setting an example that would be widely imitated. It claimed among its ancestors "the *Perroniana*, the *Thuana*, the *Scaligeriana*, the *Sorberiana*, the *Valesiana*, the *Menagiana*, etc. containing the Observations and Sayings of several great Men, whose names they bear."[82] Such ana attributed their quotable contents to their protagonists; Brown wrote his own. He had other models, too, French collections of original wit.

Never meant to be merely read, the *Maximes* of La Rochefoucauld (1665) and *Les caractères* of La Bruyère (1688) were composed to be quoted. Seventeenth-century France produced a series of notable quotable *Pensées* by Pierre Nicole, Pierre Bayle, Adrien de Montluc, prince de Chabanais, comte de Cramail, and, most famously, Pascal's *Pensées* (1657), which says: "All good maxims are in the world. We only need to apply them."[83] In 1779, to keep Boswell from interrupting him, Johnson gave him a copy of Pascal's *Pensées*. Boswell preserved it with reverence.[84]

The Wise are counted Wise because we quote them. O fond dream, to consort with the Wise and be one of them! Laconics show the way. The Reverend rascal Charles Caleb Colton enjoyed celebrity as the author of *Lacon: or, Many Things in a Few Words* (1820), a mix of classical quotations, pious thoughts, and pithy new *pensées*. *Lacon* was pitched "to those who think" and to witlings who think they do.

Colton staked his fame on economy. "That writer does the most, who gives his reader the *most* knowledge, and takes from him the *least* time."[85] He scatters quotes from his reading with his own phrases framed for quoting: "When you have nothing to say, say nothing"; "The greatest fool may ask more than the wisest man can answer"; "Man is an embodied paradox, a bundle of contradictions."[86] His book was a huge success, running into many editions and encouraging a train of imitators:

Alexander Anderson's *Laconics* (1827), John Timbs's *Laconics* (1827), John Taylor's *The Pocket Lacon* (1837; republished in 1841 as *The Manual of Laconics*), and Ben Cassedy's *Poetic Lacon* (1839).

For his antislavery *Laconic Manual* (1852) Charles Simmons arranged his laconics topically, in alphabetical order. Soon came Tryon Edwards's *World's Laconics* (1853, under the pseudonym Everard Berkeley; reprinted as *Pearls* in 1872), then J. F. Boyes's *Lacon in Council* (1865), William Tegg's *Laconics* (1875), John Otts's *Laconisms* (1888), and Hanford Lennox Gordan's *Laconics* (1910). Bending to the trend, C. G. Henderson compiled a *Shakespeare Laconics* (1853), and Henry Llewellyn Williams gathered a couple hundred of Abraham Lincoln's aphorisms and apophthegms as *Lincolnics* (1906).

ENGLISH PROVERBS

Quotation lovers love rare words. Savor, then, *paraemiography*, the collection and interpretation of proverbs, begun by Solomon, Zenobius, Confucius, and like-minded souls. Isaac Disraeli presumed, "Undoubtedly proverbs in the earliest ages long served as the unwritten language of morality, and even of the useful arts." He cited as examples Hesiod, "the sublime speech of Odin" in the *Edda*, and Solomon.[87]

John Heywood (1497?–1580?) entertained Henry VIII and Mary Tudor with verse and witty plays. In 1549 he published his *Dialogue Conteynyng the number of the effectuall proverbes in the Englishe tounge*, the first such collection known.[88] It is a masterpiece, well worth a little struggle with old spellings. Modern proverb collections are all about quantity, sources, and indexing. Heywood had other ideas. His *Dialogue* is a love story, with two stories within the story, told in rhymed proverbs.[89] What kind of wisdom is this? Full, frank, and contentious, the proverbs everywhere disagree.

Better it be done than wishe it had bene done.
As good undone (quoth I) as doo it to soone.

The *Dialogue* begins when a raw young man asks for the poet's advice: should he marry for love or for money? Heywood describes two marriages, one for love, one for money, in which husbands poke and parry with proverbs, wives match and overmatch them, proverb versus proverb.

> Olde fish and yong flesh (quoth he) dooth men best féede.
> And some say, change of pasture makth fat calves.
> As for that reason (quoth she) ronth to halves.
> As well for the coowe calfe as for the bull.

A wife knows on which side her bread is buttered; a husband knows a rolling stone gathers no moss. A wife asks the poet how to keep her husband's love. Make him a cuckold, he replies.

The poet persuades the young man not to marry at all, not yet, and having done so concludes that enough is enough, and enough is as good as a feast. The success of the *Dialogue* encouraged Heywood to prepare the 2nd edition (1562), to which he added six hundred rhymed epigrams, clever as foxes. Though not as neatly organized and easy to find as those in modern collections, Heywood's proverbs are so many, so choice, and so well versed that they come alive to sting and pinch. He is as modern as Manhattan: "Love me, love my dog."[90]

Proverbs of other nations were imported in packs. In 1578 John Florio, the first English translator of Montaigne, published *His first Fruites*, a miscellany containing an Italian phrase book, essays, poems, and Italian proverbs translated into Elizabethan English. A reader learns "Poche parole bastano fragli homini savy" (Few words suffice among wise men), "Ogni timidita é vitio" (All fearfulness is folly), and "Odi, vedi, e taci, se te vuoi vivere in pace" (Hear, see, and hold thy peace if thou wilt live in peace).[91] *Florios Second Frutes* followed in 1591, a dozen dialogues packed with proverbs and polite phrases in Italian and English. Florio wrote, "The Greekes and Latines thanke Erasmus, and our Englishmen make much of Heywood: for Proverbs are the pith, the proprieties, the proofs, the purities, the elegancies, as the commonest so the commendablest phrases of a language. To use them is a grace, to understand them a good, but to gather them a paine to me, though gaine to thee."[92] Amen to that.

George Herbert (1593–1633) gave a selection of aphorisms to Bishop

Andrews of Winchester "so remarkable for the language, and reason of it, that after the reading it, the Bishop put it into his bosom, and did often shew it to many Scholars, both of this and forreign Nations; but did always return it back to the place where he first lodg'd it, and continu'd it so near his heart, till the last day of his life."[93] We do not know the aphorisms, but we have a clue.

Herbert enjoys posterity because of his Christian poetry and because of a book published posthumously as *Jacula Prudentum*, or *Outlandish Proverbs* (1640).[94] It includes such heirlooms as "Living well is the best revenge" and "When war begins, then hell openeth."[95] The title shows the prudence of his publisher who, in England in 1640, minded his wit. A civil war was afoot, fought on religious lines, and Herbert's aphorisms rang true for the times: "The eye and Religion can beare no jesting."[96]

James Howell's *Παροιμιογραφια: Proverbs or Old Sayed Sawes* followed in 1659, then came John Ray, a pioneering naturalist and fellow of the Royal Society. Ray traveled through Britain collecting plants, birds, fishes, odd words, and proverbs. His collection of English proverbs (1670) won quick popularity and to this day remains the core collection of British proverbs. To him we owe our earliest versions of "Misery loves company" and "If wishes were horses, beggars must ride."[97]

Quoting old quotations got old. In *Polonius* (1852) Edward FitzGerald adapted Seneca the Younger:

> There is in Seneca's 114th Epistle a very remarkable passage about the fashion of speech at Rome in his day, which is unconsciously, but quite substantially, thus translated: "No man in this fashionable London of yours," friend Sauertcig would say, "speaks a plain word to me. Every man feels bound to be something more than plain; to be pungent withal, witty, ornamental. His poor fraction of sense has to be perked up into some epigrammatic shape, that it may prick into me; perhaps (this is the commonest) to be topsy-turvied, left standing on its head, that I may remember it the better. Such grinning insincerity is very sad to the soul of man."[98]

SURVIVAL OF THE SMALLEST

"There is no new thing under the sun," says the Preacher. La Bruyère began his *Characters* confessing, "Everything has been said and one comes too late." Goethe thought, "All truly wise thoughts have been thought already."[99] The vast heritage of thought can be a burden: too much to learn, too much to know, too large to ignore. The compendia approve Jonathan Swift: "Abstracts, Abridgments, and Summaries, &c. have the same Use with Burning-Glasses, to collect the diffus'd Rays of Wit and Learning in Authors, and make them point with Warmth and Quickness upon the Reader's Imagination."[100]

Cunning authors cut to be quoted. Aware that many busy readers would be happy to talk about his novels if they didn't have to read them, Samuel Richardson published extracts in *A Collection of the Moral and Instructive Sentiments, Maxims, Cautions, and Reflexions, Contained in the Histories of Pamela, Clarissa, and Sir Charles Grandison* (1755). Sensing a similar interest in Samuel Johnson's works, an enterprising publisher produced *The Beauties of Johnson: Consisting of Maxims and Observations, Moral, Critical, and Miscellaneous, accurately extracted from the Works of Dr. Samuel Johnson, and arranged in alphabetical order* (1781).[101] It was rapidly reprinted. Alexander Main made the most of George Eliot's lifetime of writing, publishing *Wise, Witty and Tender Sayings in Prose & Verse Selected from the Works of George Eliot* (1875). A long list could be made of similar exploitations.

In *A Tale of a Tub* (1704) Swift mocked the custom and its customers. Writers eager to seem learned can cheat, he said, scavenging quotations with raids on collections. "This will stand as an uncontestable Argument," says Swift, "that our *Modern* Wits are not to reckon upon the Infinity of Matter, for a constant Supply. What remains therefore, but that our last Recourse must be had to large *Indexes*, and little *Compendiums*; *Quotations* must be plentifully gathered, and bookt in Alphabet."[102] Quotographers saw a need and bent their backs to satisfy it.

The great quotation collections gradually grew in girth and prestige. They come from great universities: Bartlett of Harvard, Knowles of

Oxford, Shapiro of Yale. Speaking as they do for hundreds and thousands, compendia speak for their editors through a crowd of quotees, curious, valiant, rowdy, and risqué. The compilers display different tastes, interests, and industry: ten thousand quotations, thirty thousand, forty thousand.

Great quotation collections glean the millennia, distill essences, and battle for bragging rights about who's bigger, who's smarter, who's best. Who-knows-who-said-what has a market, a history, and a hall of fame.

They have been at a great feast of
languages, and stolen all the scraps.
Shakespeare

4

The Great Compendia

The great compendia have been great for a century or longer. There are
many now, and many more have passed away, each with its reason for
entering a crowded field. What can they do for you?

1 They initiate. Charles Noel Douglas felt his *Forty Thousand Quotations* responded to "a universal need . . . felt by the multitude of
busy men and women of to-day, who, while eager to be initiated
into the society of great masters of literature, find it impossible to
devote the time necessary to such studies as would accomplish
that result."[1]

2 They economize, reducing big books and long speeches to a few
select sentences.

3 They improve character, behavior, and the public good. The American News Company's *Book of Familiar Quotations* claimed to give
readers "inducements, frequently irresistible, to extend the scope
of their intellectual faculties, and to exercise them to their own
honor and the benefit of their fellow-men."[2]

4 They are a pleasure to read. A. Norman Jeffares and Martin Gray cheered, "Dictionaries of quotations offer their readers delight in the unexpected: they contain profundities and flippancies; remarks which, once made, become inevitable; truisms which capture collective wisdom, thoughts which survive and indeed gain in strength through the years."[3]

5 They accessorize. John T. Watson felt that "nothing adorns a composition or a speech more than appropriate *quotations*."[4]

6 They uplift. "Gnomic wisdom confers a wonderful sense of superiority."[5]

7 They rescue. Bernard Darwin's introduction to the first edition of the ODQ notes, "Though the great poets may wrangle a little amongst themselves, they do not stand in need of anything the dictionary can do for them. Very different is the case of the small ones, whose whole fame depends upon a single happy line or even a single absurd one. To them exclusion from these pages may mean annihilation."

8 They collect future antiques. Christopher Morley called BFQ a "proxy for Posterity."[6]

9 They correct their precursors, plug gaps, and admit the latest generation of quotable quotees.

In the past century there has been a gradual improvement in identifying sources, in finding reliable translations, in indexing and cross-referencing, and in increasing the number of quotations and quotees.

The great compendia share thousands of quotations. Quotations indexed under "Quotation" in the BFQ, BFQ, CDQ, HBQ, JGDQ, NCPQ, NDQ, ODQ, PDQ, and YBQ have the same core set: a couple from Emerson, smidgens from Alexander Smith and A. Bronson Alcott. All but NDQ and YBQ include a couplet from Edward Young's "Love of Fame":

Some, for renown, on scraps of learning dote,
And think they grow immortal as they quote.[7]

Quotations that appear in all or almost all modern compendia are classics of a kind. All include this from Samuel Johnson: "Classical quotation is the *parole* of literary men all over the world." It is the most quoted quotation on quotation in English.[8]

Though compendia often quote the same quotations, they do not quote alike. Since its 14th edition (1968), Bartlett's *Familiar Quotations* has included Winston Churchill's remark from *A Roving Commission*:

> It is a good thing for an uneducated man to read books of quotations. Bartlett's *Familiar Quotations* is an admirable work, and I studied it intently. The quotations when engraved upon the memory, give you good thoughts. They also make you anxious to read the authors and look for more.

The YBQ generously gives the full quotation, but the CDQ, JGDQ, ODQ, and PDQ cut the endorsement for BFQ. WNW omits the quotation altogether.[9]

Different compendia have different quotees and represent them differently. JGDQ has three quotations from the Koran, YBQ has fifteen, BFQ forty-eight, PDQ fifty-one, ODQ fifty-five, WNW fifty-eight. Only the last has this: "No creature is there crawling on the earth, no bird flying with its wings, but they are nations like unto yourselves."[10]

BFQ has nothing from Jacqueline Kennedy Onassis, ODQ has one quotation, YBQ has two, WNW has seven, and QW eight. Only the last has this: "If you bungle raising your children, I don't think whatever else you do matters very much."[11]

Sir Francis Bacon is delivered in 26 quotations by YBQ, 57 by PDQ, 72 by BFQ, 133 by JGDQ, 133 by ODQ, and 136 by WNW. Only the last has Bacon's advice to King James, "It is not granted to man to love and to be wise," in which Bacon paraphrases Publilius Syrus.[12]

The great compendia misquote and mislead.[13] BFQ 14th greatly increased the number of quotations from Lucretius, including this from *De rerum natura* (6.26–28): "[Epicurus] set forth what is the highest good, towards which we all strive, and pointed out the past, whereby along a narrow track we may strain on towards it in a straight course," citing Cyril Bailey's translation. Bailey in fact translated "viam monstravit" as "pointed out the path" rather than "pointed out the past." BFQ 15th,

16th, and 17th retained the mistranscription. The substitution of "past" for "path" escaped the notice of editor, typesetter, and proofreaders, converting a common metaphor into an Epicurean call for history.

Successive editions of Henry Bohn's *Dictionary of Quotations from the English Poets* had a section on quotations that includes these lines from Matthew Prior's tale "Paulo Purganti and His Wife":

> He ranged his troops and preached up patience,
> Backed his opinions with quotations.[14]

In two lines we have a modernized quotation, a quoox, and a misquotation that blunts Prior's irony and withers his point. The poem describes Doctor Paulo's attempts to evade his wife's ardor. All his learning lets him down.

> GROTIUS might own, that PAULO's Case is
> Harder, than any which He places
> Amongst his BELLI and his PACIS.
>
> He strove, alas! but strove in vain
> By dint of Logic, to maintain
> That all the Sex was born to grieve,
> Down to her Ladyship from EVE.
> He ranged his Tropes and preach'd up Patience,
> Back'd his Opinions with Quotations,
> Divines and Moralists; and run ye on
> Quite through from SENECA to BUNYAN.[15]

"Tropes" to "troops" smashes Prior's play on words, gives Dr. Paulo phantom allies, little lead soldiers, or panicked delusion, and overestimates his strength. His defenses exhausted, he gives up.

WHO'S WHO

The sorry habit of citing authors solely by last name misleads. Consider this endorsement for extractions:

Great books are not in everybody's reach; and though it is better to know them thoroughly than to know them only here and there, yet it is a good work to give a little to those who have neither time nor means to get more. Let every book-worm, when in any fragrant, scarce old tome he discovers a sentence, a story, an illustration, that does his heart good, hasten to give it. — Coleridge

This is all you'd read in old compendia. Who do you suppose is the quotee?[16]

Older compendia cite "Seneca," but which Seneca? If "Fuller," which Fuller? Which "Disraeli"? Current compendia won't make you guess: they give names and dates.

THE PIONEERS

The great compendia arose from collections of all types, florilegia, *Laconics*, and dictionaries of foreign phrases. Most of the great compendia began with an individual collector whose gatherings were augmented by friends and family. Watson's *Poetical Quotations* (1847), Bartlett's *Familiar Quotations* (1855), H. L. Mencken's *New Dictionary of Quotations* (1942), and Franklin Pierce Adams's *Book of Quotations* (1952) originated as private collections. Tryon Edwards's *World's Laconics* (1853) started the same way, eventually growing into the 644-page double-column *Dictionary of Thoughts* (1891). Robert Andrews's *Columbia Dictionary of Quotations* (1993) is the brawnier descendent of his father's *Quotations for Speakers and Writers* (1969). Quotation sprees like Wesley Camp's *Unfamiliar Quotations* (1990) and Robert Byrne's *The 2,548 Best Things Anybody Ever Said* (2003) continue the trend. Adams and Byrne continued another trend, taking every opportunity to mingle with the great. Adams included twenty quotes from himself; Byrne injected thirty-eight of his own sayings, more than by Homer, Goethe, or Shakespeare.

Such enterprises competed against skilled teams. Jehiel Keeler Hoyt and Anna L. Ward pooled resources to publish the 1st edition of *The Cyclopedia of Practical Quotations* (1882). Perhaps because Ward published under her own name *A Dictionary of Poetical Quotations* (1883)

and *A Dictionary of Quotations in Prose* (1889), Hoyt dropped her for the revised edition of the *Cyclopedia* (1896) and credited the expansion of the book to "a large number of talented [and unnamed] ladies."[17] John Bartlett acknowledged the help he received from his friend Rezin A. Wight as early as his 5th edition. He dedicated the 5th, 6th, 7th, and 8th editions to Wight; the 9th, dedicated to Wight's memory, acknowledged him as the "late assistant editor." BFQ 11th (1937) and 12th (1948) were coedited by Christopher Morley and Louella Everett. The 1st edition of *The Oxford Dictionary of Quotations* (1941) was built by the staff of Oxford University Press under the general editorship of Alice Mary Smyth. Fred Shapiro's *Yale Book of Quotations* (2006) employed a dozen research assistants.

All compendia are parts of a perpetual work in progress. Sarah Josepha Hale's *Poetical Quotations* (1849) arose from John Addington's *Poetical Quotations* (1829); Ward's *Dictionary of Poetical Quotations* (1883) is Bohn's *Dictionary of Quotations* (1867) rebuilt. Shapiro adapted a famous quotation: "All quotation dictionaries stand on the shoulders of their predecessors" (see p. 13). Bergen Evans acknowledged that his *Dictionary of Quotations* (1968) was "based, as all such dictionaries are, on its predecessors."[18] Few are as scrupulous as Shapiro and name them.

It makes a long list. Anna Ward supposed the first collection of extracts of English poetry to be John Bodenham's *Belvedére, or, The Garden of the Muses* (1600).[19] It was followed by Robert Allot's *Englands Parnassus* (1600), Josua Poole's *English Parnassus* (1657), Thomas Hayward's *British Muse* (1738), and *A Dictionary of Quotations from the British Poets* (three volumes, 1823–25).[20] Addington's four-volume *Poetical Quotations* vended the genre in the United States. Hale's *Complete Dictionary of Poetical Quotations* was an immediate and lasting success with multiple reprintings up through the 1880s.

In their first incarnations the great compendia favored English verse. Only gradually did English prose prevail.

The Bible excepted, quotations translated from other languages were scarce. For these, readers needed another book. For half a century the English-reading market was dominated by David Evans Macdonnel's

Dictionary of Quotations in Most Frequent Use (1797), which began as a concise 120-page book providing English translations for quotations from Italian, Greek, Spanish, Latin, and French — chiefly Latin and French.[21] Macdonnel organized his quotations alphabetically, from "Ab actu ad posse valet ilatio [*sic*]" (The induction is good, from what has been to what may be) to "Zonam perdidit" (He has lost his purse). His collection directly inspired Hugh Moore's *Dictionary of Quotations* (1831). Moore frankly acknowledged his many borrowings from Macdonnel, followed Macdonnel's alphabetical order, and supplied what Macdonnel sorely lacked: a keyword index.

The watershed for compendia was in the mid-1850s. Four new compendia appeared, one after another. In 1852 *The Book of Familiar Quotations* was published by Whittaker and Company in London. In 1853 the 1st edition of the *Handbook of Familiar Quotations: Chiefly from English Authors* was published in London by John Murray. In 1854 came J. C. Grocott's *Index to Familiar Quotations Selected Principally from British Authors*, published in Liverpool. All three enjoyed multiple editions. In Cambridge, Massachusetts, in 1855 John Bartlett privately published his

2. John Bartlett (1820–1905).

Collection of Familiar Quotations, "a modest little volume of 258 pages, bound in cardboard and the size of a postcard."[22] Bartlett (1820–1905) began as a bookseller and became a brand.

BARTLETT'S FAMILIAR QUOTATIONS

At age sixteen Bartlett took a job in the University Bookstore in Cambridge, Massachusetts. Before he was thirty he owned the store. "'Ask John Bartlett' was the customary advice when any one had difficulty in finding a book or a quotation, and Bartlett was so anxious to deserve his reputation that he began keeping a commonplace-book."[23] That book became Bartlett's *Familiar Quotations,* a success from the start. He sold out his 1st edition of 1,000 copies in three months, quickly published the 2nd edition in 1856, then the 3rd in 1858. In 1863 publication was taken over by Little, Brown and Company in Boston, which has kept it alive ever since, expanding and correcting it. Bartlett himself supervised all editions through the 9th (1891).

Bartlett died in 1905, having lived to see his namesake grow large enough to merit abridgment: Routledge and Sons, Bartlett's British publisher, created the first of these in 1889 with an "author's edition" of 523 pages, created by dropping a few Americans from the 5th edition of 1869. At the turn of the century American publishers reprinted the 1st and 4th editions as pocket-size books with decorative covers.

Bartlett never lacked competitors. New compendia regularly appeared, jostling for market share.

1858   Henry Southgate's *Many Thoughts of Many Minds*
1859   Anonymous, *New Dictionary of Quotations*
1865   H. G. Adams's *Cyclopedia of Poetical Quotations*
1865   J. Hain Friswell's *Familiar Words*
1866   Rev. William Rice's *Moral and Religious Quotations from the Poets*
1867   Henry Bohn's *Dictionary of Quotations from the English Poets*
1873   Austin Allibone's *Poetical Quotations*
1874   Theodore Taylor's *Golden Treasury of Thought*

3–6. Late nineteenth-century pocket
editions of Bartlett's *Familiar Quotations*.

1876   Adam Wooléver's *Encyclopedia of Quotations*

1877   G. W. Carleton's *Hand-Book of Popular Quotations*

1882   Allibone's *Prose Quotations*

1882   Jehiel Keeler Hoyt's *Cyclopedia of Practical Quotations*

1883   Anna L. Ward's *Dictionary of Poetical Quotations*

1884   Edward Parson Day's *Day's Collacon: An Encyclopedia of Prose Quotations*

1888   Charles Northend's *Gems of Thought*

1889   Ward's *Dictionary of Quotations in Prose*

1891   Tryon Edwards's *Dictionary of Thoughts*, repackaged as *Useful Quotations* (1933)

1893   Rev. James Wood's *Dictionary of Quotations*

1894   Agnes H. Morton's *Quotations*

1895   Josiah Gilbert's *Dictionary of Burning Words*

1896   Philip Hugh Dalbiac's *Dictionary of Quotations*, with companion volumes in 1901 and 1906

1896   Louis Klopsch's *Many Thoughts of Many Minds*, expanded by Charles Douglas into *Forty Thousand Quotations* (1904)

1900   Elford Treffry's *Stokes's Encyclopedia of Familiar Quotations*

1901   George W. Powers's *Handy Dictionary of Poetical and Prose Quotations*

1907   Sir Gurney Benham's *Book of Quotations, Proverbs, and Household Words*, repackaged as *Putnam's Complete Book of Quotations* (1926)

1908   William S. Walsh's *International Encyclopedia of Prose and Poetical Quotations*

The collections by Bohn, Hoyt, Benham, Southgate, and Walsh threatened the supremacy of BFQ but could not displace it. *Day's Collacon* was ambitious, independent, and immense: more than 40,000 quotations from 8,000 authors on 1,200 pages. Day says he "devoted almost his entire life" to the *Collacon*, a unique compendium with more Seneca than Shakespeare, more James Ellis than Emerson, more Colton than Coleridge, and a Coke, eight Bacons, and an Egg.

BFQ's first nine editions sold 300,000 copies. Little, Brown and Company could not let it die with Bartlett. A 10th edition was commissioned, revised, and enlarged by Nathan Haskell Dole and published in 1914. It too succeeded. The 10th edition was published by Macmillan in London and reprinted by Little, Brown in 1915, 1916, 1917, 1919, 1920, 1921, 1923, 1925, 1926, 1927, 1928, 1929, 1930, and 1932. The lapse in 1924 might be due to the new edition of Benham's *Book of Quotations* that appeared that year. Licensed reprints of BFQ 10th were published by the Review of Books in 1916, by Blue Ribbon Books in 1919 and 1934, and by Halcyon House in 1919 and 1936.

Bartlett's nine editions register his readings and rereadings over four decades. Dole's BFQ 10th retained almost all that Bartlett had gathered.[24] When Morley and Everett edited BFQ 11th, a major shift occurred: for the first time it was necessary to sweep out the has-beens and make room for the moderns and for older writers whom Bartlett and Dole excluded. *Familiar Quotations* ceased to be Bartlett's and became a lineage in his name.

BFQ 11th (1937), the first new edition after World War I and the first since the Great Depression, had much catching up to do. Its editors, Christopher Morley and Louella D. Everett, did their work admirably. BFQ 11th introduced many more German writers — Hegel, Heine, Kafka, Lessing, Thomas Mann, Karl Marx, Novalis, Rilke, Schopenhauer — and more political figures, past and contemporary — Cromwell, Hadrian, Hammurabi, Hitler, Mussolini, and Mutsuhito, emperor of Japan. Josh Billings, Anthony Trollope, Mary Baker Eddy, Henry James, Joseph Conrad, Willa Cather, Sir Arthur Conan Doyle, Edna St. Vincent Millay, Ernest Hemingway, Pearl Buck, and Kahlil Gibran debuted. The editors of BFQ 11th were surprised it had taken so long to add Emily Dickinson, Nathaniel Hawthorne, Herman Melville, O. Henry, and William Blake. Twenty-three years separated the 9th from the 10th, and twenty-three years separated the 10th from the 11th. Ever since, new editions have appeared almost every decade.

The number of women vastly increased in BFQ 10th and 11th; almost all were actresses, poets, novelists, or hymnodists. Madame de Pompadour

TABLE 1. Editions of Bartlett's *Familiar Quotations*

Edition	First Published	Total Pages	Pages in Index	Total Number of Quotees*	Number of Women Quotees**
1ST	1855	302	37	169	5
2ND	1856	366	48	185	6
3RD	1858	454	55	228	11
4TH	1863	494	70	240	11
5TH	1868	790	164	323	15
6TH	1874	790	164	325	15
7TH	1875	880	182	502	23
8TH	1882	920	252	642	45
AUTHOR'S EDITION	1889	532	174	310	14
9TH	1891	1,173	296	825	50
10TH	1914	1,474	398	1,058	92
11TH***	1937	1,626	442	2,280	303
12TH	1948	1,893	575	2,731	381
13TH, CENTENNIAL	1955	1,648	542	2,069	242
14TH	1968	1,770	594	2,272	177
15TH	1980	1,598	602	2,505	222
16TH	1992	1,461	609	2,589	253
17TH	2002	1,487	565	2,604	268

* I exclude subheadings (books of the Bible, Shakespeare's plays, etc.) and cross-references but include collective entries (ballads, shanties, spirituals, etc.), institutional quotees (*Punch*, *Sesame Street*, etc.), and book and document titles (Magna Carta, *Song of Roland*, etc.).

** I disregard the presumptive genders of pseudonyms. George Sand and George Eliot are counted as women, Alice Hawthorne and Fiona Macleod as men.

*** BFQ 11th was the first edition to use double-column pages for quotations and the first to arrange its index in three-column pages.

7. Emily Morison Beck (1916–2004), editor of the 14th and
15th editions of Bartlett's *Familiar Quotations*.

and Emma Willard first appeared in BFQ 8th; Elizabeth I, Jane Austen,
Charlotte Brontë, Mary Shelley, Jane Addams, Louisa May Alcott, and
Sarah Josepha Hale (the deceased competitor) debuted in BFQ 11th; Susan
B. Anthony was absent till BFQ 15th. Under the editorship of Emily Mori-
son Beck, the number of women did not much increase, but the turnover
did. Beck brought into BFQ 14th Anna Akhmatova, Anne Bradstreet,
Elizabeth Bishop, Louise Bogan, Clare Boothe Luce, Rachel Carson,
Colette, Héloïse, Beatrix Potter, Anne Sexton, and May Swenson.

Beck began her association with BFQ with the 13th edition, con-
tributing so much so well that she was named editor for the 14th and
15th. Her preface for the 14th opened with Churchill's praise for BFQ
and announced greater attention for science, better translations, and a
wider international outlook. The new edition had new needs: "For the
first time, the editor of *Familiar Quotations* has had a staff of consulting
scholars." She made only one editorial mistake and she made it only
once: she moved the author index to the middle of the book.

BFQ 15th was her masterpiece. The author index was back where it used to be, up in front and easy to find. For the first time John Heywood's quotations were given decent space. George Sand, Ayn Rand, Bertolt Brecht, Jorge Luis Borges, Woody Allen, and Bob Dylan debuted. The index was improved.

What began as a collection derived from great poets, orators, and philosophers gradually included other quotable careers. Note how many quotees from other walks of life Beck introduced in BFQ 13th, 14th, and 15th and how many by Justin Kaplan in BFQ 16th and 17th.

Actors, directors, filmmakers, and screenwriters: Ethel Barrymore, Samuel Goldwyn, Mae West, W. C. Fields (12th); Greta Garbo (13th); Groucho Marx (14th); Charlie Chaplin, Paddy Chayevsky (15th); Rodney Dangerfield, Cary Grant, George Lucas, Elvis Presley (16th); Oliver Stone (17th).

Cartoonists: Bill Mauldin (12th); Charles Schulz (15th); Robert Crumb, Walt Kelly, Elzie Segar, Joe Shuster, and Jerry Siegel (16th). Al Capp is included in the ODQ but is not yet in BFQ.

Civil rights and labor leaders: Emma Willard (8th); W. E. B. Du Bois, Booker T. Washington (11th); Eugene Debs (12th); Samuel Gompers, Martin Luther King, Jr. (14th); Susan B. Anthony, Cesar Chavez, Frederick Douglass, Malcolm X (15th); Jesse Jackson (16th).

Composers, hymnodists, and songwriters: Isaac Watts (1st); Gilbert and Sullivan, Frances Havergal (10th); Carrie Jacobs Bond, Oscar Hammerstein II, and Sabine Baring-Gould (11th); Irving Berlin (12th); Beethoven, Ira Gershwin, Wagner (14th); Lorenz Hart, Bob Dylan, Woody Guthrie, Mick Jagger, John Lennon, Ruggero Leoncavallo, Paul McCartney, Joni Mitchell, Keith Richards, Pete Seeger (15th); Paul Anka, Leonard Bernstein, Chuck Berry, the Doors, Duke Ellington, Arlo Guthrie, Michael Jackson, Elton John, Bob Marley, Phil Ochs, Helen Reddy, Lionel Ritchie, Bruce Springsteen, Peter Townshend (16th). Mozart made a brief appearance in BFQ 15th. Bartók, Berlioz, Debussy, Haydn, Ives, Mahler, and Stravinsky have yet to appear.

Entrepreneurs: Henry Ford (11th); Andrew Carnegie, John D. Rockefeller (12th); Coco Chanel, Cornelius Vanderbilt (16th).

Historians: Plutarch (3rd); Edward Gibbon (5th); Dionysius of Halicarnassus, Herodotus, Sallust, Tacitus (7th); Livy, Suetonius (8th); Thucydides (9th); Mary Ritter Beard, Allan Nevins (12th); Morison, Parkman, Polybius (13th); Ammianus Marcellinus, Guizot, Michelet, Ranke, Schlesinger (14th); Arnold Toynbee, Frederick Jackson Turner (16th).

Journalists: Horace Greeley (10th); Sime Silverman (12th); Edward R. Murrow (14th); Walter Cronkite, David Halberstam, William Randolph Hearst, Ernie Pyle (15th).

Military leaders and theorists: Oliver Hazard Perry, Vegetius (7th); Napoleon Bonaparte (8th); Ulysses S. Grant, William Tecumseh Sherman (9th); George Dewey, Ferdinand Foche, Philip Sheridan (11th); Charles de Gaulle, Dwight D. Eisenhower, William Frederick Halsey, Jr., Douglas MacArthur, George Marshall, Sir Bernard Montgomery, Chester William Nimitz (12th); Otto von Bismarck, Carl von Clausewitz, Thomas Jonathan "Stonewall" Jackson, John Pershing (13th); Simón Bolívar, Robert E. Lee, Alfred Thayer Mahan, Mao Tse-Tung, Helmuth von Moltke, George Patton (14th); Curtis Le May (15th); Alfred von Schlieffen, Sun Tzu (16th); Joseph Stilwell (17th).

Painters and sculptors: Michelangelo (8th); Zeuxis (11th); Leonardo, W. J. Turner (through 13th only), James McNeill Whistler (11th); Georges Braque, Paul Cézanne, Eugène Delacroix, Henri Matisse, Pablo Picasso, Pierre Renoir (14th); Marc Chagall, William Hogarth, Georgia O'Keeffe, Andy Warhol (15th); Edgar Degas, Kaethe Kollwitz (16th).

Scientists and mathematicians: Isaac Newton (4th); Hippocrates (7th); Charles Darwin (9th); Euclid, Johann Kaspar Lavater, Linnaeus (11th); Albert Einstein, Karen Horney, Ivan Pavlov (12th); René Descartes, Robert Oppenheimer (13th); Niels Bohr, Nicholas Copernicus, Sigmund Freud, Galileo Galilei, Carl Gauss, William Harvey, Hermann von Helmholtz, Lord William Kelvin, Pierre Laplace, Antoine Lavoisier, Gottfried Wilhelm von Leibnitz, Ernst Mach, Louis Pasteur, Linus Pauling, Carl Sagan, Benjamin Spock, Norbert Wiener (14th); Robert

Boyle, Erik Erikson, Galen, Werner Heisenberg, Johannes Kepler, Anton van Leeuwenhoek, Margaret Mead, Pythagoras, B. F. Skinner (15th); Stephen Hawking, Alan Turing, James Watson, Frances H. C. Crick (16th); Pierre de Fermat, Jacques Cousteau (17th).
Sports figures: Leo Durocher, Satchel Paige (14th); Muhammad Ali, Yogi Berra, George Gipp, Vince Lombardi, Knute Rockne (15th).

BFQ slowly grew more international. For most of its history, authors who were not American or English were pushed to the back of the book; it wasn't till BFQ 13th that all authors appeared in chronological order. Aeschylus, Cicero, Dante, and Goethe weren't quoted till BFQ 7th; Aristophanes, Livy, Suetonius, and Napoleon till BFQ 8th; Demosthenes, the Plinys, Marcus Aurelius, and Epictetus till BFQ 10th; and Homer (!), Sappho, Pindar, Statius, Lucan, Maimonides, Aquinas, Machiavelli, Spinoza, La Bruyère, Balzac, and Dostoyevsky till BFQ 11th. Confucius and Freud went missing till BFQ 14th. BFQ 14th greatly increased the number of Japanese represented, but most of those gains disappeared in BFQ 15th and 16th.

THE RIVALS

Competitors to BFQ continued to enter the field. The most important are:

1917   Charles Noel Douglas's *Forty Thousand Quotations*
1922   Kate Louise Roberts's revised and enlarged edition of Hoyt's *New Cyclopedia of Practical Quotations*
1934   Burton Stevenson's *Home Book of Quotations*; 2nd ed. 1935; 3rd ed. 1937; 4th ed. 1944; 5th ed. 1946; 6th ed. 1947; 7th ed. 1949; 8th ed. 1952; 9th ed. 1958; 10th ed. 1967
1941   *The Oxford Dictionary of Quotations*; 2nd ed. 1953; 3rd ed. 1979; 4th ed. 1992; 5th ed. 1999; 6th ed. 2004; 7th ed. 2009
1942   H. L. Mencken's *New Dictionary of Quotations*
1960   George Seldes's *Encyclopedia of the Great Quotations*
1968   Bergen Evans's *Dictionary of Quotations*

1993   *New Penguin Dictionary of Quotations*; replaced by a new edi-
        tion by Robert Andrews in 2006
1993   Robert Andrews's *The Columbia Dictionary of Quotations*
1995   A. Norman Jeffares and Martin Gray's *Collins Dictionary of
        Quotations*; reissued by Barnes and Noble in 1997 as *A Diction-
        ary of Quotations*
1997   Nigel Rees's *Cassell Companion to Quotations*
2005   *Webster's New World Dictionary of Quotations*
2006   Fred R. Shapiro's *The Yale Book of Quotations*

Each compendium sought to satisfy readers in different ways, recombining seven basic criteria: (1) number of quotations; (2) number of quotees; (3) accuracy; (4) sourcing; (5) currency; (6) topical range; and (7) ease of use. Different compilers tried different systems of organization, indexing, and cross-referencing to make their volumes stand out.

To speed searches, the compendia compilers chose different means for organizing quotations: chronological, alphabetical by author, or by topic. Keyword indexes separate the best from the next best. BFQ can vaunt its usefulness because of the excellence of its index; name and keyword indexes for Mencken's NDQ are sorely missed.

As editions followed editions, the compendia grew larger — more quotations from more authors on more pages, the size of the pages themselves enlarging from handbook to tome. Editors' prefaces bragged about corrections made and authors added.

Many compendia specialize: Bible quotations, Shakespeare quotations, film quotations, baseball quotations, business, military, inspirational, and goofy quotations, quotations by presidents, mayors, prime ministers, and comedians.

By far the most popular collections have been BFQ's. Its successive editions have kept it current, and its editorial vigilance has constantly improved its accuracy, sourcing, translations, annotation, and index. BFQ can be read as a history of quotable quotes; its entries are organized by author, and authors appear in chronological order, by date of birth. Beck liked that: "One becomes quickly aware that Pericles, Sophocles,

Euripides, Thucydides and Plato were contemporaries, as were Confucius, Lao Tzu, Aesop, Heraclitus, and the *Suttapitaka* a century earlier." The quotations for each author are also arranged chronologically to show "development."[25] Most modern compendia are organized by author, too, but in alphabetical order: if you're looking for quotees by name, you can find them faster in *JGDQ, ODQ, PDQ,* and *YBQ.*

The best British compendium is the ODQ, edited anonymously for its first three editions. About 95 percent of ODQ 1st is repeated in ODQ 2nd. ODQ 3rd threw out a third of the 2nd.[26] ODQ 4th had some 17,500 quotations by 2,500 quotees, most of them retained by ODQ 5th (20,000 quotations) and 6th ("well over 20,000"). Hymns and songs, repressed in the 3rd, returned in the 4th. ODQ 5th was the first to give significant representation of sacred texts other than the Bible and the first edition to go online. For ODQ 5th, Elizabeth Knowles introduced twenty "special categories" — advertising and political slogans, film lines and titles, epitaphs, prayers, and so on — the better to retrieve quotations by type and context.[27] The front matter of ODQ 7th updates the history of the ODQ to 2009. As a sign of the infinities beyond its thousands, the new introduction quotes notable quotations found nowhere else in its pages.

Angela Partington, editor of ODQ 4th, celebrated the inclusion of neglected women. There have been several collections devoted solely to:

Quotations about women: Henry Southgate's *What Men Have Said about Women* (1866), Maturin Murray Ballou's *Notable Thoughts about Women* (1882), G. F. Monkshood's *Woman and Her Wits* (1899), Jennie Day Haines's *Sovereign Woman versus Mere Man* (1905), and Ann Stibbs's *A Woman's Place* (1993).[28]

Quotations by women: Carol McPhee and Ann Fitzgerald's *Feminist Quotations* (1979), Jill Diane Zahniser's *And Then She Said* (1990), Rosalie Maggio's *New Beacon Press Book of Quotations by Women* (1996), and Mary Biggs's *Women's Words* (1996).

Or a mix of the two: Jilly Cooper and Tom Hartman's *Violets and Vinegar* (1983) and Stibbs's *Like a Fish Needs a Bicycle* (1992).

Elaine Partnow's *The Quotable Woman: The First 5,000 Years* (2001) surpasses the rest. QW shows how many women had been excluded from prior compendia. Other compendia have generous portions of La Rochefoucauld's *Maximes*; QW has a generous portion of La Rochefoucauld's collaborator, Madeleine de Souvré de Sablé. Other compendia have rosters of kings, courtiers, and presidents; QW recovers queens, courtesans, and countesses. Readers will look in vain in other great compendia for Marguerite of Navarre and Christine de Pisan and thus miss "I have heard much of these languishing lovers, but I never yet saw one of them die for love" and "A woman with a mind is fit for any task."[29]

BFQ has long set the standard, but for a generation it was not the largest, best sourced, or best annotated. Those distinctions belonged to Burton Stevenson's *Home Book of Quotations* (1934), by far the most comprehensive compendium since *Day's Collacon*. Stevenson was a quotologist to the marrow, willing to travel far to trace a quotation. For years, quotologists sought in vain for proof that Emerson first said the famous lines about building a better mousetrap.

8. Elaine Partnow, editor of *Quotable Women*.

Clever research by Burton Stevenson resolved the problem. He discovered a first printing, attributed to Emerson, in a strange little book called *Borrowings*, compiled by "the ladies of the First Unitarian Church of Oakland, California," and published in San Francisco in 1889. The actual compilers were Mary S. Keene and Sarah S. B. Yule, and it was Mrs. Yule who contributed the mousetrap piece. Fortunately, she was still living when this discovery was made, and was able to explain her Emerson attribution. She had copied the lines in her "handbook" from an address delivered by Emerson, in Oakland, in 1871, when she was a girl of sixteen.

Stevenson found what he had been looking for: "If a man can write a better book, preach a better sermon, or make a better mouse-trap, than his neighbor, though he builds his house in the woods, the world will make a beaten path to his door."[30] With labor like that Stevenson built a better compendium.

In most cases translations in the *HBQ* also provide the quotation in the

9. Burton Stevenson (1872–1962), editor of *The Home Book of Quotations.*

original language, a practice competitors selectively adopted. Stevenson grouped similar quotations, showing how notions were introduced and re-expressed through the centuries. He frequently annotated sources, exposing uncertain authorship. The HBQ is impressively immense: HBQ 10th has 2,366 double-column pages of quotations plus author and keyword indexes.

Even so, the HBQ has problems. Its bulk stood in the way of correction and updating; its last revision was in 1967. Thinking more of his readers than his quotees, Stevenson often modernized spelling, punctuation, and syntax. But while he lived, Stevenson assembled the best compendium ever printed.

BFQ 17th would honor any reference shelf, but it needs company. ODQ 7th, with "more than 20,000 quotations," is smaller than BFQ 17th's 25,000, but its selection of British quotees is richer and its selection of Americans independent. ODQ 7th devotes more than eighteen pages to the *Book of Common Prayer*; PDQ, five and a half; JGDQ four (peculiarly placed between "Pratchett" and "Prévert"); BFQ 17th has two. Neither the ODQ nor JGDQ has quotes from Black Elk, Ohiyesa, Standing Bear, or Chief Seattle, but BFQ does. The ODQ and JGDQ have all six Georges, and the PDQ has all but George IV; BFQ has only George V. The ODQ has almost as many American presidents as BFQ (thirty and thirty-two, respectively) and nearly as many quotations from them, including one from Barack Obama and some of the saltier squibs of Lyndon Johnson that BFQ omits, such as "Better to have him inside the tent pissing out, than outside pissing in."

For racism and misogyny, choose Mencken's NDQ.

For the best and most of Ronald Reagan, choose the YBQ, with twenty Reagan quotations; WNW has fifteen; BFQ only six, fewer than ODQ's ten. YBQ has more Lincoln, more John F. Kennedy, and more Martin Luther King, Jr., than other comprehensive compendia.

BFQ 17th has nothing from Marilyn Monroe. YBQ has eight gems. YBQ and QW include this quotable goal: "I don't care about money. I just want to be wonderful."[31]

The YBQ succeeded in tracking down many sources that the BFQ only "attributed." Edited by Fred Shapiro, a librarian at Yale, the YBQ benefited from his knowledge of prior compendia, a support staff, a dedicated listserv, and a Web site with a quote quiz. Only YBQ has a quotation from Arthur Twining Hadley: "You can always tell a Harvard man when you see him, but you can't tell him much." Only YBQ has this from W. E. B. Du Bois: "Not even a Harvard School of Business can make greed into a science."[32]

Current compendia collectively certify Muhammad Ali's claim "I'm the greatest." Only the YBQ quotes Ali's championship strategy, "rope-a-dope" (YBQ 14.6).

Shapiro's commitment to accuracy and range is unsurpassed. He recognized the quotability of films and pop songs, advertising and political slogans, cartoons, TV scripts, and performers' catchphrases. He finds more to like in contemporary poetry and fiction: BFQ 17th has six Bob Dylan quotations, YBQ has twenty-seven; BFQ 17th has two tidbits from J. K. Rowling, YBQ has seven.

10. Fred Shapiro, editor of *The Yale Book of Quotations*.

ONLINE

Nowadays quoters go first to their computers. For quick answers (not necessarily correct ones), nothing beats the Net. Web sites devoted to quotations are increasing in number and depth. Some, like Wikiquote, The Quotations Page, and Quote World, are all-inclusive and rapidly updated. Many quotation Web sites revert to a favorite organizational principle and feature topics such as children, love, cars, war, dogs, cats, money, history, and religion.

Google Books, JSTOR, ARTFL, Project Gutenberg, and a galaxy of Web sites dedicated to specific authors have made it ever easier to find quotations in context. Project Wombat, an online collective largely populated by resourceful research librarians (including Fred Shapiro), identifies quotations, quotees, and sources for stumped patrons.

Perched on their wires, monotonous crows cackle about the death of the book and anticipate the day when great compendia will go the way of parchment. Can they be right? Have the speed and breadth of online technology doomed print compendia? Why expect less when the compendia have spent decades dooming each other?

In the long history of quotation the great compendia stand like monuments of a passing era, artifacts destined to be digitized. If the sole reason for compendia were reference, they could not compete with the instant updating and ever expanding capacity of Web sites. But from the beginning the compendia have asserted their bookishness and, with it, the defenses of books against the imperious Internet. Print persists because books can live longer than the oldest trees. Books break free from power strips, relay towers, and service interruptions.

Topical compendia ignored "Electricity" till Hoyt revised his *Cyclopedia of Practical Quotations* (1896). "Electricity" first appeared in BFQ 11th and "Computer" in BFQ 15th. WNW and ODQ 6th have three quotations each that mention the Internet. YBQ adds two more and is the first to index "World Wide Web."

The 2009 edition of the ODQ is a snapshot of a database, supported by electronic monitoring of the Oxford Corpus online. The ODQ remembers the sayings of British Prime Ministers better than any other compendium. It uniquely preserves the "No! No! No!" of Margaret Thatcher.

But in seven editions the "Yes I said yes I will Yes" of James Joyce still has no place in the ODQ. It's everywhere else: BFQ, JGDQ, PDQ, WNW, YBQ, everyone but the ODQ repeats, "Yes I said yes I will Yes."[33]

For all we know we're a week away from another blackout, mad hacker, or shutdown. Scarecrow prophets warn that the Web, like all webs, will live a short life. But new networks emerge, quotations reproduce, and means for copying them multiply.

Long before compendia routed their circuits, quotations turned on and off.

It is easier to copy than to
think, hence fashion.

Wallace Stevens

5

Fashions

Quotations flash and fade. Seneca the Younger condemned those
who "chase after choice extracts," stuff their speech with sayings, and
depend upon their memories to make conversation. "It is disgraceful
even for an old man, or one who has sighted old age, to have a notebook
knowledge."[1]

At the catholic court of Charles IX (1550–74) "the princesses of the
House of France together with their ladies-in-waiting and maids of honor,
took the greatest pleasure in the sayings of the Greeks and Romans which
have been preserved by sweet Plutarch." Plutarch again, ever quotable.[2]

In 1688 La Bruyère described Herillus as a fop who "is continually quoting; he brings in the prince of philosophers to tell you that wine will make
you intoxicated, and the Roman orator to say that water qualifies it. When
he discourses of morals, it is not he, but the divine Plato who assures us that
virtue is amiable, vice odious, and that both will become habitual."[3]

Across the channel quotation was mandatory. Boswell went to Eton
with his "classical quotations very ready." Emerson copied a quotation
faulting English universities where "a knowledge of the classics connected

more with an ability to quote passages than aught else." Lord Chesterfield pleaded guilty:

> I was an absolute pedant; when I talked my best, I quoted Horace;
> when I aimed at being facetious, I quoted Martial; and when I
> had a mind to be a fine gentleman, I talked Ovid. I was convinced
> that none but the ancients had common sense; that the classics
> contained everything that was either necessary, useful, or orna-
> mental to men; and I was not without thoughts of wearing the
> *toga virilis* of the Romans, instead of the vulgar and illiberal dress
> of the moderns. With these excellent notions I went first to The
> Hague, where, by the help of several letters of recommendation, I
> was soon introduced into all the best company; and where I very
> soon discovered that I was totally mistaken in almost every one
> notion I had entertained.[4]

Lord Chesterfield and Maria Edgeworth objected that by the later
eighteenth century quotation had descended into vulgarity. Chesterfield's
blue blood heated at the sound of learned men who

> adorn their conversation, even with women, by happy quotations of
> Greek and Latin; and who have contracted such a familiarity with
> the Greek and Roman authors, that they call them by certain names
> or epithets denoting intimacy. As OLD Homer; that SLY ROGUE
> Horace; MARO, instead of Virgil; and Naso, instead of Ovid. These
> are often imitated by coxcombs, who have no learning at all; but who
> have got some names and some scraps of ancient authors by heart,
> which they improperly and impertinently retail in all companies,
> in hopes of passing for scholars. . . . Wear your learning, like your
> watch, in a private pocket: and do not pull it out and strike it; merely
> to show that you have one.[5]

Maria Edgeworth compared quotation reciters to trained pigs, *bore* and
boar being two forms of the same beast.[6] Familiar quotations were too
familiar, too common to count.

Though quotation tastes and proprieties alter over time and distance, they share two constants. (1) The ability to quote when called upon is everywhere admired, thus envied, and thus hated. (2) Unbidden quotation expostulation is as rude as spit.

QUOTATIONS AS CREDENTIALS

To rise in the imperial court of tenth-century Japan Sei Shōnagon had to memorize all ten volumes of the *Kokin Shū*. On a windy gray day she was tested.

> A man from the Office of Grounds came to the Black Door and asked to speak to me. He then approached and gave me a note which he said was from Kintō, the Imperial Adviser. It consisted of a sheet of pocket-paper on which was written,
>
> *And for a moment in my heart*
> *I feel that spring has come.*
>
> The words were most appropriate for the weather; but what concerned me was that I was bound to produce the opening lines. I asked the messenger which gentlemen were present, and he gave me their names. They were all the type of men to put me on my mettle; but it was Kintō's presence among them that made me most reluctant to give a commonplace answer. I felt very alone. . . . The man from the Office of Grounds urged me to hurry; and I realized that if, in addition to bungling my reply, I was slow about it, I should really disgrace myself. "It can't be helped," I thought, and, trembling with emotion, wrote the following lines:
>
> *As though pretending to be blooms*
> *The snow flakes scatter in the wintry sky.*
>
> I handed my poem to the messenger and anxiously wondered how Kintō and the others would receive it.

She was rewarded by appointment to the Palace Attendant's Office.[7]

The meaning of the quotation had little to do with spring or snow. What mattered was context: the surprise knock on the door and Sei Shōnagon's preparation for it, her sudden brief exam and the judgment of it made by an anonymous bureaucrat in the emperor's service.

Sei Shōnagon served a government that ranked women (or seemed to) by how well they memorized poetry. She records tests, triumphs, and humiliations of women compelled to quote.[8]

In imperial China bureaucrats memorized Confucius; in Baghdad, Cairo, Damascus, and Tehran the Koran; in the law courts of Europe, Australia, and America bits of Latin and Greek.

USE AND DISUSE

In 1797 David Macdonnel quoted an unnamed "judicious writer" who deduced:

> One Cause why the learned Languages have sunk into Disrepute of late Years has been the Disuse of Quotations from them by our most esteemed modern Authors. In the Times of James the First, and for a long Space afterwards, the Affectation of quoting from Latin and Greek Writers was carried to a most ridiculous Extreme, commonly one Part of a Sentence being in English and the Remainder in Language few Readers could understand. — At present we are deviating to the opposite point, and the Classics are supplanted by Quotations from our own Poets, or by French Phrases.[9]

Macdonnel compiled his *Dictionary* to help readers understand foreign phrases then in vogue, Latin proverbs like "Stultitiam simulare loco sapientia summa est" (To assume the garb of folly is, in certain situations, the most consummate wisdom) and a counterquotation from Horace, "Sapientia prima est, stultitiâ caruisse" (The first step to wisdom is to be exempt from folly).[10] A little help can help a lot, and Macdonnel's *Dictionary* filled a need; it went through nine editions by 1826.

HYPERQUOTATION

In 1809 Samuel Coleridge chafed, "That our elder writers to Jeremy Taylor inclusive *quoted* to excess, it would be the very blindness of partiality to deny." Coleridge then whacked hyperquotation with a quotation from John Milton's "Of Reformation": "More than one might be mentioned, whose works might be characterized in the words of Milton, as 'a paroxysm of citations, pampered metaphors, and aphorising pedantry.'"[11]

QUOTATION AS CRUTCH

Walter Savage Landor let Lucian speak for him: "Before I let fall a quotation I must be taken by surprise. I seldom do it in conversation, seldomer in composition; for it mars the beauty and unity of style, especially when it invades it from a foreign tongue. A quoter is either ostentatious of his acquirements or doubtful of his cause. And moreover, he never walks gracefully who leans upon the shoulder of another, however gracefully that other may walk."[12]

OWNING AND BORROWING

"I know the fashion of our time affects disdain of borrowing," A. Bronson Alcott wrote in an 1877 Boston book.[13] Meanwhile, elsewhere in Boston, Bartlett's *Familiar Quotations* was in its 6th edition, making good money by making borrowing easier.

To quote or not to quote? Emerson confessed, "Quotation confesses inferiority," and wrote, "The divine never quotes."[14] Ever ready to debate himself, Emerson also wrote, "Next to the originator of a good sentence is the first quoter of it," an opinion widely quoted.[15] Here's proof it's true. Landor praised Shakespeare's quotations as resurrection scenes. "He was more original than his originals. He breathed upon dead bodies and brought them into life." "More original than his originals" can be found in the compendia, but not under Landor. It's wrapped in a quotation from Emerson.[16]

Emerson said of Plutarch, "In his immense quotation and allusion we quickly cease to discriminate between what he quotes and what he invents. We sail on his memory into the ports of every nation, enter into every private property, and do not stop to discriminate owners, but give him the praise of all. 'T is all Plutarch, by right of eminent domain."[17]

HIGH BAROQUE

Isak Dinesen's "The Roads round Pisa" takes quotation to the highest refinement. Nobles from Denmark and Italy quote Shakespeare, Goethe, and opera libretti at each other. In the climax of her tale Dinesen's hero and heroine confront each other across quotations from Dante. Agnese had been ravished under conditions obliging her to keep the violence secret.

> [She] spoke very slowly to him, in her clear and sweet voice, like a bird's:

> *... da tema e da vergogna*
> *voglio che tu omai ti disviluppe*
> *e che non parli più com' uom che sogna.*

> She looked away for a moment, drew a deep breath, and her voice took on more force.

> *Sappe che il vaso che il serpente ruppe*
> *fu e non è, ma chi n'ha colpa creda*
> *che vendetta di Dio non teme suppe.*

With these words she walked away.[18] Hers was a skill few could appreciate: quotation as code.

QUOTATION GAMES

A century ago riddle books expected readers to recognize quotations from Dickens and Shakespeare. In the 1950s and 1960s, when books were in fashion, the *Saturday Review of Literature* teased its readers with quotation quizzes. Nowadays lines from hit songs, films, and TV series are in vogue; game shows rely on them.

Greeks and Latins had their day. Indeed, their centuries.

CENTOS

Centos are quotations cut from context and reassembled to tell a tale. Tatian wrote a sequel to the *Iliad* using nothing but rearranged Homer. In the fourth century Faltonia Betitia Proba retold Genesis and the life of Christ using lines from Virgil. Saint Gregory of Nazianzus (ca. 330–91) composed a drama of 2,600 verses presenting the Passion of Christ in lines plucked from Aeschylus and Euripides. It took three days to perform.[19]

When the pagan emperor Julian forbade grammar schools to teach anything but the classics — no prophets, no Gospels, no letters of apostles — it was possible to circumvent the prohibition by teaching the Creation, the life of Jesus, and the Resurrection by telling them in centos composed of lines from Homer and Virgil.[20] The reformation of pagan poetry into Christian texts busied the eminent. Eudocia Athenaïs, wife of Emperor Theodosius II (fifth century), finished the centos of Bishop Patricius presenting Christ's miracles and the Nicene Creed in lines from Homer.[21] Eudocia described Eve:

ἥ μεγὰ ἔργον ἔρεξεν ἀιδρείῃσι νόοιο	*Odyssey* 11.272
οὐλομένην, ἥ πολλὰ κάκ᾽ ἀνθρώποισιν ἐφῆκεν	*Odyssey* 17.287
πολλὰς δ᾽ ἰφθίμους ψυχὰς Ἄϊδι προΐαψεν	*Iliad* 1.3
πᾶσι δ᾽ ἔθηκε πόνον, πολλοῖσι δὲ κήδε᾽ ἐφῆκεν	*Iliad* 21.524

[She unwittingly did a monstrous deed,
and, destructive, she wrought many evils for men;
she cast many strong souls to Hades' abode,
wrought hardship for all, caused trouble for many.][22]

Quotation reassembly was a European art form. With lines from Virgil, Ausonius (fourth century) composed a "Nuptial Cento," admitting it

"was more likely to provoke your laughter than your praise."[23] A thirteenth-century cento composed entirely of Bible verses told the story
of Anne Musnier, who fought off three assassins till help arrived.[24] A
seventeenth-century cento from Paris rearranged Virgil into a dialogue
between the queen, the duc d'Orléans, the prince de Condé, and Cardinal Mazarin.[25] In a 1680 panegyric Théodore Desjardins raided the
treasuries of Latin literature to construct a cento of more than four
thousand lines celebrating the martial glory of Louis XIV.[26]

Once the delight of connoisseurs (Montaigne admired them), centos
are now as scorned as scrapbooks.[27] Erasmus compared composing
centos to braiding ropes of sand.[28] Charles Nodier described them as
"mosaic poetry" born of decadent caprice.[29] In careless hands originals
were cut to shreds and mangled beyond recognition, but in expert hands
the originals inform and illumine line after line.[30]

Once celebrated, Alexander Ross (1590–1654) composed centos with
lines from Virgil and Statius. In *Virgilius Evangelisans* (1634) he used
Virgil to tell the life of Jesus; *Virgilii Evangelisantis Christiados*, expanded
to thirteen cantos, followed in 1638. In *Psycomachia Virgiliana* (published
posthumously in 1661) he composed eight short poems, each a battle
(Faith versus Idolatry, Patience versus Wrath, Pride versus Humility,
and so on), all told in passages from Virgil.[31]

THE ART OF QUOTATION

Robert Burton considered his immense *Anatomy of Melancholy* a well-
knit cento:

> As a good hous-wife out of divers fleeces weaves one peece of Cloathe,
> a Bee gathers Wax and Hony out of many Flowers, and makes a new
> bundle of all,

> *Floriferis ut apes in saltibus omnia libant,*

> I have laboriously collected this *Cento* out of divers Writers.[32]

Holbrook Jackson's *Anatomy of Bibliomania* (1950) imitated Burton bril-
liantly with quotations about books and book lovers. Cyril Connolly's

The Unquiet Grave (1945) takes Burton's melancholy to new depths; he quotes Pascal, Chamfort, and Sainte-Beuve to dignify his misery. Cheerful Otto Bettmann's *Delights of Reading* (1987) is a quotation bundle topically arranged.

THE PHILOSOPHY OF QUOTATION

Susan Sontag quotes Hannah Arendt about Walter Benjamin's "little notebooks with black covers which he always carried with him and in which he tirelessly entered in the form of quotations what daily living and reading netted him in the way of 'pearls' and 'coral.' On occasion he read from them aloud, showed them around like items from a choice and precious collection."[33] Benjamin wrote, "Collecting is a primal phenomenon of study," a study he exemplified with quotations.[34]

Benjamin's notebooks are now praised and plumbed as an unfinished masterpiece, *The Arcades Project*. He wrote, "This work has to develop to the highest degree the art of citing without quotation marks. Its theory is intimately related to that of montage."[35] Benjamin planned to present a new theory for the collection and arrangement of quotations, a *philosophical* theory: the quotations would function like construction materials, which, in Rolf Tiedemann's words, "would have become nothing less than a materialist philosophy of the history of the nineteenth century" as seen from Paris.[36]

Benjamin's quotations mingle phantoms of money, mechanics of power, and hallucinations of bliss: photography; railway stations; parliamentary politics; world's fairs; *das Ewig-Heutige* (the eternally up-to-date) clothes, architecture, and furniture; cast-iron construction; kitsch; city streets; street narcotics; and, above all, the arcades, the shops that stood to reap the riches that grew from the wishes advertisements sowed.[37]

Despairing and fugitive, barely ahead of a Nazi roundup, Benjamin committed suicide. He left behind notebooks he'd filled for a dozen years and two "exposés," or prospectuses, from 1935 and 1939. The notebooks display the breadth of his research, the topics that intrigued him, drafts of sections, and a plan to compose with nothing but quotations.

"I needn't *say* anything. Merely show."[38] In its incomplete state, where quotations, citations, and Benjamin's commentaries mix, it is hard to see how the work could have been built with quotations alone. *The Arcades Project* resembles Emerson's notebooks and Paul Valéry's *cahiers*, vast warehouses where materials are stored, but Benjamin's are presorted and expertly selected, with a Paris focus (he zoomed in and out) and an eye for fashion.

Benjamin wrote, "Fashions are a collective medicament for the ravages of oblivion. The more short-lived a period, the more susceptible it is to fashion."[39]

TRACKING TRENDS

Fashion rides the waves, bursting and bright; learning digs and quarries. Stefan Morawski wrote, "The swing in the climate of European culture . . . to historicism, the incessant intervention of the past in various, and variously abstract, reflections about the present and the future, and the institutionalization of scholarship, more and more firmly entrenched the position of the quotation."[40] The eighteen editions of Bartlett's *Familiar Quotations* and its heavy rivals give abundant evidence of changes in quotation fashion in the United States since 1855. They occurred in at least nine measures:

1. GENRES: Obvious at a glance is the dethroning of poetry, which dominated the 1st edition of BFQ and its nineteenth-century successors and competitors. Quoting sermons has long since gone out of style. Soon after movies talked they were quoted. Its first equation, Einstein's $E = mc^2$, debuted in BFQ 14th.

2. SOURCES: BFQ became increasingly precise. While other compendia were content to cite an author's last name and perhaps the title of the work cited, BFQ tended to give act and scene, chapter, and page numbers.

Footnotes appeared in the 1st edition of BFQ and quickly multiplied. The notes pointed to comparable quotations — and sometimes gave them — with references that gradually grew more exact. BFQ 3rd added endnotes. BFQ 4th through 8th had appendixes containing phrases for which Bartlett wished to provide something more than a reference, but the rationale for their separation from other quotations was never clear. Bartlett abandoned the practice for BFQ 9th, his last.

Like a learned lord, Edward Gibbon quoted Greek and Latin sources in his notes without translation to prevent vulgar English readers from understanding nasty bits. Current great compendia translate; some give quotations in their original languages, too.

3. EPIGRAPHS: The modest epigraph of BFQ 4th quoted Montaigne in tiny type: "I have gathered a posie of other men's flowers, and nothing but the thread that binds them is mine own."[41] The epigraph moved to the title pages for the 5th through the 9th editions; the 10th and 11th dropped it; the 12th through the 16th restored it; and the 17th dropped it again.

George Eliot's line, "A book which hath been culled from the flowers of all books," adorns Edwards's *Useful Quotations* and the 1896 edition of the NCPQ.[42] The HBQ begins with a boast: "I can tell thee where that saying was born," from Shakespeare.[43]

"An opening quotation is a symphony preluding on the chords whose tones we are about to harmonize," sang Isaac Disraeli. He forbore them from his own books.[44]

According to Gérard Genette, epigraphs debuted with the 1678 edition of La Rochefoucauld's *Maximes*, quoting La Rochefoucauld himself, or with La Bruyère's *Caractères* (1688), which quoted Erasmus. The practice of adding epigraphs for every chapter began with the Gothic novels of Anne Radcliffe and Matthew "Monk" Lewis. Too busy to look for lines of poetry to suit his chapters, Sir Walter Scott wrote his own.[45]

4. LENGTH: The most constant measure in BFQ's many editions is length or, rather, brevity. The vast majority of quotations are no longer than three lines. The longest quotations in BFQ 17th are soliloquies from *Hamlet* and *As You Like It* and Lincoln's Gettysburg Address. Compendia that included long quotations, for example, Charles Little's *Historical Lights* (1886), could not compete with collections that filled their pages with quantity.

5. QUANTITY: As long as Bartlett himself supervised its editions, BFQ grew steadily (see table 1, p. 84). Quantity most immediately distinguishes quality. Anything with fewer than twenty thousand quotations is second-rate or specialized.

The number of quotations from each quotee in compendia measures their reputations through the years. In the 1st edition of the ODQ Queen Elizabeth had thirteen quotations, James I had four, Charles I had two, and Queen Victoria three; in ODQ 6th Queen Bess has nineteen, James nine, Charles eight, and Victoria nine.

6. TOPICS: Compendia organized by topic adapted to the times: typical headings in the 1800s were "Love" and "Marriage." "Divorce" first appeared in Bohn's *Dictionary of Quotations* (1867), "Adultery" in Mencken's *New Dictionary of Quotations* (1942), and "Second Marriage" in Andrews's *Columbia Dictionary of Quotations* (1993). Hoyt's *New Cyclopedia of Practical Quotations* (1922) was the first to use "Suffrage." Andrews's CDQ introduced "Birth Control," "Feminism," and "Sexism." Biggs's *Columbia Dictionary of Quotations by Women* (1996) introduced "Apartheid," "Overweight," and "Pay Equity," and Maggio's *New Beacon Press Book of Quotations by Women* (1996) introduced "Anti-Intellectualism," "Bisexuals," "Interior Decoration," and "Therapy"; Biggs and Maggio simultaneously introduced "Abortion" and "Sexual Harassment."

Watson's *Poetical Quotations* (1847) has headings for "Blacksmith," "Drinking," and "Smoking"; Stevenson's *Home Book of Quotations* (1934) has "Coal," "Ale and Beer," "Drunkenness," "Tobacco," and "Wine"; Mencken's *New Dictionary of Quotations* (1942) has "Ale," "Automobile," "Beer," "Brewery," "Cigar," "Cigarette," "Coffee," "Drinking," "Drugs," "Hops," "Rum," "Whiskey," and "Wine"; Evans's *Dictionary of Quotations* (1968) introduced "Oil" and "Television"; Andrews's CDQ introduced "Addiction," "Alcohol: Drunkenness," and "Child Abuse."

Stevenson, Mencken, and Evans have "Indian" or "Indians" as topic headings, the CDQ has "Native Americans." Stevenson, Mencken, and Evans have "Negro," the CDQ has "African Americans."

7. QUOTEES: Through three editions (1852, 1860, 1866) the *Book of Familiar Quotations* of L. C. Gent was resolutely British: the only author

admitted from the United States was Longfellow; the only translations were from Thomas à Kempis, Kotzebue, Rabelais, and the Bible. The subtitle of BFQ 4th (1865) advertised *"Chiefly from English Authors,"* a line that fit all editions till the 10th (1914), when Americans entered in large numbers.

The first African in BFQ was Saint Augustine in BFQ 3rd (1858); the first Asians (excepting Asiatic Greeks and Romans) were Firdousi and Omar Khayyam in BFQ 8th (1882); the first Arab was Ali ben Taleb in BFQ 9th (1891). The first Japanese were Emperor Mutsuhito and the Buddhist Kenko in BFQ 11th (1937); both lasted only one more edition. The first quotations from India were from Pilpay (or Bidpai) in BFQ 9th. Since Beck's BFQ 15th (1980) the sayings of the Buddha have appeared under the heading "The Pali Canon." The first Chinese were Chang Yen-Yuan, Chiang Kai-Shek, Ching Hao, Chuang Tzu, Confucius, Han Wu-Ti, Hsieh Ho, Huai-Nan Tzu, Hu Shih, Ku K'ai-Chih, Lao Tzu, Liu Shao-Ch'I, Mao Tse-Tung, and Mencius, all in Beck's BFQ 14th (1968).

Aesop, Booker T. Washington, and W. E. B. Du Bois first appeared in BFQ 11th; Frederick Douglass, Harriet Tubman, and Sojourner Truth had to wait till Beck's BFQ 15th. Black Elk, Black Hawk, Crowfoot, Charles Eastman, Flying Hawk, Geronimo, Chief Joseph, Red Cloud, Red Jacket, Seattle, Sitting Bull, Speckled Snake, Standing Bear, and Tecumseh, the first Native Americans to be quoted, entered as a group in the same edition.

8. SHAKESPEARE: Shakespeare is a special case. Emerson told readers of the nineteenth century that "the passages of Shakespeare that we most prize were never quoted until within this century."[46] Then Shakespeare quotations became the ruling presence. The *Book of Familiar Quotations* published by Whittaker in 1852 devotes 43 of its 106 pages to Shakespeare. Five of Hale's twenty-two pages on "Love" quote Shakespeare. "Shakespeare" is a topic heading in Grocott's *Index*, Bohn's *Dictionary*, Ward's *Dictionary*, the CDQ, HBQ, NCPQ, and NDQ.

The first three editions of BFQ began with the Bible and Shakespeare. BFQ 1st had twenty-five pages from the King James Bible and sixty-two from the bard. With high scruple BFQ 8th and 9th noted variant editions of Shakespeare's works. BFQ 17th has sixty-one pages of Shakespeare, forty-four of the Bible, a greater imbalance than shown by the ODQ 6th, with its forty pages from the Bible (most from the King James Version) and forty-five pages of Shakespeare.

The editors of the newest Arden *Hamlet* believe "To be or not to be" to be "the most frequently quoted (and parodied) speech in western and indeed global cultural tradition." Maria Edgeworth felt the passage "is a question we can no longer bear" because it was too much quoted.[47]

9. TABOOS: Lord Chesterfield advised his son that "proverbial expressions and trite sayings are the flowers of the rhetoric of a vulgar man. . . . A man of fashion never has recourse to proverbs and vulgar aphorisms."[48] Never? Bacon and Montaigne freely quoted proverbs, and proverbs pepper compendia. The JGDQ, ODQ, and YBQ have sections of proverbs from various nations; the BBQ, CDQ, HBQ, NCPQ, and NDQ have "Proverbs" as a topic heading.

Foul words are always in fashion, everywhere repeated and repressed. In the 2nd edition of his *Collection of English Proverbs* (1678) John Ray repented his earlier selection: "Now whereas I understand that some Proverbs admitted in the former Edition have given offence to sober and pious persons, as savouring too much of obscenity, being apt to suggest impure fancies to corrupt minds, I have in this omitted all I could suspect for such save one . . . and yet now upon better consideration I could wish that it also were obliterated."

As for matters "naming some Excrements of the body," Ray resorted to "that usual expedient of putting only the initial Letters for the uncleanly words. . . . For it is the naming such things by their plain and proper appellatives that is odious and offensive."[49] Happily, the philologist trumped the prude: some words were reduced to "a——" and "t——," but as the collection grew, "arse," "dung," "fuck," "piss," "shit," and "turd" survived, and so did homely proverbs like "It's good *farting* before one's own fire." The CDQ has "Excrement," "Pornography," and "Sexual Deviation."

STYLE

A. Bronson Alcott rebutted the opinion that "quoting often implies sterility and bad taste" by pointing to quotations in Shakespeare and Montaigne. "One must be a wise reader to quote wisely," Alcott taught.[50]

Editions of Montaigne's *Essais* are fertile ground for quotology.[51] Montaigne found models for quoting well in his favorite authors, Plutarch and Seneca, in the letters of Cicero and Pliny, and in the *Attic Nights* of Aulus Gellius. Michael Metschies's *Zitat und Zitierkunst* places Montaigne's use of quotations firmly within the classical tradition of Cicero, Seneca, Quintilian, Petrarch, and Erasmus.[52] But Montaigne was more playful than they, more mischievous, sometimes omitting quotees, sometimes citing quotations from different authors consecutively as if from a single source, and sometimes concealing quotations altogether.[53]

Montaigne supervised six editions of his *Essais* and was preparing the seventh when he slipped his mortal coil. Like Erasmus's *Adages*, the *Essais* grew larger with each new edition. By the time he died Montaigne had planted more than 1,300 quotations in them to bloom in glory though he returned to dust.[54] His multiple uses of quotations serve as a model and inventory for authors ever after.

His quotations show:

RANK: He places himself above, below, or on a par with the quotee. Montaigne quotes Lucretius deferentially, on the soul, on animal communication, on the dread of death, and always with respect.[55] Most of Montaigne's quotations are modest; he lets others say what he cannot say better.

RAW MATERIAL: Mary McKinley believes Montaigne cited precedents to improve upon them as much as French would allow, providing a more poignant or more compact expression or an entirely new way of viewing a subject.[56]

REINFORCEMENT: Montaigne calls in others to agree with them or have them agree with him. "D'un mot de Caesar" (On one of Caesar's sayings) (*Essais*, 1.53) confirms, centuries after Caesar, humanity's perpetual discontent.

PROOF: Stronger yet is proof. Montaigne quoted at length to prove "how puny and stunted is the knowledge of the most inquisitive men."[57] Quotations prove Montaigne loved Ovid, Horace, Plutarch, and Seneca the Younger. Quotations prove he was not finicky about quoting correctly.[58]

PRECEDENT: Montaigne draws upon antiquity for all kinds of examples. Lucilius (as described by Horace) wrote out his life bit by bit as honestly as he could, as Montaigne was doing. Montaigne's three good wives are classical Romans; his three excellent men are classical Greeks. Yet he concluded, "It is pure silliness which sends us chasing after foreign and textbook examples."[59]

FOIL: Montaigne was sparing of this use, so beloved of later writers: quoting a quote for the sake of quarreling with it. In a discreet example Montaigne quotes Joachim du Bellay, "But most of all I hate school-masterish erudition," in order to defend the erudition he admires.[60]

RESONANCE: Montaigne's quotations often evoke their original contexts and the traditions that sustained them. He quoted in Latin and Greek rather than translate for his readers, an exclusionary decision no longer enforced.[61] He expected his readers to have better memories than he did. He had the strange experience of hearing others quote him without recognizing the quotations as his own.[62]

PROPHYLAXIS: Montaigne knew all of the tricks of ventriloquism. He confided to his readers that "in the case of those reasonings and original ideas which I transplant into my own soil and confound with my own, I sometimes deliberately omit to give the author's name so as to rein in the temerity of those hasty criticisms which leap to attack writings of every kind. . . . I want them to flick Plutarch's nose in mistake for mine and to scald themselves by insulting Seneca in me."[63]

POINTS OF DEPARTURE: Lino Pertile considers Montaigne's quotations as "points of departure." McKinley describes Montaigne's quotations as "doors" that invite "excursions out of the text" but that also require a return trip.[64]

DISPLAY: Montaigne was less likely to present a surprising quote than a handsome one and most likely of all to present quotations that showed a writer's candor. His celebrated "On some lines of Virgil" offers Venus in Latin, "never as beautiful stark naked, quick and panting, as she is here in Virgil."[65]

Montaigne quoted Seneca against showy quoting. "I like and honour erudition as much as those who have it. When used properly it is the most noble and powerful acquisition of Man. But in the kind of men (and their number is infinite) who make it the base and foundation of their worth and achievement, who quit their understanding for their memory, '*sub aliena umbra latentes*' [hiding behind other men's shadows], and can do nothing except by book, I loathe it (dare I say it?) a little more than I loathe stupidity."[66]

He wrote this in his third and final book, when he was quoting less. The last words of his *Essais* are not his: they come from Horace:

Vouchsafe, O Son of Latona, that I might enjoy
those things I have prepared, and with my mind intact
I pray, may I not degenerate into a squalid senility,
in which the lyre is wanting.[67]

SELF-QUOTATION

Poems and slogans come and go; self-quotation stays in style. Diogenes Laertius quoted himself freely. To show words in context, Samuel Johnson quoted himself at least forty-eight times in the first two editions of his *Dictionary*: thirty-two times he clearly quotes himself; in the remaining sixteen he humbly cites "*Anon*[ymous]." In most cases he seems to have quoted and misquoted from memory.[68]

Edward Parsons Day, Franklin Pierce Adams, Sarah Josepha Hale, John T. Watson, George Seldes, and Bergen Evans included quotations from themselves in their collections. Tryon Edwards did too, under a pseudonym. Quotations from Christopher Morley first appeared in BFQ 11th, edited by Christopher Morley.

Groups gabble in quotation. Edmund Burke derided "petty cabals, who attempt to hide their total want of consequence in bustle and noise, and puffing and mutual quotation of each other."[69]

Erasmus had an adage for self-quoters: "Suum cuique pulchrum" (What is one's own is beautiful). And another, from Apostolius: "Suus cuique crepitus bene olet" (Everyone thinks his own fart smells sweet).[70] We'll soon see that some wits make up quotations and blame them on others.

II

Wisdom has this advantage, among others, — that no one can be outdone by another, except during the climb.
Seneca the Younger

Practica

The next best thing to being witty one's
self, is to be able to quote another's wit.
C. N. Bovee

6

Wit

Lighten up, loosen up, step up to a buffet of quips, cranks, cracks, con-
ceits, clinches, flashes, whimsies, and retorts, courteous and cutting.[1]
Gather rosebuds while ye may, eat, drink, and be merry, for tomorrow
. . . well, you know.

Before bathroom joke books there were al-Madâ'inî's famous farters.[2]
Before Molière's *Miser* (1668) there was Ash'ab the Greedy.[3] Before Woody
Allen, Mark Twain, and Voltaire were Lucian, Aristophanes, and Aesop
the slave. Aesop was caught playing marbles with boys. An Athenian
laughed at him, and Aesop, "who was an old man far more inclined to
laugh at others than to be laughed at himself," put an unstrung bow in
the middle of the road and asked the scoffer to explain its meaning.
The Athenian was stumped. Aesop helped him: "If you keep your bow
tightly strung at all times, it will quickly break, but if you let it rest, it
will be ready to use when you need it."[4]

Witty quotations have been collected east and west. Before the *Oxford
Dictionary of Humorous Quotations* (1995) and the *Edinburgh Encyclopedia
of Wit* (1802) there were *Wits Fittes and Fancies* (1595), *Wits Treasury*

(1598), *Politeuphuia: Wits Commonwealth* (1598), *Wit's Private Wealth* (1607), *Wits Laberynth* (1610), *Witts Academy* (1635), *Wits Recreation* (1640), *Wits Interpreter* (1655), *Wits Fancies* (1659), *Wits, or, Sport upon Sport* (1662), and *Wit's Extraction* (1664). Before these were Ibn al-Jawzî's *Akhbâr al-ḥamqâ* (History of Fools, late twelfth century), Ibn Sa'îd al-Quṭubullî's *Fiqar al-bulaghâ* (Witty Remarks of Eloquent Men), and al-Barmakî's *Maḍâḥik* (Anecdotes and Jokes). Byzantine Greeks read the *Philogelos* of Hierocles and Philagrius (fifth century?), from which come "A witty young egghead sold his books when he was short of money. He then wrote to his father, 'Congratulate me, father, I am already making money from my studies'" and "On being told that crows live 200 years and more, an egghead bought one to put it to the test."[5]

Democritus (early fourth century BC) was "the Laughing Philosopher." He despised fame, disputed with keen wit, never married, and, as I've said (it's worth repeating), lived to be 109.[6] He thought "truth lies in an abyss" and went looking for it there. He warned, "Do not try to understand everything." He observed, "The best way for a man to lead his life is to have been as cheerful as possible." He thought, "People are fools who live without enjoyment of life."[7]

La Rochefoucauld felt, "The man who lives free from folly is not so wise as he thinks." "Not even philosophy renounces wit," said Seneca. Plutarch wrote, "The height of sagacity is to talk philosophy without seeming to do so, and in jesting to accomplish all that those in earnest could."[8] In a noble example a bold quoox hoax succeeded in the House of Lords.

> Lord Belgrave having concluded a speech, and as he thought clinched his argument with a long Greek quotation, Sheridan when he rose to reply admitted the force of the quotation so far as it went: "but," said he, "had the noble lord proceeded a little further, and completed the passage, he would have seen that it applied the other way." He then delivered *ore rotundo* something which had all the *ais, ois, ous, kon* and *kos* that give the world assurance of a Greek quotation; upon which Lord Belgrave very promptly and handsomely complimented

the honourable member on his readiness of recollection, and frankly admitted that the continuation of the passage had the tendency ascribed to it by Mr Sheridan, and that he had overlooked it at the moment when he gave his quotation. On the adjournment of the House, Fox, who rather piqued himself upon his knowledge of Greek, went up to Sheridan saying, "Sheridan, how came you to be so ready with that passage? It certainly was as you say, but I was not aware of it before you spoke." Sheridan had indeed succeeded in hoaxing the House, for his "quotation" was quite impromptu — and entirely innocent of Greek.[9]

A WORLD OF WITS

Wits quote half-wits and Freudian slips for the sheer fun of it. "A man of wit," wrote La Rochefoucauld, "would often be at a loss were it not for the company of fools."[10]

Grand theories spun from threadbare quotes are the stuff of sport. Alexander Pope and Dr. Arbuthnot wrote a spoof that proved "all learning was derived from the Monkeys of Ethiopia . . . to ridicule such as build general assertions upon two or three loose quotations from the ancients."[11]

Blunders by big shots are collectible: Nigel Rees fills books with them. When Squeaky Fromme failed in her attempt to shoot President Ford, Hubert Humphrey said, "There are too many guns in the hands of people who don't know how to use them." Ford himself said, "Whenever I can I watch the Detroit Tigers on radio."[12]

For a while Vice President Dan Quayle was quoted solely for laughs. Quotations of President George W. Bush set new standards for quantity and pith. Books and Web sites gathered "Bushisms," hundreds of them, like these tattered two: "Rarely is the question asked: Is our children learning?" and "They misunderestimated me."[13]

"Wit makes its own welcome, and levels all distinctions," Emerson conceded. "No dignity, no learning, no force of character, can make any stand against good wit."[14] Wit that makes a point can sting, stab, or stitch up reputations for ages. Extending the familiar honeybee metaphor, Thomas Brown wrote in his *Laconics* (1700): "Good Wit has the Sting as well as the Honey of the Bee: It differs from *Wisdom* as the Edge of a *Razor* does from that of an *Axe*."[15]

To master witty, timely, well-aimed quotations takes years of practice and more memorization headaches than you want to remember. Spontaneity takes practice: "In *Anna Karenina*, we catch Stiva in the process of composing witticisms to be used 'spontaneously,' when the occasion warrants.'" Or F. Scott Fitzgerald: "He repeated to himself an old French proverb that he had made up that morning." Or Stanislaw Lec: "I met a man so poorly read that he had to make up his own quotations from the classics."[16] Half-wits are pleased enough with themselves; to please others, wily world-class wits compete like conquerors, with humor the sharpest arrow in their quivers.

Sir Francis Bacon, wise enough to detect flattery, was wise enough to apply it. In his *Advancement of Learning*, addressed to King James I, he praised the king's "wise and princely maxims" and quoted them.[17] In contrast, Bacon noted that "Aristotle, as though he had been of the race of Ottomans, thought he could not reign except the first thing he did he killed all his brethren," and "he never nameth or mentioneth an ancient author or opinion, but to confute and reprove."

Wits sip Champagne and spit venom. Wits tease out a reluctant smile and wag dagger tongues. Wit makes you laugh and cry. "Educated insolence" is what Aristotle called it.[18]

Shakespeare knew how to "have at you with a proverb," in the repartee of the Renaissance. He portrayed an exemplary contest of wits in *Henry V* between the Constable of France and Orleans.[19] In *Twelfth Night* the clown declares, "Those wits that think they have thee do very oft prove fools" (1.5.30), a point the play confirms.

The plays of Sheridan, Oscar Wilde, Gilbert and Sullivan, and George Bernard Shaw won praise for their witty exchanges. Sheridan's Mrs. Malaprop gave her name to a species of inadvertent wit, widely imitated and often quoted: one word misused for another. "She's as headstrong as an allegory on the banks of the Nile." "He is the very pineapple of politeness!"[20]

TOO MUCH WIT

Phaedrus warned, "Wit when temperate is pleasing, when unbridled it offends." "Wear it like your sword in the scabbard, and do not brandish it to the terror of the whole company," Lord Chesterfield admonished.[21] Wit thus whispers.

When men wore wigs, witty women were risqué. Elizabeth Montagu knew Chesterfield's metaphor:

> It is often said that wit is a dangerous quality; it is there meant that it is an offensive weapon that may attack friend, as well as enemy, and is a perilous thing in society; but wit in women is apt to have other bad consequences; like a sword without a scabbard it wounds the wearer, and provokes assailants. I am sorry to say the generality of women who have excelled in wit have failed in chastity; perhaps it inspires too much confidence in the possessor, and raises an inclination in the men towards them, without inspiring an esteem; so that they are more attacked and less guarded than other women.[22]

Yet Montagu was famous for her wit and gathered witty women around her. Samuel Johnson bragged to Boswell of having dined alone with Elizabeth Carter, Hannah More, and Fanny Burney. Boswell asked, "Might not Mrs. Montagu have been a fourth?" Johnson replied, "Sir, Mrs. Montagu does not make a trade of her wit; but Mrs. Montagu is a very extraordinary woman; she has a constant stream of conversation, and it is always impregnated; it has always meaning."[23]

Montagu was the first woman in BFQ, with three lines only, written on a window after her marriage:

> Let this great maxim be my virtue's guide, —
> In part she is to blame that has been tried;
> He comes too near, that comes to be denied.

In BFQ 3rd Bartlett recognized that her last line is a quotation from Sir Thomas Overbury's poem *A Wife*.[24] Overbury wrote it for the press; Montagu took it for herself.

Johnson enjoyed pitting women against each other. He goaded Fanny Burney to match wits with Montagu: "Down with her, Burney! — down with her! — spare her not! — attack her, fight her, and down with her at once! You are a rising wit, and she is at the top; and when I was beginning the world, and was nothing and nobody, the joy of my life was to fire at all the established wits, and then everybody loved to halloo me on."[25]

Bacon said, "They say, he is not a wise man that will lose his friend for his wit; but he is less a wise man that will lose his friend for another man's wit." William Shenstone wrote, "It is often observed of wits, that they will lose their best friend for the sake of a joke." The locus classicus is from Horace: "Dummodo risum / excutiat sibi, non hic cuiquam parcet amico" (Provided he can raise a laugh for himself, he will spare not a single friend).[26]

Dr. Thomas Fuller surely knew the proverb, but what did he do? He "had a fault which is too common with persons who abound in wit — he would rather lose his friend than his jest. Having written some verses upon a scolding wife, Dr. Cosins, master of Queen's College, Cambridge, his friend and patron, one day desired to have a copy of them; to whom Fuller impudently replied: 'It is needless to give you the copy, for you have the original.' This jest, though it happened to be a truth, gave such offence, that the doctor instantly withdrew his patronage, and was ever after Fuller's enemy."[27] Only a half-wit or wit wholly committed to wit would pay so high a price.

Elizabeth I warned, "Where might is mixed with wit, there is too good an accord."

Confucius said, "If you badger people with clever talk, they usually just end up hating you."[28]

COMIC QUOTERS

Frederic Swartwout Cozzens's *Sayings of Dr. Bushwhacker* (1867) portrays Dr. Bushwhacker as a longwinded, overweening, unstoppable quoter. Dr. Bushwhacker quotes as if to win his point by siege, on and on, pausing only to fill his glass with port, claret, or what have you. He is, it seems, a caricature, a man Cozzens created to amuse. But Cozzens outdoes the doctor. In chapter 12, after dismissing Dr. Bushwhacker to Alaska, Cozzens takes up the topic of trite quotations and proceeds:

> How much language would be left us if these estrays were returned to their lawful owners, is a question. How could we console the dying if we had to give up to Gay's twenty-seventh Fable the phrase, "while there is life there's hope?" and what could we say to the good in misfortune if we had to restore to Prior's Ode, "Virtue is her own reward?" The shopkeeper who ends his long list of fancy articles with "and other articles too tedious to mention," makes use of a sentence as old as the Latin language. . . . Mr. Achitophel Scapegrace thinks the biggest stockholders in the Roaring River Canal Co. will have the best chance, as "all the big fish will eat up the little ones," (Pericles, Prince of Tyre, Act II, Scene First), and Mr. Bombastes Linderwold talks of a "platform" in precisely the same sense as Cromwell did two hundred years ago, (Queries in Letter 97, Carlyle). It is in Cromwell's seventh letter that we find for the first time that apt conjunction, "a gentleman and a Christian," now somewhat threadbare from misuse, and if we want "mother-wit," we must look for it in Spenser's Faërie Queen, Book IV., Canto X, verse 21.[29]

Cozzens goes on like this for pages, conspicuously committing every one of The Seven Deadly Sins of Quotation:

1 Garrulity. How he does go on!
2 Pettiness. Who cares about these things?
3 Hyperbole. Consolation does not need Gay's fables or gain much from them.
4 Obscurity. He gives no clue why "platform" should require calling in Cromwell.
5 He misquotes.[30]
6 He misdates.[31]
7 And he misattributes.[32]

As a quoter Cozzens is just bad enough to be famous. We need not wonder why Dr. Bushwhacker fled to Sitka.

The type is found throughout European literature. Quoting clowns took the stage as long ago as Menander's *Aspis* (late fourth century BC). There Daos, an elderly slave, quotes a string of lines from Greek tragedies to fool a lecherous miser.

Chiding a friend who quoted too much, Petrarch warned, "It is a childish glory to show off one's memory." The proverbial advice that Polonius reels off in *Hamlet* (1604) works best as comedy. Signor Thomas de la Fuenta, in Alain-René Le Sage's *Adventures of Gil Blas of Santillane* (1715), knew "all the classics by heart. If he would keep them to himself it would be very well, but he is always quoting them in company, and that people do not like."[33]

Two of Dickens's characters are comic quoters. Richard Swiveller in *The Old Curiosity Shop* (1841) is "a literary gentleman of eccentric habits, and of a most prodigious talent in quotation." More ludicrous is Captain Cuttle in *Dombey and Son* (1848), who boasts, "I never wanted two or three words in my life that I didn't know where to lay my hand upon 'em. . . . It comes of not wasting language as some do." Captain Cuttle was ever "proud of the accuracy and pointed application" of his quotations and was notorious for botching them. He advised, "In the Proverbs of Solomon you will find the following words, 'May we never want a friend in need, nor a bottle to give him!' When found, make a note of."[34]

SECONDHAND WIT

In *Love's Labor's Lost* Shakespeare described "honey-tongued Boyet":

That fellow pecks up wit, as pigeons pease,
And utters it again when God doth please.[35]

James Quin's wit was praised in his prime and commemorated by Tobias Smollett: Quin's "*bon-mots* are in every witling's mouth."[36] Witlings need a steady supply.

One of Brown's first *Laconics* is this: "If a Witty Man starts a happy thought, a Million of sordid Imitators ride it to death."[37] A friend of Dr.

Johnson sympathized that eminent wits were "perpetually expected to be saying good things — that it was a heavy tax on them." "It is indeed, a very heavy tax on them," Johnson agreed, "a tax which no man can pay who does not steal."[38]

In *Impressions of Theophrastus Such* (1879) George Eliot described Aquila, a parasite who picks up quotations in one conversation, then replays them in the next as if his own: "To his quick eye, ear, and tongue, a few predatory excursions in conversation where there are instructed persons, gradually furnish surprisingly clever modes of statement."[39]

Thomas Higginson knew "a brilliant New York talker" who "dined through three English counties on the strength of jokes which he had found in the corners of an old American 'Farmer's Almanac.'"[40] Alexander Woolcott ran in circles "quoting Mrs. [Dorothy] Parker. I know a great many circles where, by doing just that, one can gain a reputation as a wit. *One* can? Several can. Indeed, several I know do."[41]

Because wit quickly stales, the appetite for fresh wit is insatiable. TV and radio programs, joke books, and Web sites replenish the supply. In 1930 *Reader's Digest* ran a brief series entitled Repartee that became the more general Patter in August 1931. Patter and Picturesque Speech appeared frequently in issues thereafter, accompanied by jokes, anecdotes, and the ever popular Word Power. A new version of repartee, Spiced Tongue, ran irregularly between October 1946 and April 1948. The first appearance of Quotable Quotes in May 1933 began a series that continues to this day.[42] The January 1934 issue quoted Mae West, "A curved line is the loveliest distance between two points."

In relaying a risky joke, the usual ploy is to introduce it as being said by someone else. La Bruyère saw another advantage: "We often pretend that a witticism is our own, by so doing run the risk of destroying its effect; it falls flat, and witty people, or those who think themselves so, receive it coldly, because they ought to have said it, and did not. On the contrary, if told as another's, it would meet with a better reception; it is but a jest which no one is obliged to know."[43]

Wily wits use quotations to beguile.

SECONDHAND PRAISE

Aristotle was asked, "What thing is not to be done, though it be just and true?" He answered, "A man ought not to praise himself."[44]

In a selfish world secondhand praise is good business. Benjamin Franklin's *Autobiography* quotes people praising him.[45] Samuel Smiles enjoyed fame during his lifetime chiefly as the author of *Self-Help* (1859), the book that launched a genre. He self-helped his *Autobiography* (1905) by writing about his reluctance to write it. He told a friend that his life was not worth recording. The *Autobiography* records his friend's reply, "Your books are extensively read in this country and America. They have been translated into nearly every language in Europe. They appear in many of the Indian languages, and even in Siamese and Japanese. I am quite sure that your readers would like to know much more about yourself than has yet been published by your interviewers." Smiles complied and wrote.

Halfway through his *Autobiography* Smiles admits that "it would be considered absurdly eulogistic were I to detail the many marks of sympathy and gratitude which I have received from all classes of the community, at home and abroad" and mentions "a few curious instances": a man from Dundee who named his son after Smiles; a man from Hastings who wrote to him, "I have repeatedly gained hope and courage" from *Self-Help*; a lady from Birmingham whose son wrote, "I thank God I have read it"; a gentleman who thanked him, saying, "I am now a prosperous man, and have to thank you for it all."[46]

Successful American businessmen know the trick. In the final pages of his autobiography, *Be My Guest* (1957), Conrad Hilton quotes his 1950 speech, "The Battle for Freedom," and follows with excerpts from the "thousands of letters . . . from every corner of the land" praising the speech. He then quotes a prayer he published in 1952, adding, "I was deluged with letters and requests for copies. . . . From almost every country in the world, from every state in the Union, from the old and the young, from rich and poor, from military and civilian, the cynical and the naïve, philosophers and advertising men, rabbis, ministers, from

wise men and crackpots from every level of society, from schoolteach-
ers and Sunday school teachers, from children of eight to oldsters of
ninety-two," on and on, and to top it off, he quotes from a letter that
assured him, "God read it too — with pleasure."[47]

VENTRILOQUISM

There are two modes of quotation ventriloquism: (1) Put the words
you want said into someone else's mouth. Sir Francis Bacon described
"a cunning, which we in England call 'The turning of the cat in the pan';
which is, when that which a man says to another, he lays it as if another
had said it to him."[48] Or (2) find what you want already said by someone
else, preferably someone famous and respected.

The first mode is easier. Martin Luther "was fond of the device of putting words into other people's mouths." Josephus noticed that Clearchus
put words in the mouth of Aristotle. No one has been more successful
than Plato in his treatment of Socrates.[49]

Lacking a real person, words can be placed in the mouths of theatri-
cal or fictional characters. Emerson wrote:

It is a familiar expedient of brilliant writers, and not less of witty
talkers, the device of ascribing their own sentence to an imaginary
person, in order to give it weight, — as Cicero, Cowley, Swift, Landor,
and Carlyle have done. And Cardinal de Retz, at a critical moment in
the Parliament of Paris, described himself in an extemporary Latin
sentence, which he pretended to quote from a classic author, and
which told admirably well. It is a curious reflex effect of this old
enhancement of our thought by citing it from another, that many
men can write better under a mask than for themselves.[50]

Lucian wrote *Dialogues of the Dead* (second century), Fontenelle wrote
Nouveaux dialogues des morts (1683), Matthew Prior's *Dialogues of the Dead*
(published posthumously in 1760) were admired by Alexander Pope, and
Walter Savage Landor wrote a series of *Imaginary Conversations* (1824,
1826, 1846), bringing famous people back to life to converse quotably.

More difficult but more effective is to find the words you need verifiably provided by someone of greater authority. Admitting that Pythagoras was wise, Petrarch would nonetheless denounce his doctrine of metempsychosis "if I dared. Since I do not dare, Lactantius of Formiae will speak through me more boldly."[51] Mikhail Bakhtin noticed that proverbs are used "to indicate something the speaker for whatever reason does not wish to say directly."[52]

TRANSCENDENTAL VENTRILOQUISM

Georg Christoph Lichtenberg wrote, "There exists a species of transcendental ventriloquism by means of which men can be made to believe that something said on earth comes from Heaven."[53]

Prior to and throughout the American Civil War the debate over slavery called on higher powers. In one of the most famous quotations in American history Abraham Lincoln declared, "'A House divided against itself cannot stand.' I believe this government cannot endure, permanently half *slave* and half *free*."[54] Lincoln quoted Mark 3:25, a vouched quotation so often associated with Lincoln that if it came from any other source it would have been his by now. He quoted Scripture to agree with it, to invoke its power to strengthen his own.

Slaveholders invoked it, too. L. Wesley Norton demonstrated, "There was not a significant point of view in regard to slavery that did not find its proponents to defend it or its antagonists to condemn it on the basis of the Bible." Norton observed that "certain passages became centers of argument, first of all, Genesis 9:20–27."[55]

And Noah began to be an husbandman, and he planted a vineyard; and he drank of the wine, and was drunken; and he was uncovered within his tent. And Ham, the father of Canaan, saw the nakedness of his father, and told his two brethren without. And Shem and Japheth took a garment, and laid it upon both their shoulders, and went backward, and covered the nakedness of their father; and their faces were backward, and they saw not their father's nakedness. And Noah awoke from his wine, and knew what his younger son had done unto him. And he said, Cursed be Canaan; a servant of servants shall he be unto his brethren. And he said, blessed be the Lord God of Shem; and Canaan shall be his servant. God shall enlarge Japheth, and he shall dwell in the tents of Shem; and Canaan shall be his servant.

Because Ham was believed to be the ancestor of the people of Africa and Shem and Japheth the ancestors of the people of Asia and Europe, these verses were read as biblical justification for enslaving blacks.[56]

We might gape with wonder at such an interpretive stretch: a drunk old man wakes up grumpy at his son and condemns his grandson and his grandson's progeny to slavery forever.

A secular literalist might regard Noah's outburst as the sputtering of an old man with a hangover. To read these verses as divine endorsement for whip and chain it was only necessary to believe: (1) They were a holy man's curse, words that were more than words, invested with a power that lasted for centuries. Or (2) for those too sophisticated to believe in the power of curses, Noah's words were prophetic: slavery was not a consequence of his speaking but an ordained future he foresaw. The whole incident, drink, stupor, and rude awakening, looked to a future that slaveholders dutifully fulfilled. Or (3) the fact that the words were said by Noah is subordinate to the fact that they are words in the Bible. "The word of God, as in this and all other parts of the Scriptures, do not convey false ideas, but true and immutable ones."[57] God spoke through Noah.

Abolitionists had biblical texts of their own, which did little to persuade slaveholders. Appeal to the Hebrew and Greek of the Old and New Testaments was belittled as pedantry, irrelevant to believers adamant that the King James Bible spoke for God clearly.[58] Attempts to dismiss Genesis as old law overruled by the New Testament were answered by Paul's letter to Philemon, returning the slave Onesimus to his master. A slaveholder wrote: "You preach the requirements of God's law, but constantly forget, in regard to this very matter, both the precept and example of Paul, its great expounder. . . . He does notice the subject, and gives directions for the conduct both of masters and slaves, although he did not himself own a servant. Where he says, 'Slaves, obey in ALL THINGS your masters,' you say, 'Run away' on all occasions; and more — to the extent of your ability, you aid them in so doing."[59]

The Reverend Fred A. Ross accused abolitionists of "torturing the Bible for a while" to get the testimony they wanted.[60] He knew how: Ross won a national reputation as a student of the Bible able to quote chapter and verse that proved God's approval of slavery.[61]

Lincoln read Ross with disgust.[62] Against a Bible verse what could stand except another Bible verse? So he wrote his "House Divided" speech.

But I leap ahead . . .

The nature of man, which coveteth
divination, thinks it no peril to foretell
that which indeed they do but collect.
Francis Bacon

7

Prophecy

Prophetic friends depressed Lord Byron:

> Of all the horrid, hideous notes of woe,
> Sadder than owl-songs or the midnight blast,
> Is that portentous phrase, "I told you so,"
> Uttered by friends, those prophets of the *past*.[1]

Bankers, bookies, brokers, pollsters, weather forecasters, and actuaries practice prophecy routinely. They are the latest in a long line of farsighted folk who carve their livings from the future. Publilius Syrus said, "The future fights all attempts to master her."[2] But we try. Rather than rely on gutted birds, fits and faints, or commotion of planets and stars, modern prophets keep careful records, chart cycles, study metamorphoses, and demystify cause and effect with computer models and million-dollar laboratories.

Others ask old books what will be. What must happen, and what must happen again? What did the past predict about tomorrow? What did it say about today?

And how could anything deposited thousands of years ago predict what will happen, clearly, precisely, and certainly? Only with the help of expert interpreters able to read dead languages, long ice-core cylinders, and layers of ash.

DIVINE WORDS

Priests devoutly memorized the thousand hymns of the Ṛig Veda to guarantee that mantras were accurately repeated; a single mistaken syllable could spoil everything. Getting it right, exactly right, was essential and difficult, so much so that a Vedic priest prayed for help, praying, "Within my mouth, Bṛhaspati, deposit speech lucid, vigorous, and free from weakness."[3] To quote the Veda (says the Veda) is to open heaven and call the gods. It says, "Now have we found the secret tongue of worship," saying so in Sanskrit.[4]

Correct quotation is commanded in Hebrew by the Lord of Lords. Affixed to the entryway of homes around the world is a small case containing a mezuzah, a small scroll on which are two passages, handwritten on parchment, from Deuteronomy 6:4–9 and 11:13–21. Deuteronomy 6:4–9 explains why.

> Hear, O Israel: The LORD our God is one LORD: And thou shalt love the LORD thy God with all thine heart, and with all thy soul, and with all thy might. And these words, which I command thee this day, shall be in thine heart: And thou shalt teach them diligently unto thy children, and shalt talk of them when thou sittest in thine house, and when thou walkest by the way, and when thou liest down, and when thou riseth up. And thou shall bind them for a sign upon thy hand, and they shall be as frontlets between thine eyes. And thou shalt write them upon the posts of thy house, and on thy gates.

Quotations honor and obey.

Quotations comfort and relieve. A young man in Søren Kierkegaard's *Repetition* (1843) loved the book of Job body and soul. "It is my joy to make transcripts again and again of all that he said, now in Danish characters, now in Latin script, now on a sheet of one size, now on that of another size. . . . Every one of these transcripts is laid like a so-called 'God's-hand-poultice' upon my sick heart."[5]

Quotations protect. Ottoman talismanic shirts worn under armor "were covered with Koranic verses, prayers and sequences of numbers meant to protect the wearer through spiritual efficacy. These texts also had apotropaic power. Both armour and shirts, for example, are often inscribed with the phrase from Koran 61:13 asking for help from God and a speedy victory (*naṣr min allāh wa fatḥ gharīb*) or with the opening verses of Koran 48 (*Surat al-Fath*), the chapter of Victory."[6]

"A bird that had learned to speak was being chased by a hawk, and cried out a phrase it had been taught: 'Saint Thomas, help me!' The hawk fell dead."[7]

Franz Kafka told Gustav Janouch, "Words are magical formulae. They leave fingermarks behind on the brain, which in the twinkling of an eye become the footprints of history."[8] Christopher Morley wrote for BFQ 11th: "One can melodize words for years without stopping to consider how silly they are. Who cares? The magic happens."[9]

Quotations prophesy. Skepticism neither slows nor fazes persons eager to extract the future from the *I Ching* (quoted at last in BFQ 15th) or to consult the sibylline oracles, the prophecies of Merlin and Nostradamus, and, above all, Revelation, the Apocalypse of Saint John, with its Four Horsemen, Armageddon, and angels crying "Woe!"

SKEPTICISM

In *Antigone* Sophocles complained, "Prophets as a tribe are money-lovers, each and every one."[10] Many have made their livelihood by collecting and invoking prophecies made by others. Thucydides mentions prophecy collectors happy to quote from their collections whenever disaster struck.[11]

The future is full of disasters. Take your pick: nuclear war, runaway comets, plummeting asteroids, global warming, viruses, genetics gone wild, and volcanoes rising under the sea. All have quotable prophets and redoubtable naysayers calling them fools.

Look back: collections of prophecies are among the world's oldest literature. The collections of Esarhaddon and Assurbanipal date from the seventh century BC. The Balaam text from Deir 'Allā is a century older. The prophecies of Neferti and the prophecies of Ibalpiel II are in their fifth millennium.[12] Skeptics say they are the world's oldest humbug.

"Divinations, and soothsayings, and dreams are vain," says Ecclesiasticus 34:5. "The best of seers is he who guesses well," wrote Plutarch, quoting Euripides.[13]

According to Xenophon, Socrates said that soothsayers have the reputation "of prophesying the future for others but of not being able to foresee their own." Aesop has a fable on it. Lucian called prophets "habitual liars." In crackling sarcasm Erasmus remarked, "Some persons with the gift of foreknowledge divine wonderful things about times gone by."[14]

Montaigne reported that Scythians set false prophets afire. Francis Bacon thought prophets "ought all to be despised; and ought to serve but for winter talk by the fireside. . . . They have done much mischief."[15] Thomas Hobbes warned, "Though God Almighty can speak to a man by dreams, visions, voice, and inspiration; yet he obliges no man to believe he hath so done to him that pretends it; who, being a man, may err, and, which is more, may lie." "Among all forms of mistake," wrote George Eliot, "prophecy is the most gratuitous."[16]

Enough.

Prophets do not need a vision or trance; some see the inevitable consequences of present foolishness plain as day. You don't need a crystal ball to know you don't soothsay for Scythians. You don't need a Tarot to foretell that hyped religion has hell to pay. God help you if you fail to foresee a happy future for your potentate. "Alexander dragged the Pythian priestess to the temple on a forbidden day. — She exclaimed, '*My son, thou art invincible*,' which was oracle enough for him."[17]

Souls who know sage quotations beware offending the pious wishes of the mighty. The elder Seneca quoted Fuscus quoting Virgil quoting Dido, queen of Carthage, who dared to scorn the oracles that opposed her. Dido said, "Scilicet is superis labor est, ea cura quietos sollicitat" (This is work for gods, this is to vex their peace).[18] As if: Who do you think you're fooling? Why would heaven disclose the future to *you*? Seneca says the line was a *puerum locum*, a common quotation used to reproach sanctimony. But Fuscus warned it was unwise to quote it in front of potentates. They have a killer counterquotation, "Capulo tenus abdidit ensem" (He buried the sword to its hilt).[19] *Dixit* Seneca.[20]

Fuscus, a contemporary of Virgil, already considered his poetry prophetic. Saint Augustine thought Virgil a prophet.[21] Dante did too, and many others.

DIVINE QUOTATION

Kierkegaard wrote, "Any theological student who confines his sermon to Bible quotes can be the profoundest of all, for the Bible is surely the profoundest book of all."[22] Yet with all its riches, it's strange what some people take out of it. "Scrutamini Scripturas" (Search the Scriptures), says the Gospel of John. "These two words have undone the world," wrote John Selden in 1689, heartsick over the wars of religion that bloodied England throughout his life.[23]

Joseph Smith the prophet prophesied anew by discovering old books written on gold tablets. The tablets are seen no more. Smith's English translation of them tells a quotation tale unique in Christian literature. Late in the Book of Mormon Jesus arrives, newly resurrected, to preach salvation to Native Americans. When they doubt he is the Messiah, he persuades them truly he is. How? By quoting, word for word, chapter 54 of Isaiah, the prophecy of his coming.[24] Jesus proves he is Jesus by quoting.

In the New Testament Jesus quotes Psalms, Isaiah, Hosea, and Deuteronomy. In one place he quoted in order to contradict a commandment and in another to expand one.[25]

To emphasize the words of Jesus many modern Bibles display them in red type. This innovation in Bible printing was conceived by Louis Klopsch of New York City, an enterprising Christian publisher. In 1889 Klopsch acquired the *Christian Herald* and took it from a circulation of thirty thousand to a quarter of a million, enjoying a "material prosperity" that paid for missions and famine relief.[26] In 1896 he published his own quotation collection, *Many Thoughts of Many Minds*, arranged under topics of interest to him: "Business," "Employment," "Labor," "Work," "Gold," "Money," "Riches," and "Wealth." Under the heading "Christ" the person most quoted is Napoleon. Under "Religion" Klopsch quotes H. G. J. Adam: "If we make religion our business, God will make it our blessedness," a quotation that keeps Mr. Adam in compendia.[27]

In 1899 Klopsch was stopped by Luke 22:20: "This cup is the new testament in my blood, which I shed for you." He "conceived the idea which took form in the issue of the 'Red Letter Bible.' This he designed to show, first, the words in the New Testament actually spoken by the Savior; and second, the prophetic references to Christ in the Old Testament." Klopsch "engaged the services of a number of distinguished Bible scholars, including several leading college professors in this country and abroad." The scholars marked sections of the Bible and looked at each other's markings, "so that each eminent scholar practically went over the entire Bible and annotated the work already done by others. Many months were occupied in this interchange."[28] The result first appeared in 1901: the red-letter Bible. It was a commercial triumph; printing followed printing, and imitators soon followed. Klopsch plowed his profits into missionary work.

DIVINATION BY QUOTATION

Above reproach and beyond rebuttal, in crises God is the ideal witness, called to testify, and the ideal judge, whose rule is revealed in quotations.[29] Sumerians, Egyptians, Aryans, Druids, Greeks, and Romans paid dearly to consult oracles and hear what Amun or Apollo had to say. Tarquin Superba, the last king of Rome, paid an exorbitant sum to buy old prophetic scrolls from a hard-bargaining Sibyl.[30]

The verses of Homer and Virgil were thought to have prophetic power. The *Sortes* were practiced for centuries in this way: a question was asked, and the poets' works were read at random; chance verses were interpreted as divine reply. Rabelais parodied the *Sortes* in *Gargantua and Pantagruel* and listed powerful men who took the practice seriously: Opellius Macrinus, Brutus, Hadrian, Clodius Albinus, Alexander Severus, and Claudius Augustus.[31] The *Sortes Apostolorum* claimed: "These are the sortes sanctorum which never err nor deceive; that is, ask God and thou shalt obtain what thou desirest."[32]

Christian churches combated the superstition but discovered people were doing the same thing with Bibles. Saint Anthony converted to Christianity after accidentally overhearing Matthew 19:21. In a crisis of faith Augustine opened a Bible to read whatever he found there and read Romans 13:13: "Let us walk honestly, as in the day; not in rioting and drunkenness, not in chambering and wantonness, not in strife and envying." He remembered, "A light of security infused into my heart, — all the gloom of doubt vanished away."[33]

Proud of himself for having ascended Mont Ventoux, Petrarch randomly opened the *Confessions* of Augustine and was stunned to read, "And men go to admire the high mountains, the vast floods of the ocean, and the revolutions of the stars — and desert themselves."[34] He could not believe it was coincidence and took fright. At the outbreak of civil war, Charles I consulted Virgil and read:

at bello audacis populi vexatus et armis,
finibus extorris, complexu avulsus Iuli,
auxilium imploret, videatque indigna suorum
funera; nec, cum se sub leges pacis iniquae
tradiderit, regno aut optata luce fruatur,
sed cadat ante diem mediaque inhumatus harena.

[Harassed in war by the arms of a fearless nation, expelled from his territory and torn from Iulus's embrace, let him plead for aid and see his friends cruelly slaughtered! Nor yet, when he has submitted to the terms of an unjust peace, may he enjoy his kingship or the life he longs for, but perish before his time and lie unburied on a lonely strand!][35]

Muhammad recited the Koran in suras, later gathered together, each a part of an eternal book that Muhammad quoted as it was revealed to him. Sura 39 begins: "This Book is revealed by God, the Mighty, the Wise One. We have revealed to you the Book with the Truth." Sura 43 says: "We have revealed the Koran in the Arabic tongue, that you may understand its meaning. It is a transcript of the eternal book in Our keeping, sublime, and full of wisdom."

In March 1985 Shiite Hezbollah grabbed Terry Anderson, an American reporter, off the streets of Beirut. They bound and gagged him, stuffed him in the trunk of a car, and drove him away to eighty-one months of captivity. His guards were bored and inattentive, but some were kind. One gave him a Bible, "a source of bewilderment and humility," Anderson says, "there is so much I don't understand."[36] He had other books too. "The books are a blessing, even the bad ones."[37] He prayed for answers, and when the answer was silence, he understood, "If I were God, I wouldn't talk to me, either."[38] He read "a book on prayer written by an English evangelist that is very good. He says that prayer is always answered, that the stricture, 'Ask and ye shall receive' is meant literally. I don't know about that. I'm not sure anymore that it is even right to ask for anything, except patience and strength to endure what comes, and help in understanding."[39]

He asked his captors for a radio. They went away, prayed for help, and opened a Koran at random. They read, decided the Koran said no, so no, no radio. Anderson told them, "Well, go do it again." They asked again, the Koran answered, and this time Anderson's prayer was granted. He got his radio.[40]

QUOTING GOD

In any language the Bible is a textbook for quotology. Peter quotes Leviticus, Psalms, and Isaiah. Paul quotes Exodus, Job, Isaiah, and Hosea.

Chapters 36 through 39 of Isaiah quote chapters 18 and 19 of 2 Kings. Much of Chronicles is word-for-word iteration of 1 and 2 Kings.

God himself is quoted in Genesis, Exodus, Leviticus, Numbers, Deuteronomy, Joshua, Judges, 1 and 2 Samuel, 1 and 2 Kings, 1 and 2 Chronicles, Job, Psalms, Isaiah, Jeremiah, Ezekiel, Hosea, Joel, Amos, Obadiah, Jonah, Micah, Nahum, Zephaniah, Haggai, Zechariah, and Malachi. "The Lord said" introduces quotations that lay down the law and storm in anger. "The LORD spake thus to me," says Isaiah. "Sanctify the LORD of hosts himself; and let him be your fear, and let him be your dread" (8:11, 13). "The fear of the LORD is the beginning of wisdom," says Proverbs, then says it again (1:7, 9:10).

Maimonides' magnificent *Guide of the Perplexed* proceeds through the prophecies of Ezekiel to the grace and glory of creation and the mysteries of what will be. He concludes, "The final end of all that exists is not to be sought."[41]

FALSE PROPHETS

The bitter exchange between King Ahab and the prophet Micaiah ben Imlah is told in 1 Kings 22 and again in 2 Chronicles 18. It is worth reading twice.

Ahab hated Micaiah because Micaiah always foretold trouble. Four hundred prophets told Ahab his planned military campaign would succeed, but Ahab asked for Micaiah's prophecy, too. Micaiah first gave Ahab the reassurance he wanted, but Ahab was suspicious and asked again. Then Micaiah said:

> I hear the word of the LORD; I saw the LORD sitting upon his throne, and all the host of heaven standing on his right hand and on his left.
>
> And the LORD said, Who shall entice Ahab king of Israel, that he may go up and fall at Ramoth-gilead? And one spake saying after this manner, and another saying after that matter.
>
> Then there came out a spirit, and stood before the LORD, and said, I will entice him. And the LORD said unto him, Wherewith?

And he said, I will go out, and be a lying spirit in the mouth of all his prophets. And the LORD said, Thou shalt entice him, and thou shalt also prevail: go out, and do even so.

Now therefore, behold, the LORD has put a lying spirit in the mouth of these thy prophets.

So Micaiah said, but how could Ahab believe him? Micaiah said he saw God in heaven consult with spirits; he told Ahab that the Lord commanded a spirit to make his prophets lie. Was Micaiah telling the truth or making up a story to defame rival prophets and threaten the king? Ahab decided he'd been right in the first place: Micaiah prophesied nothing but trouble.[42] Ahab threw Micaiah in prison, went on with his war plan, and died at Ramoth-gilead, just as Micaiah said he would.

This episode is much more than another sorry instance of a willful king ignoring a prophetic warning: it is a glaring example of the difficulty the powerful have in detecting who is a pious fraud and who a holy terror.

The truth of prophecy is contested in the Micaiah episode: four hundred prophets had been wrong because they felt a spirit within them, a spirit sent by God, says Micaiah. If we take Micaiah at his word, the four hundred lying prophets did not know they were wrong; they mistook because God sent them a lying spirit. Four hundred errant prophets prove inspiration cannot be trusted.[43]

And what if you were Ahab? Micaiah's story *sounds* like a story. Ahab would be dumb not to see it that way and dumber still if he failed to see what a story can say. Maimonides wrote: "God is too exalted than that He should turn His prophets into a laughing-stock and a mockery for fools by ordering them to carry out crazy actions. . . . Undoubtedly it has become clear and manifest that the greater part of the prophecies of the prophets proceeds by means of parable."[44] Whether speaking literal truth or parable, Micaiah clearly warned Ahab, do not go to war.

When another prophet demanded that Micaiah tell Ahab why the king should believe Micaiah, he replied that events would prove him right. They do, but this exasperates the problem rather than solves it: since the truth of a prophecy can only be confirmed after the fact, how to tell in advance whether a prophecy is true or false?

The past record of a prophet is no guarantee. Ahab distrusted Micaiah because he *always* foresaw trouble, and until Ramoth-gilead Ahab had succeeded well enough.

Consensus is no guarantee. The episode exposes the error of trusting a supermajority, those four hundred mistaken prophets. It gives every solitary maniac with a wild idea a scriptural precedent for denouncing everyone else.

Not even apparent contradiction by a greater prophet is a guarantee. According to 1 Kings 21:19, no less a prophet than Elijah had foretold that dogs would lick Ahab's blood in Jezreel, far from Ramoth-gilead. Rabbis resolved the contradiction by noting that dogs in Jezreel licked Ahab's bloody chariot days after he died.[45]

What is most arresting about the episode is that here, in the midst of God's word, is a life-or-death example that throws into doubt those who presume to know God's will. A heaven-sent message could come from a lying spirit, serving God as it was commanded to do. In the times of Jeremiah and Micah lying prophets had become a public problem. The Bible is emphatic: some lies come directly from God. Ezekiel, quoting the Lord, said, "And if the prophet be deceived when he hath spoken a thing, I the LORD have deceived that prophet."[46] True and false prophets alike believed they were truly quoting God. Their faith was sometimes right, sometimes not.

We can be sure that some false prophets knew they were faking it, plying credulity for whatever they could get. The credulous get worse than they ever supposed, failing to foresee that in matters as perilous as war and the word of God a quoter had better be able to tote more than quotation. A lifetime reputation for honesty would help. Otherwise, the link to the quotee in heaven could be hollow as a smoke ring.[47]

Micaiah exposed Ahab as four hundred times a fool because he put his faith in four hundred prophets.

LATTER PROPHETS

The words of Abraham Lincoln are cast in bronze, incised on marble, and publicly venerated. Lincoln's fame rose like a flame from a Bible quotation.

In 1858 Lincoln said, "A House divided against itself cannot stand," quoting Mark 3:25.[48] Lincoln told Horace White of the *Chicago Press and Tribune* that "some of his friends had scolded him a good deal about the opening paragraph and the 'house divided against itself' and wanted him to change it or leave it out altogether, but that he had studied this subject more deeply than they had and that he was going to stick to that text whatever happened."[49]

The quotation was already deeply embedded in American politics. Thomas Paine had alluded to it in *Common Sense*. Andrew Jackson cited it often. Sam Houston, Daniel Webster, and abolitionists had applied it directly to slavery. The quotation was a lightning rod for the Lincoln-Douglas debates.[50] It stirred Douglas's indignation. He raged against Lincoln's use of it in Jonesboro and Charleston.

Lincoln's vouched quotation is now treated as prophetic. What then of Douglas, who said, "This is the inevitable and irresistible result of Mr. Lincoln's argument, inviting a warfare between the North and the South, to be carried on with ruthless vengeance until one section or the other shall be driven to the wall and become the victim of the rapacity of the other."[51]

Like the warnings of Jeremiah and Amos, Cassandra and Tiresias, Douglas's warnings were futile. They could not prevent the disaster they predicted. War came, but not because Lincoln's quotation invited it.

As Lincoln foresaw, war came because the House divided.

My imagination doesn't require anything
more of the book than to provide a
framework within which it can wander.
Alphonse Daudet

8

Meditations

When true principles have once been etched into the mind, even
the briefest commonplace will suffice to recall the futility of regrets
or fears; such as, for example,

What are the children of men, but as leaves
That drop at the wind's breath.

Marcus Aurelius[1]

How wisely was it said *Ducunt volentes fata, nolentes trahunt.* There are so many daily proofs of it, that, so far as I am concerned, truer words were never spoken.

Francesco Guicciardini[2]

Our patrons of learning are so farre now adaies, from respecting the *Muses,* and giving that honour to Schollers, or reward which they deserve, & are allowed by those indulgent priviledges of many noble Princes, that after all their paines taken in the *Universities,* cost and charge, expenses, irksome houres, laborious tasks, wearisome daies, dangers, hazards (barred *interim* from all pleasures which other men have, mewed up like hawkes all their lives) if they chance to wade through them, they shall in the end be rejected, contemned, & which is their greatest misery, driven to their shifts, exposed to want, poverty and beggary. Their familiar attendants are,

Pallentes morbi, luctus, curaeque laborque
Et metus, & melesuada fames, & turpis egestas,
Terribiles, visu formae —
Griefe, labour, care, pale sicknesse, miseries,
Feare, filthy poverty, hunger that cryes,
Terrible monsters to be seene with eyes.

If there were nothing else to trouble them, the conceipt of this alone were enough to make them all melancholy.

Robert Burton[3]

What a strange lecture comes next in your letter! You say I must familiarize my mind with the fact, that "Miss Austen is not a poetess, has no 'sentiment' (you scornfully enclose the word in inverted commas), no eloquence, none of the ravishing enthusiasm of poetry," — and then you add, I *must* "learn to acknowledge her as *one of the greatest artists, of the greatest painters of human character,* and one of the writers with the nicest sense of means to an end that ever lived."

The last point only will I ever acknowledge.

Can there be a great artist without poetry?

What I call — what I will bend to, as a great artist then — cannot be destitute of the divine gift.

Currer Bell (pseudonym of Charlotte Brontë)[4]

"The eternal Silence of these infinite spaces TERRIFIES ME."

This eloquent phrase, which the powerful impression it seeks to produce on our minds and the magnificence of its form have made one of the most famous sayings ever uttered, is a Poem *and not a* Thought *at all.*

For Eternal *and* Infinite *are symbols of nonthinking. Their impact is entirely emotional.*

Paul Valéry[5]

And quietly — heavily — like an irrevocable sentence, there came, breathed to him as it were from that winter cold and loneliness, words that he had read an hour or two before, in the little red book beside his hand — words in which the gayest of French poets has fixed, as though by accident, the most tragic of human cries —

"Quittez le long espoir, et les vastes pensées."

He sank on his knees, wrestling with himself and with the bitter longing for life, and the same words rang through him, deafening every cry but their own.

"Quittez — quittez — le long espoir, et les vastes pensées!"

Mrs. Humphrey Ward[6]

The development of mankind has made us so delicate, sensitive, and ailing that we need the most potent kind of cures and comforts — hence arises the danger that man might bleed to death from the truth he has recognized. Byron expressed this in his immortal lines:

Sorrow is knowledge: they who know the most
Must mourn the deepest o'er the fatal truth,
The tree of knowledge is not that of life.

There is no better cure for such cares than to conjure up the festive frivolity of Horace, at least for the worst hours and eclipses of the soul, and with him to say to yourself:

Why do you torture your poor reason
for insight into the riddle of eternity?
Why do we not simply lie down under the high plantane?
or here under this pine tree?

    Friedrich Nietzsche[7]

Years later, he frequently read that what he had seen had not lasted more than half a dozen seconds. But Dad forever maintained otherwise. The light, three times brighter than midday, simply persists. At the moment that Oppenheimer, a few miles west, speaks to himself those often-quoted words from the Bhagavad Gita, *"I am become Death, the destroyer of worlds," my father hears, at his back, the unchanged chatter of card players, Sinatra's sinners still smooching angels, in an early and unexplained sun-shower.*

Richard Powers[8]

A party of us were looking one autumn afternoon at a country church. Over the western door was a clock with, " THE HOUR COMETH," written in gold, upon it. Polonius proceeded to explain, rather lengthily, what a good inscription it was. "But not very apposite," said Rosencrantz, "seeing the clock has stopped." The sun was indeed setting, and the hands of the clock, glittering full in his face, pointed up to noon. Osric however, with a slight lisp, said, the inscription was all the more apt, "for the hour would come to the clock, instead of the clock following the hour." On which Horatio, taking out his watch, (which he informed us was just then more correct than the sun,) told us that unless we set off home directly we should be late for dinner. That was one way of considering an Inscription.

Edward FitzGerald[9]

9

Confucius went to Chou, intending to ask Lao Tzu about the rites. Lao Tzu said, "Those of whom you speak have already rotted away, both the men and their bones. Only their words are here."
Ssu-ma Ch'ien

Last Words

Edward Le Compte wrote: "Death can make even triviality momentous, and delirium oracular. Last words have an aura about them, if not a halo."[1]

Famous last words can record words said immediately before they proved to be dead wrong: Tony "Two-ton" Galento said, "I'll moider de bum," before Joe Louis beat him up.[2]

Or they can be the last words uttered before death. Dying, Frederick the Great consoled, "We are over the hill, we shall go better now."[3]

Or they can be both. At the battle of Spotsylvania (1864) Gen. John Sedgwick uttered his famous last words: "They couldn't hit an elephant at this dist . . ."[4]

Last words form in art, law, and ceremony: requiems, valedictions, last wills and testaments, tomb inscriptions, last chapters, last acts, last words written, last words spoken, last words spoken coherently.

The ODQ and Tsouras's *Military Quotations* devote separate sections to last words; the CDQ, HBQ, NCPQ, NDQ, and ODQ have pages of epitaphs; Bartlett's *Familiar Quotations* had an epitaphs section from its 11th through its 14th editions. Great writers — Pope, Dryden, Johnson, Coleridge, Scott, Burns, and many more — wrote epitaphs. In *The Arabian Nights* Shahrazad recites the epitaph of Majd al-Din:

> You were created from earth, becoming a live creature;
> You were taught to speak with eloquence.
> You have returned to earth, becoming a dead thing.
> It is as though you never left the earth at all.[5]

Emily Dickinson's epitaph: "E.D. Called Back."

The last words of Shakespeare's heroes are quoted profoundly. Hamlet said, "The rest is silence." Lear wailed, "Never, never, never, never, never." Anyone with a spark of drama enjoys supposing Prospero's last speech is Shakespeare's farewell to the stage. Villains die quotably: Richard III bargaining for a horse, Macbeth fighting for his life. At the moment of his execution cruel Aaron of *Titus Andronicus* is asked if he has anything to repent. He says:

> I am no baby, I, that with base prayers
> I should repent the evils I have done;
> Ten thousand worse than ever yet I did
> Would I perform if I might have my will.
> If one good deed in all my life I did
> I do repent it from my very soul.[6]

If the very soul of evil were to die someday, it would say something like that.

The first books of last words were collections of the dying words of converts and martyrs. In his *Actes and Monuments of Martyrs* (1653) John Foxe quotes Dr. Weston of Oxford, who quotes Augustine: "When the last words of one lying on his death-bed are heard which is ready to go to his grave, no man saith that he hath made a lye."[7]

"Dying speeches" made good reading in Britain and her colonies. *The Dying Speeches of Several Excellent Persons, who Suffered for their Zeal against Popery* (1683) and John Eliot's *Dying Speeches of Several Indians* (1685?) collect last words. "For the encouragement of piety in other children," Cotton Mather assembled *A Token* (1700), a short book commemorating the last days and last words of six Puritan children.

The anonymous compiler of *The Dying Speeches and Behaviour of the Several State Prisoners that have been Executed the last 300 years* (1720) doubted the probity of last words.

> But 'tis with great difficulty, if ever the contrary Party will admit, that the Constancy, Serenity, or even the Exultation of the Sufferer at his Execution, are any signs he is the right; or that the Justification of the Enterprize of the last Gasp adds any weight to the Justice of his Cause. . . . Indeed, we find Men of the most distant principles have dy'd, not only with equal Intrepidity, but equal Hopes of future Joys: We find the Cavalier looking on the Cause of God's Vice-regent as the Cause of God, and bravely embracing Death and Sufferings, in Defence of his Lawful King, and the ancient Constitution: Soon after we behold the Regicide, at his Execution, in Raptures at the Thoughts that God had been so gracious to permit him to imbrue his Hands in Royal Blood. . . . Whatever else may be concluded from such Scenes as these, we easily discern from hence, how far natural Courage, Education, and a Familiarity with Dangers, or the Spirit of Enthusiasm, can carry a Man.[8]

Contrite, defiant, protesting, and baffled last words of the condemned. "Last words were indeed an important part of public executions for centuries. . . . In Elizabethan England and later, hundreds, perhaps thousands, of broadsides and pamphlets, chapbooks, and even ballads were printed and reprinted that reported the last words (usually, but not always, carefully prepared and conforming to a formula allowing for little spontaneity or originality) spoken by traitors and highwaymen, pirates and murderers, royalty and dissenting ministers literally under the gallows or in front of the executioner's block."[9]

Last words edify. Solon said, "We should always learn." When he lay in bed dying, two friends came to say good-bye but fell into arguing. Solon rose to listen to their arguments, applauded one for the reasons he gave, then said his dying words, "I thank heaven, that I finish my days in this manner, and have not left the world without knowing this, what I have just learned."[10]

Last words admonish: "The great Saladin died in 1193, and by his express direction his winding-sheet was displayed on high by his standard-bearer with these awful words, 'See here all that is left in possession of the mighty Sultan Saladin, conqueror of the East.'"[11]

Last words disappear. Elizabeth I repined, "All my possessions for a moment of time," words that have vanished from the ODQ.[12]

Last words give a glimpse of heaven. Charles Reade expired ecstatic, "Amazing, amazing glory!"[13] Thomas Edison died saying, "It's very beautiful over there."[14] Elizabeth Barrett Browning said, "Beautiful."[15] Frances Willard said, "How beautiful to be with God." Saint Teresa said, "Over my spirit flash and float in divine radiancy the bright and glorious visions of the world to which I go." Mary Anne Schimmelpenninck said, "O, I hear such beautiful voices, and the children's are the loudest." Mary Wollstonecraft said, "I know what you are thinking of, but I have nothing to communicate on the subject of religion."[16]

Some say only farewell, remember me.

Last words bestow a last blessing, pray for mercy, or call the name of a loved one. By some accounts Napoleon expired saying, "Josephine," and Josephine died saying, "Napoleon."[17] Gustav Mahler cried "Mozart!" as if meeting him.[18]

Rabelais died saying, "I go to seek the great Perhaps." Martin Luther died affirming, "Yes." John Greenleaf Whittier died denying, "No. No!"[19]

Beethoven died quoting, "Plaudite amici, finita est comedia" (Applause, friends, the play is finished), a line compared to the words of the dying

Augustus. Tragic to the last, Nero died reciting the *Iliad*.[20] Lucan died quoting his own *Pharsalia*. Edmund Waller died quoting Virgil. Filippo Strozzi died inscribing a line from Virgil with the point of his sword: "Exoriare aliquis nostris ex ossibus ultor" (Arise from my ashes, unknown avenger).[21] The great historian Guizot died quoting Corneille.[22]

Augustine died quoting Jesus, "Into Thy hands, I commend my spirit."[23] So did Charlemagne, Thomas à Becket, Columbus, Lady Jane Grey, Jan Hus, Torquato Tasso, Anne Boleyn, Mary, Queen of Scots, and Cardinal Newman. "Untold Christians have departed this life with these words."[24]

Denis Diderot died quoting Montaigne, "I lower my head and plunge, devoid of sensation, into death, neither contemplating it nor exploring it, as into some voiceless, darkling deep, which swallows me up at one jump and in a instant overwhelms me with a powerful sleep entirely lacking in any sensation or suffering."[25]

Last words cannot rest in peace. According to another source, Diderot's last words were "The first step towards philosophy is incredulity."[26] *Credo.*

The saints of *The Golden Legend* died praying. Zeuxis and Sir Thomas Urquhart died laughing. William Blake died singing. Paganini played his violin. Vespasian said, "Vae, puto deus fio" (I believe I'm becoming a god).[27]

John Calvin died in silence. Confucius, too.

Wordsworth affirmed:

> Strongest minds
> Are often those of whom the noisy world
> Hears least.[28]

It is difficult to remember all,
and ungracious to omit any.

Cicero

Acknowledgments

I must first thank Phil, my twin. He was answering my questions before
we were born. He still does, kindly and quickly. He gave this book its
longest quotation.

For sister Diane, whose library set a threshold for mine, and for Margot, who gave me lilies of the valley, I offer two quotations and a thesis.
The thesis: sisters know everything. Quotation 1: from Diane (quoting
W. S. Gilbert), "Of that there is no manner of doubt — no probable,
possible shadow of doubt, no possible doubt whatever." Quotation 2:
from Margot (quoting herself), "Mom loves me best."

Dad, thanks for Mom. Mom, thanks for Dad.

When Bill Kohlhaase and I were teens, we copied quotations from
Nietzsche and Pascal on index cards and taped them to our walls to
puzzle our parents. Bill was the first reader to plough through a draft of
Quotology and the first to clear away weeds and litter. He read another
draft, too, and reacted. Readers can thank him that a long and ugly
chapter on polemics and war manuals is kaput.

Dependable friends and candid critics Steve Lehmann and Warren Motte (the most insatiable reader I know) coaxed me through draft five.

Rex Wallace, chair of classics at the University of Massachusetts, read draft six. Then he read it again. His encouragement was vital.

The readers for the University of Nebraska Press, Jordan Stump and Robert Con Davis-Undiano, gave draft eight strong critiques and every benefit of the doubt.

Brother Phil read draft after draft, with generous corrections and no complaints. None to me, anyway.

William Germano and Diane Gibbons are real live ideal readers. I've kept them in mind from beginning to end, sparing them till now.

Like an Atticus, Bill Sisler helped me with Cicero. Bill and Elaine Sisler relax anxieties faster than butter melts on pancakes.

Dimitri Gutas opened up Arabic *sententiae* for me. Rick Powers led me to Terry Anderson's *Den of Lions* and to the *Gita* of Robert Oppenheimer.

William Kinderman and Katherine Syer disrupted my popcorn and coffee diet with salads, salmon, and wine. For years I've owed many of my best days to Bill and Katherine.

Valerie Hotchkiss, rare books librarian of the University of Illinois, welcomed me to other worlds in the University Library's rare books room. Paula Kaufman, the head of the library, gave me space to work in a library I love like a cloud afloat in paradise. Bruce Swann, Illinois' classics librarian, is an angel there.

The reference librarians of the Project Wombat Web site amaze me. If I can please them a little, I'll grin a lot.

Dr. Dominique Chéenne and Dr. Julia Laurer-Chéenne have been stalwart friends through thick, thin, and bleeding. No two know more than they do about turning a frown around or about turning the tiniest good news into feast and celebration.

Now and then Amy Howland McDavid distracted me from my books and papers. Amo Amy.

Day after day the men and women of the University of Illinois Press remind me how much care goes into bringing a book about. I thank them for their diligence, intelligence, and grace. I thank the faculty and administration of the University of Illinois for valuing their press. *Quotology* was written during the Rod Blagojevich years, coincident with the George W. Bush years. As the University of Illinois deals with the consequences it is a blessing to have Dr. Meena Rao, vice president for academic affairs, as my boss and counselor.

I thank the University of Nebraska for prizing its press and thank the University of Nebraska Press for its time and talents. UNP has made the Platte River Road a highway to the world. Ladette Randolph, now with *Ploughshares*, was more certain than I that *Quotology* had a future. Kristin Rowley took the prospectus from pupa to cocoon to a book that some summer day may open before you like a sunning butterfly. Mary M. Hill's copyediting of *Quotology* saved me from serious blunders. For remaining faults blame me and thank Mary. Without her they would have been worse.

Quotology got its final trim and polish from its project editor, Sara Springsteen, and its cover, type, and page design from Nathan Putens. I thank them both for making the book better and better every step of the way.

One last quote, from Elizabeth Barrett Browning's *Aurora Leigh*, then back to the library:

> . . . how God laughs in heaven when any man
> Says, "Here I'm learned; this I understand;
> In that, I am never caught at fault or doubt."

NOTES

For economy's sake, I use short-form citations. Complete bibliographic information is in the works cited section. Abbreviations to the major compendia cite their most recent editions. References to BFQ, for example, refer to *Bartlett's Familiar Quotations*, 17th ed. (2002), and references to ODQ refer to *Oxford Dictionary of Quotations*, 7th ed. (2009). References to prior editions are abbreviated as BFQ 1st, ODQ 2nd, and so on.

For certain works — Greek and Latin classics, Erasmus, Shakespeare, Robert Burton, and others — I follow established citation conventions. When I cite novels, plays, and poems available in multiple editions, I cite chapter, scene, and line numbers rather than pages. I only include such works in the works cited if the edition matters. In any case, I have tried to make it as easy as possible to locate a source precisely.

Notes indicate whenever quotations appear in one or more of the great compendia. Checking them was a chore, and new editions of living compendia will make the citations archival, but the task answered basic questions about how compendia borrow and trade.

I often had to choose between competing translations. The great compendia do not agree; when it matters, I've noted that.

Volume epigraph: Dr. Richard Bentley, quoted in Walpole, *Walpoliana*, 2:31.
Chapter epigraph: Lincoln, in Fehrenbacher and Fehrenbacher, *Recollected Words*, 273.

1. Horace, *Epistles*, 1.2.40; JGDQ 334.82; NDQ 95; ODQ 410.5. BFQ 81 attributes the quotation to Aristotle, *Politics*, 5.3.2 (1303b). Like ODQ 646.13, BFQ recognizes that the phrase was already proverbial by the time Aristotle wrote his Greek version, more literally translated as "The beginning, as the proverb says, is half the whole," HBQ 146. Plato, "ἀρχὴ γὰρ λέγεται μὲν ἥμισυ παντός," *Laws* 6 (753e), NDQ 95. The passage was translated by R. G. Bury for Loeb's *Plato* and by A. E. Taylor for Princeton's *Collected Dialogues* as the familiar "Well begun is half done." Erasmus treats another version, "Principium dimidium totius," in *Adages*, 1.2.39, *Collected Works*, 31:181–82. NCPQ 65.21 remarks that Horace's version can be traced back to Hesiod with no further detail. Erasmus identifies the sources in Horace, Plato, and Aristotle and notes that the line from Hesiod (*Works and Days*, 40) was quoted by Lucian in *Hermotimus*, 3.

2. Emerson, "All mankind love a lover," "Love," *Essays*, 328; BFQ 455.21; HBQ 1177.2; JGDQ 246.15; NCPQ 468.20; YBQ 243.13. Heraclitus, "All is flux," "πάντα χωρεῖ," as quoted by Plato, *Cratylus*, 402a; BBQ 477; BFQ 64.1; JGDQ 316; ODQ 393.3; PDQ 535; YBQ 356. *La vida es sueño* titles a play by Calderón de la Barca; BFQ 254.18; JGDQ 133; ODQ 193.7; PDQ 250; YBQ 127; HBQ 1121.7 gives fifteen parallels.

3. Aeschylus, fragment 223, *Aeschylus*, 2.501; HBQ 787.10. Aesop, "Hercules and the Driver," *Aesop's Fables*, 222; BFQ 61.5; PDQ 8.5. In his *Adages* (1.6.17, *Collected Works*, 32:15) Erasmus traces the Latin version, "Dii facientes adiuvant," to Varro, *Res rusticae*, 1.1.4; see also "Industriam adiuvat deus," *Adages*, 3.9.55, *Collected Works*, 35:339.

4. Brinkelow, *Complaint of Roderick Mors* (ca. 1540), HBQ 1633.8. ODQ 632.19 cites this as a French proverb from the late thirteenth century but gives no source.

5. Marcus Aurelius, *Meditations*, 5.23, quoted by Matthew Arnold in "Marcus Aurelius," *Essays*, 373. T. S. Eliot, "These fragments I have shored against my ruins," *The Waste Land*, line 431.

6. Disraeli, *Curiosities*, 3:376, quoting a proverb from James Kelly's *Complete Collection of Scottish Proverbs* (1721), 110; HBQ 1628.7. Mencken tracked the quotation to Samuel Palmer's preface to *Moral Essays on Proverbs* (1710), NDQ 988.

7. Smiles, *Character*, 291.

8. NCPQ 850.4.

9. Emerson, *Journals*, 11:73.

10. Erasmus, *De Ratione Studii, Literary and Educational Writings 2*, 671. I have replaced "even in" with "even on."

11. Isaiah 5:21. For a list of the fifty-seven quotations, see the appendix to Montaigne, *Oeuvres complètes*, 1419–25.

12. Field, *Love Affairs*, 34–35. Field gives no source. The eldest I've found is in a footnote in Colton, *Lacon*, 387–88.

13. "Doing the Backstroke," episode 1 of *Weeds* 3 (Showtime 2007), quoting Virgil, *Georgics*, 3.284; BBQ 671, 870; BFQ 96.18; HBQ 2009.2; JGDQ 725.29; NCPQ 839.1; NDQ 1197; ODQ 833.2; PDQ 1118.15; YBQ 791.21.

14. Landor, "Southey and Porson," *Imaginary Conversations*, 3.200; HBQ 1667.11. The lines are from Catullus, *Carmen*, 61, but out of order: "stretching his baby hands from his mother's lap, with lips half-parted." For a defense of Latin quotations, see Drexler, "On Latin Quotation."

15. Huxley, *Crome Yellow*, 39.

16. Timbs, *English Eccentrics*, 429, 432.

17. I quote Xenophon quoting Socrates quoting Homer: "ὁμοκλήσασκέ τε μύθῳ: / δαιμόνι, ἀτρέμας ἧσο, καὶ ἄλλων μῦθον ἄκουε, / οἳ σέο φέρτεροί εἰσι," Xenophon, *Memorabilia*, 1.2.58; Homer, *Iliad*, 2.188–91, 198–202, in Walter Leaf's translation, 2.229–32.

18. Evans, Nadjari, and Burchell, "Quotational and Reference Accuracy," 242; Fenton et al., "Accuracy of Citation," 40.

19. Ingleby, *Oscar Wilde*, 67. Field, *Love Affairs*, 183–84; Boswell, *Life of Johnson*, 1:228–29. Jacobs, *History*, 15.

20. Yogi Berra, *Sports Illustrated*, March 17, 1986, 18; YBQ 58.16.

21. Cozzens, *Sayings*, 3.

22. Erasmus, *Praise of Folly*, chap. 18; CDQ 669.5.

23. *Edinburgh Encyclopaedia of Wit*, 62–63. Lady Chudleigh (1656–1710) "was a lady of much repute in the eighteenth century for her writings in both prose and verse," Reynolds, *Learned Lady*, 146.

24. Moers, *Literary Women*, 23.

25. Quotation in music is widespread, for example, national anthems in works by Beethoven and Tchaikovsky. For hip-hop and rap sampling, see Keyes, *Rap Music*. Salvador Dalí and Otis Kaye boldly quoted other painters. New churches reverently reset windows, traceries, or cornerstones from older churches. The exterior of the Chicago Tribune Tower has inset fragments from the Great Wall of China, the great pyramid, the Roman Coliseum, Petra, the Parthenon, the Taj Mahal, and other famous buildings.

26. Auden, "Reading," *The Dyer's Hand*, 9. In 1788 the Reverend Vicesimus Knox wrote, "It often happens that the quotations constitute the most valuable part of a book and the reader may rejoice in such a case, that he has not spent his money and time in vain; which, peradventure, he might have done, had the author inserted nothing but the production of his own brain," *Winter Evenings*, 1:92.

27. Benjamin, "ein Autor, von dem ein Zitat, wo immer es sich findet, den Leser das Buch vergessen macht, in dem er es antrifft," *Das Passagen-Werk*, 1:584 (N6, 2), *Arcades Project*, 468. Benjamin quotes Michelet often in *The Arcades Project*.

1. ELEMENTS

Part epigraph: Confucius, *Analects* (15.37), 179.
Chapter epigraph: Coleridge, *The Friend*, 1:53.

1. Smiles, *Character*, 100–101.

2. Smith, *Dreamthorp*, 148; CDQ 758; HBQ 1667; NDQ 1001; PDQ 1021.

3. Barzun to Arthur Krystal, "Age of Reason," 94. The full quotation is more precise: "Whoever wants to know the heart and mind of America had better learn baseball, the rules and realities of the game — and do it by watching first some high school or small-town teams," Barzun, *God's Country*, 159; BFQ 776.16. The *Yale Book of Quotations* gives him one more: "If it were possible to talk to the unborn, one could never explain to them how it feels to be alive, for life is washed in the speechless real," which is the sole Barzun quotation in the ODQ; see YBQ 46; ODQ 60.14. WNW has seven Barzun quotes (63.32–38).

4. The major texts are Frege, "On Sense and Reference," *Translations*, 56–78; Tarski, "The Concept of Truth in Formalized Languages," *Logic, Semantics, Metamathematics*, 152–278; Geach, "Quotation and Semantics," *Logic Matters*, 189–211; and Quine, *Mathematical Logic*, chap. 4, and *Word and Object*, 143, 212ff.

5. Davidson, "Quotation," 79. Davidson's essay (1979) eclipsed Nelson Goodman's "Some Questions Concerning Quotation" (1974), though Goodman raises other important questions, particularly about how other means of expression — paintings, photographs, music — quote.

6. Davidson, "Quotation," 81. On this "famous" quotation, see Recanati, "Open Quotation," 638.

7. Heywood, *Proverbs and Epigrams*, 18, 21. I have modernized his spelling.

8. Ellis, *Dance of Life*, 86; BFQ 617.24. Emerson, *Journals*, 10:293.

9. Wells, *Outline of History*, 608; BFQ 644.16; JGDQ 739.17; ODQ 846.23; PDQ 1138.9; WNW 898.89; YBQ 806.7. Ronell, *Telephone Book*, xv.

10. Madame de Pompadour; JGDQ 518; NCPQ 305.17; NDQ 273; ODQ 611.12; PDQ 862; QW 588.3; WNW 658.46. BBQ 713 notes that "there is an old Greek proverb to the same effect, denounced by Cicero ('De Finibus,' 3.19) as an inhuman and disgraceful saying"; BFQ 337.6 calls the saying "an old French proverb"; HBQ 1632.14 says the proverb was "applied to spendthrifts"; YBQ 598 notes that Mirabeau had earlier written "Après moi le déluge"; for sources, see Fournier, *L'esprit*, 339–40, and Latham, *Famous Sayings*, 85–86. Khrushchev, BFQ 741.7; ODQ 462.9; PDQ 646.4; WNW 466.99; YBQ 426. Philip Regier informed me:

> Khrushchev uttered words that have been given the translation, "We will bury you," on at least three occasions. The first was at a reception at the Polish embassy in Moscow on November 18, 1956. The usual form of the quotation most often

cited in Russian, "Мы вас похороним," is not exactly Khrushchev's original wording ("Мы вас закопаем"). The popular misquote in Russian is apparently due to the dire interpretation promulgated by the western media. Both verbs (похороним and закопаем) mean "We will bury," but похоронить means "to bury a dead person," while закопать means "to hide in the earth." That is, the western media took it as a death threat, but Khrushchev was alluding, as he later explained, to the succession of socialism over capitalism, just as capitalism had replaced feudalism. Nothing personal, just Marxist inevitability. On the other two occasions, the Kitchen Debate with Vice President Richard Nixon in Moscow on July 24, 1959, and the shoe-banging incident at the U.N. on October 12, 1960, Khrushchev used the expression, "Показать кузькину мать," which means literally "to show somebody Kuzka's mother" and is approximately equivalent to "to teach somebody a lesson." The unfamiliarity of the idiom led interpreters first to say something about Kuzka's mother, then to speculate that кузька is also a term for an earth-dwelling grain pest (*Anisoplia austriaca*), so one would have to be speaking about burying somebody in order to show him the mother of a кузька. Khrushchev later told his interpreter, Viktor Sukhodrev, that he meant that he would show Americans things they had never seen before. Yuri Gagarin's spaceflight took place just a few months later, April 12, 1961. (E-mail, August 4, 2008)

Frost, "Fire and Ice," BFQ 669.11; CDQ 1005.7; JGDQ 267; ODQ 344.13; PDQ 453.18; WNW 338.97; YBQ 294.10.

11. Nostradamus, *Complete Prophecies*, 139 (4.85).

12. For the dispute about quotation marks, see Davidson, "Quotation." For a formidable demonstration of what is marked by quotation marks, see Derrida, *Of Spirit*, 23–30, 65–68.

13. Rouse and Rouse, *Preachers, Florilegia and Sermons*, 31.

14. *American Heritage Dictionary*, 3rd ed., 1487.

15. Parkes, *Pause and Effect*, 21–22, 57–61.

16. McMurtrie, "Concerning Quotation Marks," 6–7.

17. Compagnon, *La seconde main*, 41.

18. Newhall, "Indication of Quotations," 427. See also *Science*, April 8, 1927, 355, and July 8, 1927, 38.

19. Wittgenstein, *Philosophical Remarks*, 306.

20. Quoted by Morley in the preface to BFQ 11th, xiii.

21. Emerson, "Quotation and Originality," *Letters*, 156.

22. Haskins, *Renaissance*, 113.

23. 1 Timothy 6:10; BFQ 46.26; HBQ 1337.2; JGDQ 76.549; NCPQ 523.23; NDQ 802; ODQ 115.23; PDQ 166.13; WNW 124.79; YBQ 76.377.

24. Dalbiac, *Dictionary of Quotations (English)*, iii.

25. Locke, *Essay*, 2:259. The quotation has been modernized.

26. Boswell, *Life of Johnson*, 3:29.

27. Knox, *Winter Evenings*, 1:91.

28. Colton, *Lacon*, 360n.

29. Bacon, *Major Works*, 372. Diogenes Laertius, *Lives*, 10.123.

30. Sand, "*Il n'y a qu'un sexe.* Un homme et une femme, c'est si bien la même chose, que l'on ne comprend guère les tas de distinctions et de raisonnements subtils dont se sont nourries les sociétés sur ce chapitre-là," Flaubert, *Correspondance* (January 15, 1867), 3:594; Sand, *The George Sand–Gustave Flaubert Letters*, 49.

31. La Bruyère, "Une femme cependant regarde toujours un homme comme un homme; et réciproquement un homme regarde une femme comme une femme," *Les caractères*, 137, *The Characters*, 86.

32. Saint Paul quoted Hebrew scripture when writing to Greek churches. Could Greeks appreciate Old Testament quotations? Would they even recognize them? See Stanley, *Arguing with Scripture*.

33. It is remembered in Latin (as in Shakespeare, *Julius Caesar*, 3.1.77), though it was uttered in Greek: καὶ σὺ τέκνον, "You, too, my child?" Suetonius, "Julius Caesar," §82; BFQ 92.6; HBQ 984.16; JGDQ 132.7; ODQ 193.3; PDQ 249.7; WNW 184.27; YBQ 126.

34. The quotation was not remembered in ODQ 2nd, 3rd, 4th, 5th, or 6th but was again recalled in ODQ 7th, 217.1.

35. Franklin, "Poor Richard Improved, 1758," *Writings*, 1294–95.

36. Fournier, *L'esprit*, 436.

37. Fournier, "Si le *mot* en valait la peine, il laissait dire et ne reniait pas la paternité," *L'esprit*, 438. Bartlett translated *mot* as "Good thing," BFQ 4th, 399; HBQ 147.20.

38. Confucius, *Analects* (5.4, 7, 18). "I don't know" were also the last words of Abelard; see Guthke, *Last Words*, 68.

39. Fuller, *Holy and Profane States*, 180; HBQ 1292.11; NCPQ 506.23.

40. Modern compendia credit Fuller as the source rather than the intermediary.

41. Lewis, *Margaret Thatcher*, 51.

42. Ling, *Politeuphuia*, 48.

43. Pope, "Essay on Criticism," 420–21, *Poems*, 156.

44. Koestler, *Ghost in the Machine*, 115.

45. Gratzer, *Eurekas and Euphorias*, 38. Another supposed reply is, "Why sir, there is every possibility that you will soon be able to tax it!" ODQ 341.12; YBQ 250.

46. For detailed studies of this bon mot, see Chapin, "A Legendary Bon Mot?" and especially Cohen, "Faraday."

47. Voltaire, "Le mieux est l'ennemi du bien," translating "le meglio è l'inimico del bene," BFQ 316.16; JGDQ 728.21; WNW 883.47. Voltaire introduced the phrase twice, in his *Dictionnaire philosophique* (1770) and in his "La Bégeule" in *Contes* (1772), ODQ 834.2. Shapiro found an earlier instance in a letter Voltaire wrote to the duc de Richelieu, June 18, 1744, YBQ 791. PDQ 1121.22 cites this as "an Italian proverb" and NDQ 99 as "an English proverb not recorded before the XIX century."

48. Lowell, "For an Autograph," *Poetical Works*, 353; BFQ 515.12; HBQ 1507.5; YBQ 475. Lowell thought well enough of the phrase to use it again in his essay on Dryden in *Literary Essays*, 3:143.

49. Newton made the remark in a letter to Robert Hooke, February 5, 1675. Merton's *On the Shoulders of Giants* traces the trope back through Burton's *Anatomy of Melancholy* to Bernard of Chartres in the early twelfth century. See also Garber, *Quotation Marks*, 8.

50. Thomas à Kempis, "Non quaeras quis hoc dixerit: sed, quid diciatur attende," *Imitation of Christ*, 1.5.1; ODQ 804.14; PDQ 1086.

51. Morson, "Bakhtin," 219.

52. CDQ viii–ix. But "the idea of quotation is linked irresistibly with, above all, a knowledge of sources," Morawski, "Basic Functions," 690.

53. Churchill actually said, "I have nothing to offer but blood, toil, tears and sweat," speech to House of Commons, May 13, 1940. This is one of the most quoted quotations in modern English: BFQ 665.19; JGDQ 163.11; ODQ 229.12; PDQ 295.19; WNW 216.75; YBQ 152.12; Keyes, *Nice Guys*, 53–54, and *Quote Verifier*, 15–16; Rees, *Brewer's Quotations*, 93.2, *Cassell Companion*, 162.6, *Sayings*, 101–2, and *Why Do We Quote?* 29.

54. Byron, "Age of Bronze," *Poetical Works*, 176; the last two lines are quoted with different punctuation in BFQ 665n4; ODQ 185.7; YBQ 125.28.

55. See BFQ 665n4 and YBQ 209.4, 648.3.

56. BFQ 13th, 869.

57. Borges, "Un gran escritor crea sus precursors," *Nueva antología personal*, 243. Borges felt this was important enough to repeat: see "Nathaniel Hawthorne" and "Kafka and His Precursors," *Other Inquisitions*, 57, 108.

58. Rufinus, "Inveniet tam brevem ut videat singulis versiculis ingentes explicare sensus, tam vehementem ut unius versus sententia ad totius possit perfectionem vitae sufficere," in Chadwick, *Sentences of Sextus*, 10. I base my translation on Henry Fremantle's.

59. In *Quotology* "apophthegm" will be reserved for the genre exemplified by Erasmus: a "quick, witty reply" concluding an anecdote. For example, when Lady Astor told Winston Churchill, "If I were your wife, I'd put poison in your coffee," he replied, "If I were your husband, I'd drink it," Keyes, *Nice Guys*, 52, and *Quote Verifier*, 26; Rees, *Cassell Companion*, 161.4.

60. "The Compilers to the Reader," ODQ 1st, x.

61. Dole, preface to BFQ 10th, v.

62. Cozzens, *Sayings*, 73.

63. Lamb, BFQ 654.1. The Ninon de L'Enclos quotation is "attributed" without a source in BFQ 276.6; Partnow provides six L'Enclos quotations and traces this one to *La coquette vengée* (1659), QW 439.1; but see La Rochefoucauld, "L'enfer des femmes, c'est la vieillesse," *Maximes*, #562; "elle avait été addressée par La Rochefoucauld à Ninon de Lenclos," *Maximes*, 173n. Guinan, BFQ 704.1. Díaz, BFQ 544.1.

64. Stevenson's quotability is to blame. BFQ retains quotes from other competing editors of compendia, Sarah Hale, H. L. Mencken, and F. P. Adams. Henry Bohn was included in BFQ 13th to 17th, and George Seldes was included from BFQ 12th through 16th.

65. Morley, preface to BFQ 11th, xiii.

66. Ouida, *Wanda*, 399. Elizabeth I, quoted in Hume, *History of England* in the third person, "that God might pardon her, but she never could," 713; but in the first person in JGDQ 244.17; ODQ 312.12; and as "God may forgive you" in BFQ 151.17 and HBQ 709.14.

67. Borges, "Pierre Menard, autor del *Quijote*," *Ficciones*, 47–59, and *Labyrinths*, 36–44. See Compagnon, *Le seconde main*, 376–77.

68. Ṣiddīqī, *Ḥadīth Literature*, 77.

69. Cicero, *De natura deorum*, 1.5.10; HBQ 897.11; ODQ 231.20; NCPQ 741.12; YBQ 156.

70. Horace, *Odes*, 1.11.7; BFQ 99.12; HBQ 1600.8; JGDQ 332.13; NCPQ 795.3–4; ODQ 411.16; PDQ 560.24; WNW 413.19; YBQ 371.17. Also Goethe (Mephistopheles speaking): "Doch der den Augenblick ergreift, / das ist der rechte Mann" (The right man is the one who seizes the moment), *Faust*, 1.2017–18, *Werke*, 2:799; NDQ 875; and George Washington, "*Carpe diem, carpe noctem* . . . to conquer and make love," Deltiel, *Lafayette*, 61; HBQ 2121.11.

71. Augustine, *City of God*, bk. 18, chap. 44.

72. Cited by Montaigne, "De l'institution des enfans," *Oeuvres complètes*, 145 (*Essais*, 1.26), *Complete Essays*, 165.

73. BFQ 476.7. Evans, *Dictionary*, 268.12, had previously done so.

74. Darwin made his first appearance in BFQ 9th (1891), with three quotations from chapter 3 of *The Origin of Species*. In a note Bartlett reminded readers that "the Survival of the Fittest" was taken from Herbert Spencer, BFQ 9th, 622.

75. Browne, *Religio Medici*, 29. Pineda was author of *Monarchia Ecclesiastica o Historia Universal del Mundo* (1588). Pineda quoted "one thousand and fortie authors."

76. Dionysius of Halicarnassus, *Roman Antiquities*, 8.8.

77. Smyth, *Streaks of Life*, 135.

78. Paine, *Collected Writings*, 79; YBQ 575.

79. Colton, *Lacon*, 185–86.

80. Edgeworth, "Thoughts on Bores," *Tales and Novels*, 9.223.

2. TYPES

Epigraph: Emerson, "Plato; Or the Philosopher," *Representative Men, Essays*, 634; NDQ 1001. In shorter form, HBQ 1667.4.

1. For other typologies, see the four "functions" of Morawski, "Basic Functions," 692–96; the four "stages" of Compagnon, *La seconde main*, 10–11; and the six "categories" of Boller, *Quotesmanship*, 32.

2. Selden, *Table Talk*, 92.

3. Frege, "On Sense and Reference," *Translations*, 65.

4. Cappelen and Lepore, "Varieties of Quotation," 429–30.

5. Shakespeare, *Henry IV, Part 1*, 5.4.121. Beaumont and Fletcher, *A King and No King*, 4.3.63. Hazlitt, *Characteristics*, 138. Powers, *Gold Bug Variations*, 622.

6. Parker, in Keats, *You Might As Well Live*, 46; JGDQ 504.19; ODQ 596.17; PDQ 839.22; WNW 638.72.

7. Parker in Drennan, *Algonquin Wits*, 121; YBQ 581.37.

8. Boswell, *Life of Johnson*, 1:427.

9. Cerquiglini, *In Praise*, 39. For the three versions of *Hamlet*, see the 3rd edition of the Arden Shakespeare edited by Thompson and Taylor, 91–94.

10. Woolf, *Room of One's Own*, 5. I take the phrase "cryptic quotation" from Meyer, *Poetics of Quotation*, 7. Yaeger calls Woolf's allusion a "cryptic citation"; see her "Editor's Column," 440–41, 447n4.

11. Van Doren, introduction to ODQ 1st, vi.

12. Betty Radice, introduction to *Praise of Folly, Collected Works of Erasmus*, 27:79.

13. Bakhtin, *Dialogic Imagination*, 68–69.

14. Baudelaire, "To the Reader," *Les fleurs du mal*, 5; Lowell, "To the Reader," *Imitations*, 46. The original French reads:

Nos péchés sont têtus, nos repentirs sont lâches;
Nous nous faisons payer grassement nos aveux,
Et nous rentrons gaiement dans le chemin bourbeux,
Croyant par de vils pleurs laver toutes nos taches.

15. France, *Oxford Guide*, 475.

16. Standing Bear's address to the federal court in April 1879, as recalled in Tibbles, *Buckskin and Blanket Days*, 201. "The newspaper accounts do not mention the 'skin of a different hue' passage alluded to in Standing Bear's address to the court (this speech is much embroidered in [Tibbles's] *Buckskin and Blanket Days*). . . . While

this does not mean that Tibbles invented Standing Bear's orations, it does suggest that he elaborated on them," Kay Graber, in her "Note on the Text," in Tibbles, *The Ponca Chiefs*, 140. Shakespeare, *Merchant of Venice*, 3.1.

17. Cozzens, *Sayings*, 59–68.

18. Johnson, *Rambler*, no. 143 (July 30, 1751), *Works*, 4.394.

19. Jonson, *Timber*, §121.

20. Apuleius, "Ut te videam, aliquid et loquere," *Florida*, §2. Petrarch, "Alterum adolescentem cum vidisset ingenuo vultu atque habitu sed tacitum: 'Loquere,' inquit, 'ut te videam,'" *Rerum memorandarum libri*, 159 (3.71.24). Erasmus, *Apophthegmes*, 134 (3.47).

21. Molière, "La parole a été donnée à l'homme pour exprimer sa pensée," *Le mariage forcé*, 4.1.186; both quotations in HBQ 1901.15, 1902.4. Bartlett cited Edward Young, "Men talk only to conceal their mind," and Voltaire, "Ils n'emploient les paroles que pour déguiser leurs pensées." Bartlett adds, "It is impossible to trace this saying to any particular source. The germ of the thought is to be found in Jeremy Taylor; Lloyd, South, Butler, Young, and Goldsmith have repeated it after him," BFQ 3rd (1858), 179, 383. Bartlett got around to specifying the sources for South, Lloyd, and Goldsmith in BFQ 7th (1875), 283. The Fournier passage was first disclosed in the "Miscellaneous" section of BFQ 4th (1863), 400. Only Voltaire survives in BFQ 17th, 316.18.

22. "Il mit ainsi, dans *le Nain jaune*, toujours sous le couvert de M. de Talleyrand, sa fameuse phrase: 'La parole a été donnée à l'homme pour déguiser sa pensée.' Puis, la réputation du *mot* une fois faite, il voulut le réclamer: peine perdue!" Fournier, *L'esprit*, 441. In a note Fournier adds that M. Michaud *jeune* "l'attribue positivement à M. de Talleyrand." Stevenson cites an earlier instance, "The true use of speech is not so much to express our wants as to conceal them," Oliver Goldsmith, *The Bee*, 66; HBQ 1901; JGDQ 287.42; ODQ 364.29.

23. Coleridge, *Biographia Literaria*, 1:147–48. Coleridge's editors provide the original German from Schelling's *Darlegung des wahren Verhältnisses der Naturphilosophie* (1806): "Wer nur die Geschichte der Wissenschaften in den letzen Jahrhunderten kennt, wird darin einstimmen müssen, dass unter den Gelehrten derselben eine Art von geheimem und stillschweigendem Vertrag stattzufinden schien, über eine gewisse Gränze in der Wissenschaft nicht hinauszugehen." For more, see the editors' introduction, 1:cxiv–cxxvii; Fruman, *Coleridge*; and McFarland, "Coleridge's Plagiarisms."

24. The critical literature is vast. Particularly worthwhile are White's *Plagiarism and Imitation*, Lindey's *Plagiarism and Originality*, and Randall's *Pragmatic Plagiarism*.

25. Linkletter, *Kids Say the Darndest Things*, 126. Rājashekhara, quoted in Keith, *History*, 342. Stravinsky (attributed), JGDQ 678. Evans, *Dictionary*, xii.

26. Arendt, *Willing*, 129.

27. Nietzsche, *Twilight of the Idols, Portable Nietzsche*, 510.

28. Huxley, *Ends and Means*, 114.

29. Derrida, "Il y aurait de la légèreté à penser que 'Descartes,' 'Leibniz,' 'Rousseau,' 'Hegel,' etc., sont des noms d'auteurs, les noms des auteurs de mouvements ou de déplacements que nous désignons ainsi," *De la grammatologie*, 148, *Of Grammatology*, 99.

30. Ronell, *Stupidity*, 183. Readers of Dostoevsky will recall that his 1872 novel was titled *The Possessed*.

31. Shestov, *Dostoevsky and Nietzsche*, 155.

32. BFQ 832.6; CDQ 349.27; JGDQ 393; ODQ 473.18; PDQ 664; YBQ 437.

33. Marx, BFQ 744.17; in a different form, ODQ 526.1; WNW 557.91; YBQ 498. Benchley, quoted in Drennan, *Algonquin Wits*, 42.

34. Dickinson, letter of July 1862, quoted in Higginson, *Carlyle's Laugh*, 260.

35. Nietzsche, "Jeder tiefe Geist braucht eine Maske: mehr noch, um jeden tiefen Geist wächst fortwährend eine Maske," *Beyond Good and Evil*, §40; *Sämtliche Werke*, 2.604; *Basic Writings*, 241.

36. Austen, *Northanger Abbey*, chap. 15.

37. Gutas, *Greek Wisdom Literature*, 50, 76–79, 252–56. Everything I've seen confirms Chadwick's remark, "Of all literary forms aphorisms are the most loosely attached to their original inventors," *Sentences of Sextus*, 149.

38. The first occurrence of "misquote" cited in the *Oxford English Dictionary* is from Shakespeare's *Henry IV, Part 1*, 5.2.13 (1596); the first occurrence of "misquotation" is from Samuel Johnson's *Notes on Shakespeare* (1773).

39. Colton, *Lacon*, 358n. Colton dropped a word; the original reads, "Qui sedens adversus identidem, te / Spectat et audit" (Who, sitting opposite you, gazes at you and hears you), Catullus, 51.3–4, *Poems*, 58–59; Catullus here adapts a poem by Sappho. The misattribution persisted in editions throughout Colton's lifetime; the quotation and attribution were finally corrected in William Tegg's edition (London, 1866).

40. "A.L.," *Letter*, 43.

41. Cioran, *Anathemas*, 166.

42. Bierce, *Devil's Dictionary*, 106.

43. Longinus, *On the Sublime*, 9.9, conflating the Septuagint Genesis 1:3 and 1:6. "Longinus, in almost all his quotations, differs from his authors," Francis Lockier, quoted in Spence, *Anecdotes*, 66.

44. Burke, *Philosophical Enquiry*, 59, 65–66. Thanks to Mark Canuel for these examples.

45. Knox, *First Greek Anthologist*, 6.

46. Frost, *Notebooks*, 231. Holmes, *Autocrat*, 71.

47. Unamuno, "la verdad forma parte de la dicha en un sentido tertulianesco, de *credo quia absurdum*," *Del sentimiento trágico*, 83; *Tragic Sense*, 104. Tertullian, "Certum est, quia impossible est," *De carne Christi*, 5; BFQ 116.20; HBQ 152.14; NCPQ 390.16; ODQ 802.12; WNW 849.83.

48. These are by now standard examples. See George and Boller, *They Never Said It*, 8–9, 47; Keyes, *Nice Guys*, 2, 7, 138–39, and *Quote Verifier*, 54, 166–67; Knowles, *What They Didn't Say*, 30, 87; Rees, *Quote*, 38, 39; ODQ 547.11, 548.14; YBQ 215.39, 260.42.

49. Heywood, *Proverbs*, 51; HBQ 1151.12.

50. For a collection of found poems, see Dillard, *Mornings like This*. In an early instance of a found poem Carl Sandburg arranged Lincoln quotations as verse; see §57 of *The People, Yes* (1936).

51. Aristotle, *Art of Rhetoric*, 1.15.13–17.

52. Bruce, *English Bible*, 108–9.

53. Charles Caleb Colton, *Lacon* (Philadelphia: Porter & Coates, 1849), 223. Cerquiglini characterized the problem: "The printed text was anything but certain: grievances were commonplace, and old books repeat a long litany of '*Errata, si quae occurrent, benevolus Lector,*' to plead not guilty in a rather offhanded manner that represented little respect for what was being published," *In Praise*, 4.

54. "A.L.," *Letter*, iii–iv.

55. Schopenhauer, "On Authorship and Style," 505; NCPQ 654.19.

56. Natalie Clifford Barney, quoted in Vicinus, *Intimate Friends*, 175.

57. Pearson, *Common Misquotations*, 10, 13. Morson gives other examples of misquoters misquoted in "Bakhtin," 217–18.

58. George and Boller, *They Never Said It*; Keyes, *Nice Guys*; Knowles, *What They Didn't Say*; and Pearson, *Common Misquotations*.

59. Pearson, *Whispering Gallery*, 124.

60. Waller, "Democrats Usher in an Age of Treason," *Insight Magazine*, December 23, 2003. Waller blamed his editor. Despite Waller's correction, the quotation was recited by Gaffney in the *Washington Times*, February 14, 2007, and by Young the same day. When confronted about the misquote, Young responded that he stood by it.

61. Boller, *George Washington*, 3–23, 38–39, and *Quotesmanship*, 329–41.

62. Pseudo-Philo, in Charlesworth, *Old Testament Pseudepigrapha*, 2:373.

63. "Dans tous les pays et à toutes les époques, les supercheries littéraires sont fréquentes. Pour mieux déconcerter la critique, les auteurs de pastiches ont souvent cherché dans les temps anciens des noms célèbres, afin d'étayer leurs écrits d'une autorité imposante" (In every country and in all epochs, literary frauds are frequent. To better confound criticism, authors of pastiches have often looked for celebrated names from ancient times to prop up their writings with imposing authority), Delepierre, *Supercheries littéraires*, 31–32.

64. Hamilton, *Federalist*, no. 15, December 1, 1787, *Writings*, 223; BFQ 370.13; NDQ 482; YBQ 332.6. Junius, *Letters* (#35), 160, December 19, 1769; BFQ 360.7.

65. Hazlitt, *Characteristics*, 39.

66. Herodotus, *Histories*, 2:4.

67. Bettina Gozzi, quoted in Casanova, *History*, 1:86.

68. Rees, *Word of Mouth*, 14, and *Quote*, 35.

69. Neihardt, *Black Elk Speaks*, 207. Ray DeMallie noted, "Although these are Neihardt's words, not Black Elk's, this is the most frequently quoted passage from the book," *Sixth Grandfather*, 55n82.

70. Tacitus, *Annals*, 13.3.

71. Much of the research, writing, and revision was done by a group of assistants — Gordan Allen, Norman Brook, William Deakin, Lord Ismay, Denis Kelly, and Sir Henry Pownall — informally called the "Syndicate." "No reviewer seemed to guess that the memoirs were the work of many hands, even if Churchill was their presiding genius," Reynolds, *In Command*, xxi, 137.

72. In Drennan, *Algonquin Wits*, 62.

73. Arendt, *Eichmann in Jerusalem*, 48.

74. Woetzel, *Nuremberg Trials*, 268.

75. Arendt, *Eichmann in Jerusalem*, 49.

76. Balzac, *Old Goriot*, 114. Wilde, *Picture of Dorian Gray* (chap. 2), 20.

77. BBQ 474; BFQ 85; HBQ 189; JGDQ 133; ODQ 193.17. It is an indirect quotation from Athenaeus: "Callimachus the grammarian used to say that a big book is a big nuisance," *Deipnosophists*, §72a. Burton translates: "A great Booke is a great mischiefe," "Democritus to the Reader," *Anatomy*, 1:10.

78. YBQ 231.

79. Elms, "Apocryphal Freud," 95–101.

80. Kant, "What Is Enlightenment?" 3. It was also the motto of the Earl of Macclesfield; see Macdonnel, *Dictionary of Quotations* 9th, 348.

81. Quoted by Ascheim, *Nietzsche Legacy*, 274.

82. Wollstonecraft, *Vindication*, 56–57.

83. Boller further divides such quotations into "adversary-as-authority quotes" and seven types of "confrontation quotes," *Quotesmanship*, 32, 83–219.

84. Luther, *Table Talk*, #78, quoting Luke 19:22.

85. Boswell, *Life of Johnson*, 4:274 (May 15, 1784).

86. Grafton, "Violence," 5.

87. Burke, Letter 1, *Three Letters Addressed to a Member of the Present Parliament, on the Proposals for Peace with the Regicide Directory of France, 1796–7, Works*, 5:335.

88. Emerson, *Journals*, 11:110; CDQ 757; JGDQ 248.82; ODQ 315.20; YBQ 244.

89. BFQ 454; PDQ 418.36, and in the misleading form on ix.

90. Augustine, *City of God*, bk. 3, chap. 16.

91. It is uncertain that issue 200 was written by Steele (1672–1729); there is reason to suppose the author was Henry Martyn (1665–1721). Steele later used "Vincit amor Patriae" as an epigraph for the *Englishman*, no. 32 (December 15, 1713), but without a translation.

92. *Spectator*, October 19, 1711, 3:122.

93. Sites, *Inscriptions and Quotations*, 13. The foisted translation is attributed to Virgil by Jones, *Dictionary of Foreign Phrases*, 124; by Edwards, *Dictionary of Thoughts*, 366; by Christy, *Proverbs, Maxims, and Phrases*, 2:308; and many others. The editors of BBQ, BFQ, CDQ, JGDQ, NCPQ, NDQ, ODQ, PDQ, WNW, and YBQ were not fooled.

94. Milton Mayer, *Progressive*, April 25, 1942, in Boller, *Quotesmanship*, 283, who devotes all of chapter 7 to quooxes.

95. Tolstoy, *Anna Karenina*, 696 (pt. 8, chap. 1).

96. Einstein, *Essays in Humanism*, 85.

97. Demosthenes, "First Philippic," 47.25, *Demosthenes*, 1:83.

98. Coulter, "Another Liberal Noos-ance," October 17, 2007, http://www.anncoulter.org/cgilocal/article.cgi?article=216.

99. Garber, *Quotation Marks*, 24–29.

100. Brantôme, *Lives*, 391.

101. Seneca, *Epistles*, 81.14.

102. BFQ 17th, 138.18, reduces the roll to four, based on Fortescue.

103. Cervantes, "Las comparaciones que se hacen de ingenio a ingenio, de valor a valor, de hermosura a hermosura y de linaje a linaje son siempre odiosas," *Don Quixote*, pt. 2, chap. 1. Bartlett quotes Motteux's translation.

104. Heywood, *A Woman Killed with Kindness*, 1.2.20–21.

105. Burton, *Anatomy*, 3.3.1.2.

106. Fortescue actually wrote, "*Comparationes* vero, *Princeps*, ut Te aliquando dixisse recolo, *odiosae reputantur*" (I remember a saying of yours, *my Prince*, that *Comparisons are odious*), *De Laudibus Legum Angliae*, chap. 19. Bartlett quotes John Selden's translation.

107. Shakespeare, *Much Ado about Nothing*, 3.5.15.

108. Cervantes, *Don Quixote*, pt. 2, chap. 23. Bibota, *Lippincott's Monthly Magazine*, November 1888, 725. Bibota attributes the quotation to Boiardo, though he's aware that scholars attribute the line to Francesco Berni's *Rifacimento* (6:4) of Boiardo's poem; Dalbiac and Harbottle cite Berni in their *Dictionary of Quotations (French and Italian)*, 351.

109. Wollstonecraft, quoted in Todd, *Mary Wollstonecraft*, 387; Dickens, *Barnaby Rudge*, chap. 45; Gilman, *Herland*, title of chap. 6.

110. HBQ 290.1, 2; NCPQ 125.17; Evans, *Dictionary*, 118.19; see also Hazlitt, *Characteristics*, #223.

111. ODQ 629.16 and YBQ 609.51 treat it as a proverb. Also Bohn, *Hand-book*, 80, and Speake, *Oxford Dictionary of Proverbs*, 56.

112. Gutas, *Greek Wisdom Literature*, 115; the quotation is repeated as a saying of Plato's, 137, 328.

3. COLLECTIONS

Epigraph: Ecclesiasticus 6:35.

1. Brihadāranyaka Upanishad, "yo ha vai jyeṣṭhaṃ ca śreṣṭhaṃ ca veda jyeṣṭhaśca śreṣṭhaśca svānāṃ bhaṣati," 16.1.1, Upanishads, 245. Democritus, "σοφίν ἄθαμβοσ ἀξίν πάντων," fragment 216; Diels, *Fragmente*, 2:189, Freeman, *Ancilla*, 111. Swift, *Tale of a Tub*, introduction, *Prose Works*, 1:40. Marcus Aurelius, *Meditations*, 7.59.

2. Butler, *Hudibras*, 1.3.1011–12; BFQ 271.12; HBQ 250.6; NCPQ 109.4.

3. Proverbs 8:10–12, 13:3, 18:7. On Wisdom as a woman, see also Wisdom of Solomon 6.

4. Ahiqar, *Aramaic Proverbs*, 73. On Pythagoras, see Seneca, *Epistles*, 52.10. Lao Tzu, *Tao te Ching*, §56; BFQ 59.9; ODQ 480.8; PDQ 1068.10; YBQ 442.7. Japanese proverb, NDQ 1098; cf. Thomas Hardy, "That man's silence is wonderful to listen to," *Under the Greenwood Tree*, 118; CDQ 840.9. Sextus, "Sapiens vir etiam cum tacet honorat deum," Chadwick, *Sentences of Sextus*, #427; Chadwick adds, "For an excellent survey of the ancient idea of the religious value of silence see Odo Casel, *De philosophorum graecorum silentio mystico* (Giessen, 1919)," 180. Abba Poemen, in *Sayings of the Desert Fathers*, 84. Gracián, "Es el recatado silencio sagrado de la cordura," *Oráculo manual*, 162, *Art of Worldly Wisdom*, 2; NDQ 1097. James 1:19. Lavater, *Aphorisms*, #22.

5. Beckett, *Watt*, 62.

6. Tan, *Opposite of Fate*, 9–10, 293–94.

7. Marie de France, prologue to her *Lais*; QW (2001 ed.), 191.1; WNW 550.49:

Qui Deus a duné esciënce
e de parler bone eloquence,
ne s'en deit taisir ne celer,
ainz se deit voluntiers mustrer.

8. Chāndogya Upanishad, "Puruṣya vāgraso," 1.1.2, Upanishads, 284. Jonson, *Timber*, §119; HBQ 1896.12.

9. The collection altered considerably as it moved from language to language. By the time Caxton published his edition it included sayings of Saint Gregory. See *The Dicts and Sayings of the Philosophers*, ed. Bühler, x–xi.

10. *The Dicts and Sayings of the Philosophers*, ed. Bühler, 96, 97, see also 286, 287. Bühler's edition has two different translations on facing pages, thus the dual citations. I have modernized the English.

11. Solon, quoted by Diogenes Laertius, *Lives*, 1.58; BFQ 57; HBQ 1897.3. Dionysius of Halicarnassus, *Roman Antiquities*, 1.1.3–4. Ray, "Speech is the picture of the mind," *Collection of English Proverbs*. Erasmus, *Adages*, 1.6.50, *Collected Works*, 32:36; see also "Stultus stulta loquitur," *Adages* 1.1.98, *Collected Works*, 31:141–42. Seneca, *Epistles*, 114.1; see also Cicero, *Tusculan Disputations*, 5.47. *Mahābhārata*, "Yādṛśaḥ puruṣasyātmā, tādṛśaṃ saṃprabhāṣate," 5.3.1. "Verbum excogitatum [ostendit] hominis cordis," Ecclesiasticus 27:6. Ibn 'Aṭā'illāh, *Ṣūfī Aphorisms*, 50.

12. Ibn 'Aṭā'illāh, *Ṣūfī Aphorisms*, 35. Plutarch, "The Education of Children," 10e–f, *Moralia*, 1:51; BFQ 111.14; HBQ 1824.13. Emerson, "Circles," *Essays*, 408.

13. Pascal, "Voulez-vous qu'on croie du bien de vous, n'en dites pas," *Pensées*, #44; HBQ 1823.10. Lincoln, HBQ 1823.10; an attributed quote, see Keyes, *Quote Verifier*, 145–46. Eliot, *Impressions*, 48; BFQ 513.15; NDQ 1098; PDQ 411.65; QW 955.33; YBQ 233.19.

14. Miller, "The True Poet," *In Classic Shades*, 71.

15. Aristotle, "χρὴ δ᾿ οὔποθ᾿ ὅστις ἀρτίφρων πέφυκ᾿ ἀνήρ παῖδας περισσῶς ἐκδιδάσκεσθαι σοφούς" and "οὐκ ἔστιν ὅστις πάντ᾿ ἀνὴρ εὐδαιμονεῖ," *Art of Rhetoric*, 1394a, 1395b, quoting Euripides, *Medea*, 294, and fragment 661.

16. *Rhetorica ad herennium*, 4.17.

17. Quintilian, *Institutio oratoria*, 8.5.3–4. Quoted by Erasmus in *De Copia, Literary and Educational Writings 2*, 627.

18. Seneca, *Controversiae*, 1.preface 23, *Declamations*, 1:22–25.

19. Sextus, "Magnam scito esse sapientiam per quam ferre potes ineruditorum inperitiam," Chadwick, *Sentences of Sextus*, #285.

20. In E. M. Sanford's survey of 415 *libri manuales* from the seventh through the fourteenth centuries, 79 contain Cato's stichs. Thomas Baldwin found Cato's *Disticha de moribus* and the *Sententiae pueriles* of Leonhardus Culmannus in use in the schools of Renaissance England, *William Shakspere's Small Latine & Lesse Greeke*, 1:581–606.

21. Mishnah, Aboth, 1.17. Quoted by Maimonides, *Guide of the Perplexed*, 2:629.

22. Gutas, *Greek Wisdom Literature*, 103; this gnome of Abū Sulaymān Muḥammad b. Ṭāhir b. Bahrām al-Sijistāni al-Manṭiqī (late tenth century).

23. Bacon wrote this in Latin: "Neque tantum in usu erat apud Hebraeos, sed alibi etiam priscorum sapientibus frequentissimum; ut si cujuspiam observatio in aliquid incidisset quod vitas communi conducibile fuisset, id redigeret et contraheret in brevem aliquam Sententiam, vel Parabolam, vel etiam Fabulam," *De Augmentis Scientiarum*, bk. 8, chap. 2, *Works*, 3:86 (translated in *Works*, 9:266).

24. Evans, *Dictionary*, vii. Lec, *Unkempt Thoughts*, 125; BFQ 783.1; YBQ 448.

25. Proverbs 26:4–5, and Ecclesiastes 9:16, 18. On quotation in Ecclesiastes, see Gordis, *Koheleth*, 95–108.

26. Maimonides, *Guide of the Perplexed*, 1:19, quoting Tractate Shabbath, 30a.

27. See Bühler, *Zenobii Athoi proverbia*. The collections of Zenobius and Diogenianus of Heraclea are newly edited and translated into Italian in Lelli, *I proverbi greci*.

28. Proverbs 8:17–19.

29. Watson, *Poetical Quotations*, vi, quoting Sir William Jones's translation of "A Persian Song by Hafiz." Hale, *Complete Dictionary*, iii. Ward, *Dictionary of Quotations in Prose*, v.

30. "Si utile est, ibi inventitur. Et cum ibi quisquis invenerit omnia quia utiliter alibi didicit" (If useful, it is found there. And one will find there everything useful learned elsewhere), Augustine, *On Christian Doctrine*, 2.42.63.

31. Photius's *Bibliotheca*, Codex 232, mentions a sixth-century work by Stephanus Gobarus organized in the same fashion, though responding to questions some steps below high theology (e.g., whether Thomas cut off the soldier's ear or Peter did; and at what age — thirty, thirty-three, forty, almost fifty — was Jesus crucified). See Harnack, "The 'Sic et Non.'"

32. Citing Saint Jerome, Abelard asserted, "Nonnulla in ipsis divinorum testamentorum scriptis scriptorum vitio corrupta sunt" (In places even the holy scriptures are corrupted by the folly of scribes), prologue to *Sic et non*.

33. Colish, *Peter Lombard*, 1:51.

34. Colish, *Peter Lombard*, 1:86.

35. Bakker and Schabel, "*Sentences* Commentaries," 435–61. Petrarch lamented that Lombard's *Sentences* "has been the victim" of thousands of commentators, "On His Own Ignorance," 108–9.

36. Photius's *Bibliotheca*, Codex 167, our sole source for what is known about Stobaeus, is included in Gaisford's edition of Stobaeus, *Florilegium*, 1:lxxxi–xciv.

37. Grotius, "Ego cum alia, quae apud Stobaeum extant, fragmenta veneratus sum semper, tum pro meo in artem poeticam affectu singulariter dilexi, quas ipsius beneficio servatas habemus, poetarum reliquas," in Gaisford's edition of Stobaeus, *Florilegium*, 1:xliii.

38. Pfeiffer, *History of Classical Scholarship*, 141.

39. Rouse and Rouse, *Preachers, Florilegia and Sermons*, 156.

40. Stobaeus, "Περί Βραχυλόγιας" (On Brevity in Speech), *Florilegium* (Gaisford ed.) (35.10), 2:38–40, citing Epictetus, *Encheiridion*, *Discourses*, 2:472–73. Surviving manuscripts of the *Encheiridion* lack this passage.

41. Knox, *First Greek Anthologist*, 13–14. Knox adds, "I would regard the loss of Lucian's works as a far greater tragedy than the loss of Plato's."

42. Rouse and Rouse, *Preachers, Florilegia and Sermons*, 210–11.

43. Rouse and Rouse, *Preachers, Florilegia and Sermons*, 129.

44. Rouse and Rouse, *Preachers, Florilegia and Sermons*, 125.

45. I am here entirely in debt to the edition of Santa Cruz's *Floresta* prepared by Cuartero and Chevalier.

46. Santa Cruz, *Floresta española*, 1.15. Aristotle, quoted in Diogenes Laertius, *Lives*, 5.18. See also Bacon, quoting Queen Isabella, it is "'like perpetual letters commendatory,' to have good forms," "Of Ceremonies and Respects," *Essays*, #52, *Major Works*, 441.

47. Walsh, *Poetical Quotations*, vi; Adams, *Cyclopedia*, vii; Southgate, *Many Thoughts*, vi.

48. Proverbs 7:16, 5:2. Ecclesiasticus 24:19–21. Seneca, *Epistulae ad Lucilium*, #84, *Epistles*. For the honeybee metaphor, see also Plutarch, "On Listening to Lectures," 41f, *Moralia*, 1:224–25; Isocrates, *Ad demonicum*, 51f; and Petrarch, *Rerum familiarum libri*, 1.8.

49. Edwards, *World's Laconics*, 232. Salmond, prologue to the Damascene's *Exposition*, vii.

50. Plutarch, *Table Talk*, 8.8.728, *Moralia*, 9:175.

51. Macrobius, *Saturnalia*, 26–28 and preface.

52. Macrobius, *Saturnalia*, 181–83, 187–88.

53. Macrobius, *Saturnalia*, 385–86.

54. Holmes, *Autocrat*, 7. The book succeeded so well that he followed it with *The Professor at the Breakfast Table* (1859) and *The Poet at the Breakfast Table* (1862). Rabelais, "Je t'aime du bon du foye," *Gargantua and Pantagruel*, bk. 3, chap. 21.

55. Pliny, *Natural History*, 14.141; BBQ 867; BFQ 57n5; HBQ 2215.9; JGDQ 516; NDQ 1299; WNW 655.6.

56. Luther, *Table Talk*, #67; BBQ 882 also cites Burton, Herbert, Defoe, and Ray; BFQ 144.14 cites Burton and Herbert; HBQ 272.13–273.2 cites six more; ODQ 6th, 715.6, cites Defoe and Thomas Becon; WNW 258.13 cites only Defoe; YBQ 477 cites only Luther.

57. Luther, *Table Talk*, §§122, 469, 3814. On Noah, see §3476.

58. Coleridge, *Collected Letters*, 6:561, 656; quoted in Coleridge's *Table Talk*, 1:88n15.

59. Coleridge, Aphorism XV, *Aids to Reflection*, 299–300.

60. Coleridge, *Table Talk*, 1:xli, xlv.

61. John T. Coleridge, in Coleridge's *Table Talk*, 1:li.

62. Coleridge, *Table Talk*, 1:405.

63. Coleridge, Essay VII, *The Friend*, 1:52–53.

64. Orme and Maxwell quoted by Boswell, *Life of Johnson*, 3:284 (April 15, 1778), 2:117 (1770). Johnson quoted by Boswell, *Life of Johnson*, 3:375 (March 26, 1779); BFQ 328.18; PDQ 613.119.

65. Boswell, *Life of Johnson*, 1:421.

66. Emerson, *Society and Solitude*, 167.

67. Havens, *Commonplace Books*, 36, 46, 55, 9.

68. Petrarch, *Rerum memorandarum libri*, xxxv–liii.

69. Erasmus, dedicatory letter to Pieter Gillis, *Parabolae, Literary and Educational Writings 1*, 130.

70. Huizinga, *Erasmus*, 39.

71. Erasmus, *Adages*, 2.10.49, *Collected Works*, 34:146. See also "Battologia. Laconismus," *Adages*, 2.1.92, *Collected Works*, 33:70–71.

72. Erasmus, *Adages*, 3.10.91, *Collected Works*, 35:392.

73. Montaigne, "De l'institution des enfans," *Oeuvres complètes*, 145–46 (*Essais*, 1.26), *Complete Essays*, 165–66.

74. Baldwin, *William Shakspere's Small Latine & Lesse Greeke*, 2:342–50.

75. Bacon, *Advancement of Learning*, bk. 2, *Major Works*, 229.

76. Bacon, *Works*, 7:208.

77. Bacon, *Promus*, 269–371.

78. Chesterfield, February 5, 1750, *Letters to His Son*, 1:291.

79. Swift, "A Letter of Advice to a Young Poet" (1721), *Prose Works*, 9:334, quoted in Timbs, *Laconics*, 1.248. The proverb about "Great wits" recurs in Chesterfield, November 12, 1745, *Letters to His Son*, 2:427, and Shenstone, *Essays*, 97.

80. Swift, *Tale of a Tub*, §10, *Prose Works*, 1:134.

81. Simmons, *Laconic Manual*, 3.

82. Brown, *Laconics*, A4. Volume 10 of *Constable's Miscellany* (1827), titled *Table Talk*, took extracts from *Menagiana, Huetiana, Gasconiana, Voltairiana, Johnsoniana, Omniana, Foggiana*, and the like.

83. Pascal, "Toutes les bonnes maximes sont dans le monde; on ne manqué qu'à les appliquer," *Pensées*, #380.

84. Boswell, *Life of Johnson*, 3:380.

85. Colton, *Lacon*, xii.

86. Colton, *Lacon*, 111, 170, 198 (but "imbodied"); BFQ 412.4; JGDQ 176; ODQ 244.9–10, 12; PDQ 314; WNW 228.53, 55.

87. Disraeli, *Curiosities*, 3:256–57.

88. That is, the first in English. Latin proverb collections circulated throughout the Middle Ages. See Werner's *Lateinische Sprichwörter* and Singer's fourteen-volume *Thesaurus proverbiorum medii aevi*.

89. Archer Taylor cites several similar works made up of proverbs in *The Proverb*, 180–82. To his list add Michael Drayton, "To Proverb," from *Idea* (1593), *The Barons' Wars*, 245; Evans, *Dictionary*, 562.12.

90. Heywood, *Proverbs*, 132, 140.

91. Florio, *First fruites*, 31–33.

92. Florio, *Florios Second Frutes*, xiii; PDQ 437.

93. Walton, *Life of Mr. George Herbert*, 273.

94. Isaac Disraeli reminds English readers that *Jacula* means "Darts or Javelins! something hurled and striking deeply," *Curiosities*, 3:359.

95. Herbert, *Jacula*, #524, 306, 1141, *Works*, 339, 331, 360. "All is not gold that glisters," "Comparisons are odious," and others signal that some aphorisms are not original with Herbert.

96. Herbert, *Jacula*, #158, *Works*, 326.

97. Ray actually wrote, "It's good to have company in trouble" and "If wishes would bide, beggars would ride," but see Bohn, *Hand-book*, 4, 143; Bohn is based on Ray. BFQ 17th mistakenly attributes "Blood is thicker than water" to Ray; it appears in Bohn, *Hand-book*, 231. BBQ 764, 806; BFQ 281.7, 9–10; HBQ 118.18, 1320.4, 2169.18. JGDQ, ODQ, PDQ, WNW, and YBQ have no entries for Ray.

98. FitzGerald, *Polonius*, xxiii–xxiv, 28. Lord Lennox's *Lacon* was an invention of *Punch*.

99. Ecclesiastes 1:9. La Bruyère, "Tout est dit, et l'on vient trop tard," *Les caractères*, 67. Goethe, "Alles Gescheite ist schon gedacht worden," *Sprüche in Prosa*, #1, *Werke*, 2:229. The English translation as given appears in Douglas, *Forty Thousand Quotations*, 1423, and Edwards, *Dictionary of Thoughts*, 572, from which it entered many other books. Dalbiac translates "Gescheite" as "cleverness," *Dictionary of Quotations (German)*, 9.

100. Swift, "A Letter of Advice to a Young Poet," *Prose Works*, 9:334. This quoox appeared on the title page of Edwards's *World's Laconics*, in the preface of Tegg's *Laconics*, as the first of Timbs's *Laconics*, and often elsewhere, always hiding an excision. Between the "etc." and "have the same use" is this: "& which are admirable Expedients for being very learned with little or no *Reading*." Louis Landa doubted whether the "Letter" was written by Swift, *Prose Works*, 9:xxiv–xxvii.

101. See Boswell, *Life of Johnson*, 1:214, 4:148–51.

102. Swift, "Digression in Praise of Digressions," *Tale of a Tub*, §7, *Prose Works*, 1:93.

4. THE GREAT COMPENDIA

Epigraph: Shakespeare, *Love's Labor's Lost*, 5.1.37. This was an epigraph for Hoyt and Ward's *Cyclopedia*. An adapted version, with "He has" rather than "They have," was the epigraph for successive editions of Macdonnell's *Dictionary of Quotations*.

1. Douglas, *Forty Thousand Quotations*, 7.

2. *Book of Familiar Quotations*, iii–iv.

3. Jeffares and Gray, *Dictionary*, vii.

4. Watson, *Poetical Quotations*, v. The fourth of Morowski's four functions of quotation was "ornament."

5. Evans, *Dictionary*, vii.

6. Morley, preface to BFQ 11th, xi.

7. Young, "Love of Fame: Satire 1," *Poetical Works*, 270; BBQ 405; BFQ 305.16; CDQ 759; HBQ 1668.6; JGDQ 774; NCPQ 654.25; ODQ 876.10; PDQ 1179; WNW 935.79.

8. In Boswell, *Life of Johnson*, 4:102 (May 8, 1781); BBQ 177; BFQ 329.7; CDQ 758.18; HBQ 1667.9; JGDQ 361.223; NCPQ 654.10; NDQ 1000; ODQ 443.6; PDQ 613.134; WNW 446.51; YBQ 405.100. The runner-up is also from Johnson: "Every quotation contributes something to the stability or enlargement of the language," preface to his *Dictionary* (1755); CDQ 758.17; HBQ 1667.9; JGDQ 354; NCPQ 654.9; NDQ 1000; ODQ 435.18; PDQ 608.30; WNW 442.41; and quoted as a blurb for ODQ 4th. It is a quoox: JGDQ notes that Johnson means only "every quotation" in his *Dictionary*.

9. Churchill, *A Roving Commission*, 116; BFQ 665.10; CDQ 757.7; JGDQ vii, 164.45; PDQ 294.10; YBQ 152.7. Churchill read BFQ in the late 1890s and so would have read the 8th edition, or the so-called author's edition, published by Routledge. The only other author in BFQ to cite Bartlett is Samuel Hoffenstein, who wrote, "I play with the bulls and the bears; / I'm the Bartlett of market quotations." This appeared in BFQ 12th, 970, and disappeared after BFQ 13th.

10. WNW 478.59, quoting the Koran, Arthur Arberry translation, 6:38.

11. QW 2676.1.

12. WNW 46.52, quoting Bacon's *Advancement of Learning*, bk. 2, *Major Works*, 175. Publilius Syrus, "Amare et sapere vix deo conceditur" and "Cum ames non sapias aut cum sapias non ames."

13. For fifty-four examples, see McIntyre, "Study," 64–84.

14. Bohn, *Dictionary of Quotations*, 492. The quoox appeared as early as 1865 in H. G. Adams's *Cyclopedia*, 524, with "tropes"; Allibone, HBQ, NCPQ, and PDQ have it. The ODQ had it from its 1st edition (1941). It was absent from BFQ till Beck put it in BFQ 14th (1968).

15. Prior, "Paulo Purganti and His Wife," *Poems*, 91, referring to Hugo Grotius's *De Jure Belli ac Pacis* (*The Rights of War and Peace*) (1625).

16. Hartley, not Samuel Taylor, Coleridge, *Biographia Borealis*, 322n. Collections that attribute this quote to "Coleridge" include Allibone, *Prose Quotations*, 601; Ballou, *Treasury of Thought*, vii; Gilbert, *Dictionary of Burning Words*, iv; Sinclair, *Kaleidoscope*, 1; Southgate, *Many Thoughts*, epigraph; Edwards, *Dictionary of Thoughts*, i, 460; and Douglas, *Forty Thousand Quotations*, 1423.

17. Hoyt, *Cyclopedia*, v. Later editions of the *Cyclopedia* were updated by Kate Louise Roberts. Topically arranged, each edition began with "Abhorrence," an irony that did it no harm: the *Cyclopedia* stayed in print for half a century.

18. YBQ xiv. Evans, *Dictionary*, xv.

19. Ward, *Dictionary of Poetical Quotations*, iv. She refers to it as *Belvidere*.

20. Bohn cites these as the precedents for his own *Dictionary of Quotations*, vii–ix.

21. It enjoyed instant success, and a quick sequence of new editions grew rapidly larger: the 2nd edition (1798) has 215 pages; the 3rd (1799) 278 pages; the 4th (1803) 408 pages; by the publication of the 9th edition (1826) it had grown to 432 pages, plus advertisements.

22. Beck, "Long, Happy Life," 102.

23. Bowerman, "John Bartlett," 6.

24. Dole deleted only Dinah M. Mulock, Thomas Oliphant, Frances S. Osgood, and Mrs. C. B. Wilson.

25. BFQ 14th, xv.

26. ODQ 3rd, iii, vi.

27. ODQ organizes its quotations by author's last name. For readers who prefer subject rubrics, there are *The Oxford Dictionary of Phrase, Saying, and Quotation* (1st 1997; 2nd 2002; 3rd 2006) and *The Oxford Dictionary of Thematic Quotations* (2000), alias *The Oxford Dictionary of Quotation by Subject* (2004).

28. Haines edited three other books of quotations, *Ye Gardeyne Boke* (1906), *Christmasse Tyde* (1907), and *Weather Opinions* (1907).

29. QW 289.2, 244.11.

30. YBQ 532 and QW (2001 ed.), 2323.7, citing different sources. JGDQ 469 has three quotations from Marilyn Monroe; ODQ 553.17–18 and WNW 591.59–60 have two each; PDQ 783–84 has six, three of them performance quotations. Each set has at least one quotation unique to it. With eleven quotations, none of them attributed or performance, QW (2001 edition) 2323.1–11 gives Monroe more space than any other compendium.

31. Starrett, *Books Alive*, 316–17.

32. YBQ 328, 218, http://yalepress.yale.edu/yupbooks/qyd (November 15, 2009).

33. For Thatcher, ODQ 804.4. "Yes I said yes I will Yes" are the famous last words of Joyce's *Ulysses* (1922); BFQ 696.13; JGDQ 367.29; PDQ 622.32; WNW 452.96; YBQ 410.22.

5. FASHIONS

Epigraph: Stevens, "Adagia," *Opus Posthumous,* 176.

1. Seneca, "Certi profectus viro captare flosculos turpe est et fulcire se notissimis ac paucissimis vocibus et memoria stare; sibi iam inniatur. . . . Turpe est enim seni aut prospicenti senectutem ex commentario sapere," *Epistles,* 33.7.

2. Brantôme, *Lives,* xviii.

3. La Bruyère, "*Hérille,* soit qu'il parle, qu'il harangue ou qu'il écrive, veut citer: il fait dire au Prince des philosophes que le vin enivre, et à l'Orateur romain que l'eau le tempère. S'il se jette dans la morale, ce n'est pas lui, c'est le divin Platon qui assure que la vertu est aimable, le vice odieux, ou que l'un et l'autre se tournent en habitude," "Des jugements," §64, *Les caractères,* 371, *Characters,* 352.

4. Boswell, *Letters,* 2:380. Emerson, *Journals,* 10:246, quoting Victor Aimé Huber, *The English Universities,* trans. Francis W. Newman (London, 1843), 2:304. Chesterfield, June 24, 1751, *Letters to His Son,* 2:30; see also December 19, 1751, 2:44.

5. Chesterfield, February 22, 1748, *Letters to His Son*, 1:53.

6. Edgeworth, "Thoughts on Bores," *Tales and Novels*, 9:210, 222.

7. Sei Shōnagon, *Pillow Book*, 130. The *Kokin Shū* is an anthology of 1,111 poems. Sei Shōnagon also knew two other poetry anthologies, the *Ko Manyō* and *Gosen Shū*, *Pillow Book*, 79.

8. Sei Shōnagon, *Pillow Book*, 42, 100, 108–9.

9. Macdonnel, *Dictionary of Quotations* 9th, iii.

10. Macdonnel, *Dictionary of Quotations* 9th, 373, 349, quoting Horace, *Epistles*, 1.1.41–42.

11. Coleridge, *The Friend*, 1:52.

12. Landor, "Lucian and Timotheus," *Imaginary Conversations*, 1:306.

13. Alcott, *Table-Talk*, 8.

14. Emerson, "Quotation and Originality," *Letters*, 151, 161; HBQ 1667.4. Despite Emerson's definition of the divine, the Bible, Koran, and Vedas quote extensively.

15. Emerson, "Quotation and Originality," *Letters*, 154; BFQ 457.20–21; HBQ 1667.5; JGDQ 248.74–75; NCPQ 550; NDQ 1001; PDQ 419.61; YBQ 245.45 quotes a variant from Emerson's journal.

16. Landor, "The Abbé Delille and Walter Landor," *Imaginary Conversations*, 3:304; BFQ 457.21; HBQ 1805.9; JGDQ 248.75.

17. Emerson, *Lectures*, 285. This view follows a distinguished line: "Quamquam quid ego alienum aliquid dixerim, licet ab aliis elaboratum, cum Epycuri sententia sit ab eodem Seneca relata, quicquid ab ullo bene dictum est, non alienum esse sed nostrum?" (How can I say that something another wrote is not mine, when Epicurus's opinion, as recorded by Seneca himself, is that anything said well by anyone is our own?), Petrarch, *Rerum familiarum libri*, 1.8.

18. Dinesen, *Seven Gothic Tales*, 208–10. The passages are from Dante's *Purgatorio* 33.31–36, Anthony Esolen's translation. Beatrice speaks:

> I wish that you would now
> loose yourself from your fear, be free of shame,
> and speak no longer as a dreamer does.
> Know that the vessel broken by the snake
> once was, and is no more. Let him trust well,
> God's judgment does not shy for sop or cake.

19. Delepierre, *Tableau*, 2:296–97.

20. Green, "Proba's Cento," 555–60. Jerome's condemnation of Christian centos blames their compilers for pride and distortion.

21. Usher, "Prolegomenon," 305, 308. Editions of Eudocia's centos were published by Aldus and Stephanus.

22. Eudocia altered Homer's ἢ μέγα ἔργον to ἢ μεγὰ ἔργον and his ἀνθρώποισι δίδωσι to ἀνθρώποισιν ἐφῆκεν. I take the example and translation from Usher, *Homeric Stitchings*, 13.

23. Ausonius, "quod ridere magis quam laudare possis," "Cento Nuptialis," *Ausonius*, 2:370–71.

24. Delepierre, *Tableau*, 1:147–53.

25. Delepierre, *Tableau*, 2:302.

26. Delepierre, *Tableau*, 2:114–22.

27. Montaigne, "De l'institution des enfans," *Oeuvres completes*, 146 (*Essais*, 1.26), *Complete Essays*, 166.

28. Erasmus, "Ex arena funiculum nectis," *Adages*, 2.6.51, *Collected Works*, 33:317; see also "Farcire centones," *Adages*, 2.4.58, *Collected Works*, 33:221–22.

29. "Genre de poésie en mosaïque, enfanté au milieu des caprices d'une littérature en décadence," quoted by Delepierre, *Tableau*, 1:9.

30. Usher, *Homeric Stitchings*.

31. Delepierre, *Tableau*, 2:59–97.

32. Burton, "Democritus to the Reader," *Anatomy*, 1:11. The Latin quotation is from Macrobius, "We ought in some sort to imitate the bees," *Saturnalia*, 27. Johnson told Boswell that Burton's *Anatomy* "is a valuable work. It is, perhaps, overloaded with quotation," *Life of Johnson*, 2:440.

33. Sontag, *On Photography*, 75, quoting Arendt's "Walter Benjamin," introduction to Benjamin, *Illuminations*, 45. The essay also appeared in Arendt, *Men in Dark Times*.

34. Benjamin, "Das Sammeln ist ein Urphänomen des Studiums," *Passagen-Werk*, 1:278 (H4, 3), *Arcades Project*, 210.

35. Benjamin, "Diese Arbeit muß die Kunst, ohne Anführungszeichen zu zitieren, zur höchsten Höhe entwickeln. Ihre Theorie hängt aufs engste mit der der Montage zusammen," *Passagen-Werk*, 1:572 (N1, 10), *Arcades Project*, 458.

36. Tiedemann, "Dialectics at a Standstill," 261.

37. Benjamin, *Passagen-Werk*, 2:674 (S1, 2), *Arcades Project*, 543.

38. Benjamin, "Ich habe nichts zu sagen. Nur zu zeigen," *Passagen-Werk*, 1:574 (N1a, 8), *Arcades Project*, 460. Sontag made a modest attempt at the project with her "Brief Anthology of Quotations" in *On Photography*, 183–207.

39. Benjamin, "Moden sind ein Medicament, das die verhängnisvollen Wirkungen des Vergessens, im kollektiven Maßstab, kompensieren soll. Je kurzlebiger eine Zeit, desto mehr ist sie an der Mode ausgerichtet," *Passagen-Werk*, 1:131 (B9a, 1), *Arcades Project*, 80.

40. Morawski, "Basic Functions," 690.

41. Montaigne, "J'ay seulement faict icy un amas de fleurs estrangeres, n'y ayant fourny du mien que le filet à les lier," "De la phisionomie," *Oeuvres complètes*, 1033 (*Essais*, 3.12), *Complete Essays*, 1196. BFQ uses the John Florio translation.

42. Eliot, "The Spanish Gypsy," bk. 2, *Poetical Works*, 149; NCPQ 654.4. The "book" in Eliot's poem is the thirteenth-century *Siete partidas* of King Alfonso X of Castile, "Alfonso the Wise."

43. Shakespeare, *Twelfth Night*, 1.5.9.

44. Disraeli, "Quotation," *Curiosities*, 3:173.

45. Genette, *Paratexts*, 145–47.

46. Emerson, "Quotation and Originality," *Letters*, 156.

47. Thompson and Taylor, introduction to Shakespeare, *Hamlet*, 15. Edgeworth, "Thoughts on Bores," *Tales and Novels*, 9:223.

48. Chesterfield, September 27, 1749, *Letters to His Son*, 1:218. See also Disraeli, *Curiosities*, 3:355.

49. Ray, *Compleat Collection*, vi–viii. The apologetic preface reappeared in the 1742 reimpression of the 3rd edition (1737).

50. Alcott, *Table-Talk*, 8; BFQ 444.16; CDQ 757.1; HBQ 1666.21; NDQ 1001; PDQ 10; YBQ 12.

51. The most worthwhile of many studies of Montaigne's quotations are Villey, *Sources & l'évolution*, vol. 1; Metschies, *Zitat und Zitierkunst*; Cave, *Cornucopian Text*, 271–321; Compagnon, *La seconde main*; and McKinley, *Words in a Corner*.

52. Metschies, *Zitat und Zitierkunst*, 9–37. The first volume of Villey's *Sources* provides an extensive list of Montaigne's wide reading.

53. Metschies, *Zitat und Zitierkunst*, 65, 55. See also *Oeuvres complètes*, 822, 841 (*Essais*, 3.5), *Complete Essays*, 952, 975.

54. The metaphor is Montaigne's: "Les formes de parler, comme les herbes, s'amendent et fortifient en les transplantant" (Locutions are like seedlings: transplanting makes them better and stronger), "Sur des vers de Virgile," *Oeuvres complètes*, 851 (*Essais*, 3.5), *Complete Essays*, 988.

55. Montaigne, "Apologie de Raimond Sebond," *Oeuvres complètes*, 524, 431, 422 (*Essais*, 2.12), *Complete Essays*, 608–9, 506, 496.

56. McKinley, *Words in a Corner*, 14, 76–78.

57. Montaigne, "Combien chetive et racourcie est la cognoissance des plus curieux!" "Des coches," *Oeuvres complètes*, 886 (*Essais*, 3.6), *Complete Essays*, 1028.

58. Metschies, *Zitat und Zitierkunst*, 50–51.

59. Montaigne, "De la praesumption," *Oeuvres complètes*, 615 (*Essais*, 2.17), *Complete Essays*, 719. "De trois bonnes femmes" and "Des plus excellens hommes," *Oeuvres complètes*, 722–36 (*Essais*, 2.35, 2.38), *Complete Essays*, 842–57. "C'est pure sottise qui nous fait courir après les exemples estrangers et scholastiques," "De l'experience," *Oeuvres complètes*, 1059 (*Essais*, 3.13), *Complete Essays*, 1227.

60. Montaigne, "Mais je hay par sur tout un sçavoir pédantesque," "Du pedantisme," *Oeuvres complètes*, 132 (*Essais*, 1.25), *Complete Essays*, 150.

61. Metschies, *Zitat und Zitierkunst*, 5–6.

62. Montaigne, "De la praesumption," *Oeuvres complètes,* 635 (*Essais,* 2.17), *Complete Essays,* 740.

63. Montaigne, "Ès raisons et inventions que je transplante en mon solage et confons aux miennes, j'ay à escient ommis parfois d'en marquer l'autheur, pour tenir en bride la temerité de ces sentences hastives qui se jettent sur toute sorte d'escrits. . . . Je veux qu'ils donnent une nazarde à Plutarque sur mon nez, qu'ils et s'eschaudent à injurier Seneque en moy," "Des livres," *Oeuvres complètes,* 387–88 (*Essais,* 2.10), *Complete Essays,* 458.

64. Pertile, "Paper and Ink," 203; McKinley, *Words in a Corner,* 24, 103–4.

65. Montaigne, "Venus n'est pas si belle toute nue, et vive, et haletante, comme elle est icy chez Virgile," "Sur des vers de Virgile," citing *Aeneid,* 8.387–92, *Oeuvres complètes,* 826 (*Essais,* 3.5), *Complete Essays,* 958.

66. Montaigne, "J'ayme et honore le sçavoir autant que ceux qui l'ont; et, en son vray usage, c'est le plus noble et puissant acquest des hommes. Mais en ceux là (et il en est un nombre infiny de ce genre) qui en establissent leur fondamentale suffisance et valeur, qui se raportent de leur entendement à leur memoire, '*sub aliena umbra latentes,*' et ne peuvent rien que par livre, je le hay, si je l'ose dire, un peu plus que la bestise," "De l'art de conferer," *Oeuvres complètes,* 905 (*Essais,* 3.8), *Complete Essays,* 1050. "Sub aliena umbra latentes" is from Seneca, *Epistles,* 33.8.

67. Horace, *Odes,* 1.31.17–20:

Frui paratis et valido mihi,
Latoe, dones, et, precor, integra
cum mente, nec turpem senectam
degere, nec cythara carentem.

68. Wimsatt and Wimsatt, "Self-Quotations."

69. Burke, *Reflections on the Revolution in France, Works,* 3:343–44.

70. Erasmus, *Adages,* 1.2.15, *Collected Works,* 31:155–61, and 3.4.2, *Collected Works,* 35:4; the second was adapted by Montaigne as "Stercus cuique suum bene olet" (Everyone thinks his own shit smells sweet), "De l'art de conferer," *Oeuvres complètes,* 907 (*Essais,* 3.8), *Complete Essays,* 1053; quoted by Emerson in *Journals,* 6:139.

6. WIT

Part epigraph: Seneca, "Inter cetera hoc habet boni sapientia; nemo ab altero potest vinci, nisi dum ascenditur," *Epistles,* 79.8. Compare Blake, "I cannot think that Real Poets have any competition. None are greatest in the Kingdom of Heaven; it is so in Poetry," "Annotations to 'Poems' by William Wordsworth," *Complete Writings,* 783. *Chapter epigraph:* Bovee, *Intuitions and Summaries of Thought,* 2:124.

1. I take most of this list from Jerrold, *Book of Famous Wits,* 16.

2. Rosenthal, *Humor in Early Islam*, 6n3.

3. For Ash'ab, see Rosenthal, *Humor in Early Islam*, 15–33.

4. Aesop, *Aesop's Fables*, 247; from Phaedrus, *Fabularum*, 3.14. Also, "Neque semper arcum tendit Apollo" (Apollo does not always keep his bow bent), Horace, *Odes*, 2.10.19, quoted by Bacon, *Advancement of Learning*, bk. 1, *Major Works*, 155; and "Arcus tensus rumpitur" (The bow breaks if strung too tight), Erasmus, *Adages*, 4.5.78, *Collected Works*, 36:192.

5. Thierfelder, *Philogelos*, §§55, 255; Baldwin, *Philogelos*, 11, 48.

6. Diogenes Laertius, *Lives*, 9.43.

7. Freeman, *Ancilla*, 104, 107, 109, 110.

8. La Rochefoucauld, "Qui vit sans folie n'est pas si sage qu'il croit," *Maximes*, #209; BFQ 273.25. Seneca, "Neque enim philosophia ingenio renuntiat," *Epistles*, 75.3. Plutarch, "Table-Talk I," *Moralia*, 8:15.

9. Jerrold, *Book of Famous Wits*, 153.

10. La Rochefoucauld, "Un homme d'esprit serait souvent bien embarrassé sans la compagnie des sots," *Maximes*, #140; BBQ 731; HBQ 2173.5; NDQ 1308.

11. Pope, quoted in Spence, *Anecdotes*, 114.

12. Rees, *Word of Mouth*, 263, 209.

13. Florence, South Carolina, January 11, 2000, and Washington DC, August 4, 2004. These are two of the top ten "Bushisms" at http://politicalhumor.about.com/cs/georgewbush/a/top10bushisms.htm (June 12, 2008). YBQ 121.2.

14. Emerson, "The Comic," *Letters*, 131; HBQ 2170.16; NDQ 1310.

15. Bacon, *Advancement of Learning*, bk. 2, *Major Works*, 204, 194. Brown, *Laconics* (I.CXXXVI), 24.

16. Morson, "Bakhtin," 223. For Stiva, see Tolstoy, *Anna Karenina*, 12. Fitzgerald, *The Crack-Up*, 125. Lec, *Unkempt Thoughts*, 66.

17. Bacon, *Advancement of Learning*, bk. 2, *Major Works*, 172–73, 206.

18. Aristotle, "εὐτραπελία πεπαιδευμένη ὕβρις," *Rhetoric*, 2.12.16; CDQ 984; NDQ 1308.

19. Shakespeare, *Comedy of Errors*, 3.1.51, and *Henry V*, 3.7.109–18.

20. Sheridan, *The Rivals*, 3.3; BFQ 367.8, 10; JGDQ 651.11; ODQ 748.12; PDQ 1011.12, 14; YBQ 707.

21. Phaedrus, "Temperatae suaves sunt argutiae: Immodicae offendunt" (Witticisms, though pleasing in moderation, are offensive in excess), *Fabularum*, 4.epilogue; HBQ 2171.9. Chesterfield, "Art of Pleasing," 15; HBQ 2170.12; see also his *Letters*, July 21, 1752, 2:111–12.

22. Elizabeth Montagu, "Letter to Mrs. Donnellan," 1749, *Letters*, 2:167–68; QW 82.

23. Boswell, *Life of Johnson*, 4:275 (May 15, 1784).

24. BFQ 3rd, 383. The quotation survived through BFQ 12th, when Montagu reached a peak with six quotations. Beck reduced her to four. The ODQ allows her eleven (554.3–13); QW (2001 ed.) has thirty-six; QW (2010 ed.) only nine (585.1–9).

25. Burney, *Diary*, 1:42.

26. Bacon, *Apophthegms*, #249, *Works*, 13:398. Shenstone, *Literary Miscellany*, 93, quoted in Timbs, *Laconics*, 1:234. Horace, *Satires*, 1.4.34–35, quoted by Boswell, *Life of Johnson*, 2:79. Also Herbert, "Some had rather lose their friends than their Jest," *Jacula*, #1170, *Works*, 361. Lord Henry of Wilde's *Picture of Dorian Gray* was willing to sacrifice anybody "for the sake of an epigram" (226).

27. For Fuller, see *Dictionary of Anecdotes*, 2:74–75.

28. Elizabeth, letter to Mary, Queen of Scots, August 22, 1556, QW (2001 ed.), 331.16. Confucius, *Analects* (5.4), 44.

29. Cozzens, *Sayings*, 76–77.

30. Shakespeare's *Pericles* reads "great" fish rather than "big" ones; the phrase was proverbial long before Shakespeare.

31. The OED cites two instances of "mother-wit" elder than Spenser.

32. It is not to Gay but to Cicero that we owe "where there's life, there's hope" (dum anima est, spes esse dicitur); *dicitur* = "it is said," as if proverbial, *Letters to Atticus* (9.10), 3.56. BFQ 90.24 abbreviates the Latin to "dum anima est, spes est."

33. Menander, *Aspis*, 407–32, *Menander*, 1:68–75. Petrarch, "Memoriam ostentare puerilis est gloria," *Rerum familiarum libri*, 4.15. Shakespeare, *Hamlet*, 1.3.57–79. Le Sage, *Gil Blas*, 119 (bk. 2, chap. 9).

34. Dickens, *Old Curiosity Shop*, chap. 73; *Dombey and Son*, chaps. 4, 15.

35. Shakespeare, *Love's Labor's Lost*, 5.2.334, 5.2.316–17.

36. Smollett, *Humphrey Clinker*, 64.

37. Brown, *Laconics*, A6.

38. Croker, *Johnsoniana*, 317.

39. Eliot, *Impressions*, 94–95.

40. Higginson, *Carlyle's Laugh*, 375.

41. Woolcott, *While Rome Burns*, 152.

42. An assortment was collected in *Quotable Quotes*.

43. "C'est souvent hasarder un bon mot et vouloir le perdre que de le donner pour sien: il n'est pas relevé, il tombe avec des gens d'esprit ou qui se croient tels, qui ne l'ont pas dit, et qui devaient le dire. C'est au contraire le faire valoir que de le rapporter comme d'un autre: ce n'est qu'un fait, et qu'on ne se croit pas obligé de savoir," La Bruyère, "Des jugements," §65, *Les caractères*, 371–72, *Characters*, 352–53.

44. *Dicts and Sayings*, 168, 169, see also 286, 287. I have modernized the spelling and punctuation.

45. Franklin, *Writings*, 1421.

46. Smiles, *Autobiography*, 2, 224–26.

47. Hilton, *Be My Guest*, 268–74.

48. Bacon, "Of Cunning," *Essays*, #22, *Major Works*, 385.

49. Tappert's introduction to Luther's *Table Talk*, xxvi; Josephus, *Against Apion*, Josephus, 1:176.

50. Emerson, *Letters*, 157.

51. Petrarch, "On His Own Ignorance," 92.

52. Jan Mukařovský, *Cestami poetiky a estetiky* (On the Pathways to Poetics and Esthetics), translation from Penfield, *Communicating with Quotes*, 3.

53. Lichtenberg, *Sudelbücher*, Notebook F, #84, *Aphorisms*, 93.

54. Lincoln, in Springfield, Illinois, June 16, 1858, *Speeches and Writings*, 1:426; BFQ 474.9; JGDQ 411.4; NCPQ 332.15; ODQ 493.10; PDQ 699.11; WNW 510.34; YBQ 460.11. Lincoln had used the "house divided" quotation in an 1843 circular for the Illinois Whig Party (*Collected Works*, 1:315).

55. Norton, "The Bible in the Slavery Dispute," 1–2, 3. Norton gives no examples because they are abundant: Jones, *Slavery Sanctioned*, 11; Ross, *Slavery Ordained of God*, 30–31, 50; Brookes, *A Defence of Southern Slavery*, 21–22; and Tyson, *The Institution of Slavery*, 4–5.

56. Citing Coptic and Adam Clark, Reverend Priest asserted that "*Ham*, in the original Hebrew, or Noachian language, was the word for that which was *black*," *Bible Defence of Slavery*, 36. *The Arabian Nights* traces its racism to the curse of Ham, *Arabian Nights*, 2:87, Night 335.

57. Priest, *Bible Defence of Slavery*, 317.

58. For example, whether *doulos* means "slave" or "servant" in Ephesians 6:5, where Paul directed, "Servants, be obedient to them that are your masters according to the flesh, with fear and trembling." See Harrill, "Use of the New Testament," 150–51.

59. A Texan, *Yankee Slave-Dealer*, 330–31.

60. Ross, *Slavery Ordained of God*, 96.

61. He addressed the General Assembly of New York in 1856.

62. Lincoln, "On Pro-Slavery Theology," *Speeches and Writings*, 1:685.

7. PROPHECY

Epigraph: Bacon, "Of Prophecies," *Essays*, #35, *Major Works*, 414.

1. Byron, *Don Juan*, 14.50.1–4, *Poetical Works*, 827; HBQ 1622.17; PDQ 247.162.

2. Publilius Syrus, "Futura pugnant ne se superari sinant," *Sententiae*, #207.

3. There are 1,028 hymns in the Rig Veda. "Asme dhehi dyumatīṃ vācam āsan bṛhaspate anamīvām iṣirām," Rig Veda, 10.98.

4. "Yajñasya jihvam avidāma guhyām," Rig Veda, 10.53.3.

5. Kierkegaard, *Repetition*, 109. Translation slightly revised.

6. Blair, *Islamic Inscriptions*, 201.

7. Jacobus de Voragine, *Golden Legend*, 1:62.

8. In Janouch, *Conversations with Kafka*, 59.

9. Morley, preface to BFQ 11th, v.

10. Sophocles, *Antigone*, 1053. See Erasmus, "Vatum genus avarum" (Prophets are a greedy tribe), *Adages*, 5.1.92, *Collected Works*, 36:594.

11. Thucydides, *The Peloponnesian War*, 2.8.2, 2.21.3, *Landmark Thucydides*, 93, 103.

12. Nissinen, *Prophets and Prophecy*, 4–9. For Neferti, see Lichtheim, *Ancient Egyptian Literature*, 139–45.

13. Plutarch, "Obsolescence of Oracles," 432c, *Moralia*, 5:469, quoting Euripides fragment 973; see also Cicero, *De divinatione*, 2.5; NCPQ 636.21; and Erasmus, "Qui bene conjiciet, hunc vatem" (He who guesses right is the prophet), *Adages*, 2.3.78, *Collected Works*, 33:177.

14. Xenophon, *Symposium*, 4.5; Lucian, "Menippus and Tiresias," in *Lucian*, 7:49; Lucian also wrote the life of Alexander of Abonoteichus, "the False Prophet," *Lucian* 4:174–253. Aesop, "The Soothsayer and the Theft," *Aesop's Fables*, #316 (Perry #161). Erasmus, "Veterata vaticinari," *Adages*, 4.10.8, *Collected Works*, 36:489. See also "Sapiens divinat" and "Hoc iam et vates sciunt," *Adages*, 4.6.84, 4.8.50, *Collected Works*, 36:270, 388.

15. Montaigne, "Des cannibales," *Oeuvres complètes*, 206 (*Essais* 1.31), *Complete Essays*, 235. Bacon, "Of Prophecies," *Essays*, #35, *Major Works*, 414. In addressing King James, Bacon cited a prophecy of Daniel (Daniel 12:4) that foretold the great age unfolding around them, but this seems less an endorsement of Daniel than flattery for the king, *Advancement of Learning*, bk. 2, *Major Works*, 184.

16. Hobbes, *Leviathan*, chap. 32. Eliot, *Middlemarch*, chap. 10; CDQ 742; ODQ 307.22; PDQ 409.38; WNW 304.4; slightly misquoted in BFQ 513.8 and QW (2001 ed.), 930.54.

17. Colton, *Lacon*, 51, referring to an incident described in Plutarch, "Life of Alexander," §14.4.

18. Virgil, *Aeneid*, 4.379–80.

19. Virgil, *Aeneid*, 2.553.

20. Seneca, *Suasoriae*, 4.4–5, *Declamations*, 2:548–51. Plutarch, *Moralia*, 7:151, and Aristides, *Orations*, 49.108, cite another classical killer quotation: "δυστήνων δέ τε παῖδες ἐμῷ μένει ἀντιόωσιν" (Unhappy they whose sons oppose my power), Homer, *Iliad*, 6.127.

21. Augustine, *Epistles*, #137, §12.

22. Kierkegaard, *Papers and Journals*, 161 (43, IV A 164).

23. Selden, *Table Talk*, 11, quoting John 5:39.

24. Book of Mormon, 3 Nephi, chap. 22.

25. Matthew 5:21–22, 27–28.

26. Pepper, *Life-Work of Louis Klopsch*, 9–10.

27. Klopsch, *Many Thoughts of Many Minds*, 250. Also Ballou, *Treasury of Thought*, 439; Douglas, *Forty Thousand Quotations*, 1450; Edwards, *Dictionary of Thoughts*, 477; Wooléver, *Encyclopedia of Quotations*, 336; and Goodman, *Forbes Book of Business Quotations*, 529.

28. Pepper, *Life-Work of Louis Klopsch*, 324–25.

29. "God is a witness that cannot be sworn," Beckett, *Watt*, 9.

30. Gellius, *Attic Nights*, 1:19.

31. Rabelais, *Gargantua and Pantagruel*, bk. 3, chaps. 10–12; see Meyer, *Poetics of Quotation*, 52–53. For Opellius Macrinus, see Cassius Dio Cocceianus, *Dio's Roman History*, 88.40; for Brutus, see Plutarch, *Life of Brutus*, §24; for Hadrian, Clodius Albinus, Alexander Severus, and Claudius Augustus, see *Scriptores historiae augustae*, 1:6–7, 468–69, 2:204–5, 3:170–71.

32. McNeill, "Folk-Paganism," 454.

33. Augustine, *Confessions*, 8.12.29. Augustine cites the example of Saint Anthony in the same passage.

34. Petrarch, "Ascent of Mont Ventoux," 44, quoting Augustine, *Confessions*, 10.8.15.

35. Virgil, *Aeneid*, 4.6.15–20. For the source of this anecdote, see Yeames, "On Teaching Virgil," 10.

36. Anderson, *Den of Lions*, 14–15, 125–26, 184.

37. Anderson, *Den of Lions*, 264. He made an exception for Barbara Cartland romances: "I can't read them, and I'll read anything," *Den of Lions*, 311.

38. Anderson, *Den of Lions*, 75.

39. Anderson, *Den of Lions*, 264. The evangelist quotes Luke 11:9; see also Matthew 7:7, 21:22, and 1 John 14:13, 16:23.

40. Anderson, *Den of Lions*, 265.

41. Maimonides, *Guide of the Perplexed*, 2:449.

42. In Homer, King Agamemnon told Chalcas:

Prophet of ill! Thou never speak'st to me
But words of evil omen; for thy soul
Delights to augur ill, but aught of good
Thou never yet hast promised, nor performed.

Iliad, 1.124–26; Grocott, *Index*, 356.

43. Cogan, *I Kings*, 497. Augustine asserts that one must possess the spirit in order to interpret the word, begging the question about how to know whether the spirit is lying or true.

44. Maimonides, *Guide of the Perplexed*, 2:405, 407.

45. Ginzberg, *Legends of the Jews*, 6:312.

46. See Jeremiah 14:14, 23:25, 32, 27:9–10, 14, 29:9; Ezekiel 14:9; also Micah 3:5–7; Zephaniah 3:4.

47. On false prophets, see Crenshaw, *Prophetic Conflict*, 83–84; Carroll, *Wolf in the Sheepfold*, 43–33; Moberly, "Does God Lie"; and especially De Vries, *Prophet Against Prophet*, 33–47, 78. De Vries minutely analyzes the Hebrew text within the prophetic tradition; Moberly faults others for taking the passage out of context. See also Hobbes, *Leviathan*, chap. 32.

48. Delivered in Springfield, Illinois, on June 16, 1858.

49. White, in Fehrenbacher and Fehrenbacher, *Recollected Words*, 488.

50. Mieder, *House Divided*. Mieder devotes pages 74–92 to the role the quotation played in the Lincoln-Douglas debates.

51. Davis and Wilson, *Lincoln-Douglas Debates*, 94, see also 12–13, 17. Prophecies of forthcoming civil war were abundant in the 1850s.

8. MEDITATIONS

Epigraph: Daudet, *In the Land of Pain*, 8.

1. Marcus Aurelius, *Meditations*, 10.34, quoting Homer, *Iliad*, 6.147.

2. Guicciardini, *Maxims and Reflections*, 115 (B80), quoting Seneca the Younger quoting Cleanthes, "Fates lead the willing, the unwilling they drag along," *Epistles*, 107.11.5. Seneca's text differs slightly: "Ducunt volentem fata, nolentem trahunt," Cleanthes, fragment 527.

3. Burton, *Anatomy*, 1:307 (1.2.3.15), adapting Virgil, *Aeneid*, 6.274–77.

4. Currer Bell was the pseudonym Brontë used in her early career. Brontë quotes George Henry Lewes in a letter to him, January 18, 1848, quoted in Gaskell, *Life of Charlotte Brontë*, 241.

5. Le Silence éternel de ces espaces infinis M'EFFRAYE.

   Cette phrase, dont la force de ce qu'elle veut imprimer aux âmes et la magnificence de sa forme ont fait une des paroles les plus fameuses qui aient jamais été articulées, est un Poème

   et point du tout une Pensée.

   Car Éternel et Infini sont des symboles de non-pensée. Leur valeur est tout affective.

Valéry, "Variation sur une Pensée," *Oeuvres*, 1:458; "Variations on a Pensée," *Masters and Friends*, 86, quoting Pascal, *Pensées*, #206.

6. Ward, *Robert Elsmere*, 592; "Abandon inflated hope and great thoughts," quoting Jean de La Fontaine's "Le vieillard et les trois jeunes hommes," *Oeuvres complètes*, 1:441 (*Fables*, bk. 11, no. 8).

7. Nietzsche, *Human, All Too Human*, §109, *Sämtliche Werke*, 2:108, quoting (in English) Lord Byron's *Manfred*, 1.1.10–12 and (in Latin) Horace's *Odes*, 2.11.13–14:

> Die Entwicklung der Menschheit so zart, reizbar, leidend geworden ist, um Heil- und Trostmittel der höchsten Art nötig zu haben; woraus also die Gefahr ensteht, daß der Mensch sich an der erkannten Wahrheit verblute. Die drückt Byron in unsterblichen Versen aus. . . .
> Gegen solche Sorgen hilft kein Mittel besser, als den feierlichen Leichtsinn Horazens, wenigstens für die schlimmsten Stunden und Sonnenfinsternisse der Seele, heraufzubeschwören und mit ihm zu sich selber zu sagen:
>
> > quid aeternis minorem
> > consiliis animum fatigas?
> > cur non sub alta vel platano vel hac
> > pinu jacentes — .

8. Powers, *Prisoner's Dilemma*, 321, quoting Oppenheimer, quoting *Bhagavad-Gītā*, 11.32. Oppenheimer follows the Arthur Ryder translation. Krishna says, "Kālo'smi loka-kṣaya-kṛt pravṛddho" (Time am I, wreaker of the world's destruction); see Hijiya, "The *Gita* of J. Robert Oppenheimer," 132. Compare Ovid, "Tempus edax rerum" (Time devours everything), *Metamorphoses*, 15.234; BFQ 105.20.

9. FitzGerald, *Polonius*, xxni. "The hour cometh," John 4:21, 23, 16:32.

9. LAST WORDS

Epigraph: Ssu-ma Ch'ien, *Grand Scribe's Records*, 7:21.

1. Le Compte, *Dictionary of Last Words*, vii.

2. On June 28, 1939. BFQ 784.14; YBQ 297.

3. "La montagne est passée; nous irons mieux," quoted by Carlyle, *History of Friedrich II. of Prussia*, 10:192.

4. Robinson, *Famous Last Words*, 31. I could trace this back no further than Sandburg, *Abraham Lincoln: The War Years*, 3:49. Sandburg allows General Sedgwick to complete his sentence.

5. *Arabian Nights*, 2:36.

6. Shakespeare, *Titus Andronicus*, 5.3.185–90.

7. Foxe, *Actes*, 2:1433, quoting Augustine, "Cum verba novissima hominis morientis audiantur itur ad inferos, nemo eum dicit esse mentitum," *On the Unity of the Church*, chap. 11, §28.

8. Guthke, *Last Words*, 19.

9. *Dying Speeches and Behaviour*, A2–3.

10. Valerius Maximus, *Memorable Doings and Sayings*, 8.7.14.

11. Pettit, *History*, 1:198.

12. ODQ 4th, 274.19. The quotation lives on in QW 334.4.

13. Green, *Famous Last Words*, 103.

14. Robinson, *Famous Last Words*, 3.

15. Green, *Famous Last Words*, 9.

16. Marvin, *Last Words*, 306, 279, 249, 310.

17. Egbert, *Last Words*, 14. Guthke, *Last Words*, 68.

18. Green, *Famous Last Words*, 102.

19. Bega, *Last Words*, 121. Marvin, *Last Words*, 176. Green, *Famous Last Words*, 136.

20. Breuning, *Memories of Beethoven*, 101. Suetonius, "Augustus," §2.99, *Lives*, 1:302; "Nero," §6.49, *Lives*, 2:173. Both Augustus and Nero spoke in Greek.

21. Marvin, *Last Words*, 175, 295, 269. Lucan quoted *Pharsalia*, 3.638–41. On Waller, see Johnson, *Lives*, 2:43, "Waller repeated some lines of Virgil, and went home to die"; the lines from Virgil are not recorded. Strozzi's Virgil quotation is from the *Aeneid*, 4.625.

22. Egbert, *Last Words*, 78.

23. Bega, *Last Words*, 14, quoting Luke 23:46.

24. Guthke, *Last Words*, 50, 159, 188.

25. Bega, *Last Words*, 75–76. Diderot quotes Montaigne's "De la vanité": "Je me plonge la teste baissée stupidement dans la mort, sans la considerer et recognoistre, comme dans une profondeur muette et obscure, qui m'engloutit d'un saut et accable en un instant d'un puissant sommeil, plein d'insipidité et indolence," *Oeuvres complètes*, 949 (*Essais*, 3.9), *Complete Essays*, 1099.

26. Egbert, *Last Words*, 93, citing Diderot's daughter as his source.

27. Bega, *Last Words*, 97. Suetonius, "Vespasian," §23.

28. Wordsworth, "The Wanderer," *The Excursion*, 1.91–93, *Poetical Works*, 592.

ACKNOWLEDGMENTS

Epigraph: Cicero, "Difficile non aliquem, ingratium quenquam praeterire," *Oratio post reditum in Senatu*, 12.30; quoted by Bacon, *Advancement of Learning*, bk. 1, *Major Works*, 170–71.

WORKS CITED

Epigraph: Herbert, *Jacula*, #1146, *Works*, 360; BFQ 252.18; HBQ 181.6. Isaac Disraeli calls "Cave ab homine unius libri" (Beware the man of only one book) an "old Latin proverb," but I can find no appearance of it prior to his "The Man of One Book," *Curiosities*, 4:245; BBQ 504; BFQ 123.12; HBQ 181.6; NCPQ 77.13; YBQ 22.4. Hoyt cites Aquinas for "Homo unius libri," NCPQ 75.17.

Woe be to him that reads but one book.

George Herbert

WORKS CITED

Dates of earliest known publication are given in brackets.

Abailard, Peter. *Sic et Non: A Critical Edition*. Edited by Blanche B. Boyer and Richard McKeon. Chicago: University of Chicago Press, 1976 [ca. 1130].

Adams, Franklin Pierce. FPA: *Book of Quotations*. New York: Funk and Wagnalls, 1952.

Adams, H. G. *A Cyclopedia of Poetical Quotations Consisting of Choice Passages from the Poets of Every Age and Country*. Glasgow: Robert Forrester, 1865.

Addams, Jane. *The Long Road of Woman's Memory*. Urbana and Chicago: University of Illinois Press, 2002 [1916].

Addington, John. *Poetical Quotations, being A Complete Dictionary of The Most Elegant Moral, Sublime, and Humorous Passages in The British Poets*. 4 vols. Philadelphia: John Grigg, 1829.

Aeschylus. *Aeschylus*. Translated by Herbert Weir Smyth. 2 vols. Cambridge MA: Harvard University Press, 2006.

Aesop. *Aesop's Fables*. Translated by Laura Gibbs. Oxford: Oxford University Press, 2002.

Ahiqar. *The Aramaic Proverbs of Ahiqar*. Translated by James M. Lindenberger. Baltimore: Johns Hopkins University Press, 1983 [7th century BC?].

"A.L." *A Letter to a Friend, touching Dr. Jeremy Taylor's Disswasive from Popery. Discovering above an hundred and Fifty False, or Wretched Quotations, in it*. N.p.: n.p., 1665.

Alcott, A. Bronson. *Table-Talk*. Boston: Roberts Brothers, 1877.

Ali Yezdi, Sharfuddin. *Political and Military Institutes of Tamerlane*. Translated by Major Davy. Delhi: Idarah-i Adabiyat-i Delli, 1972 [1780].

Allibone, S. Austin. *Poetical Quotations from Chaucer to Tennyson*. Philadelphia: J. B. Lippincott, 1873.

———. *Prose Quotations from Socrates to Macaulay*. Philadelphia: J. B. Lippincott, 1882.

Allot, Robert. *Englands Parnassus, or, The Choysest Flowers of our Moderne Poets: with their Poeticall Comparisons: Descriptions of Bewties, Personages, Castles, Pallaces, Mountaines, Groves, Seas, Springs, Rivers, & c.: whereunto are annexed other various discourses, both pleasaunt and profitable*. London: For N. L., C. B. and T. H., 1600.

Anderson, Alexander. *Laconics: Or Instructive Miscellanies, Selected from the Best Authors*. Philadelphia: W. Brown, 1827.

Anderson, Terry. *Den of Lions: Memoirs of Seven Years*. New York: Crown Books, 1993.

Andrews, Robert, ed. *The Columbia Dictionary of Quotations*. New York: Columbia University Press, 1993.

———. *The Concise Columbia Dictionary of Quotations*. New York: Columbia University Press, 1989.

———. *New Penguin Dictionary of Quotations*. Harmondsworth: Penguin, 2006.

Ansen, Alan. *The Table Talk of W. H. Auden*. Princeton: Ontario Review Press, 1990.

Apuleius. *Apologia and Florida*. Translated by H. E. Butler. Oxford: Oxford University Press, 1909.

———. *Florida*. Edited by Vincent Hunink. Amsterdam: J. C. Gieben, 2001.

Arabian Nights: Tales of the 1001 Nights. Translated by Malcolm C. Lyons with Ursula Lyons. 3 vols. London: Penguin Classics, 2008 [8th–18th centuries].

Arendt, Hannah. *Eichmann in Jerusalem: A Report on the Banality of Evil*. Harmondsworth: Penguin, 1994 [1963].

———. "Walter Benjamin: 1892–1940." In *Men in Dark Times*, 153–206. Orlando FL: Harcourt Brace Jovanovich, 1968.

———. *Willing*. New York: Harcourt Brace Jovanovich, 1978.

Aristotle. *Art of Rhetoric*. Translated by J. H. Freese. Cambridge MA: Harvard University Press, 1926 [ca. 330 BC].

———. *Metaphysics I–IX*. Translated by H. Tredennick. Cambridge MA: Harvard University Press, 1933 [ca. 340 BC].

Arnold, Matthew. *Essays in Criticism*, 1st series. London: Macmillan, 1903 [1865].

Ascheim, Steven E. *The Nietzsche Legacy in Germany, 1890–1990*. Berkeley: University of California Press, 1992.

Athenaeus. *The Deipnosophists*. Translated by Charles Burton Gulick. 7 vols. Cambridge MA: Harvard University Press, 1927–57 [ca. AD 228].

Auden, W. H. *A Certain World: A Commonplace Book*. New York: Viking Press, 1971.

———. *The Dyer's Hand and Other Essays*. New York: Random House, 1962.

Augustine. *The City of God*. Translated by Rev. Marcus Dods. In Schaff, *Nicene and Post-Nicene Fathers*, 2:xi–511.

———. *The Confessions*. Translated by J. G. Pilkington. In Schaff, *Nicene and Post-Nicene Fathers*, 1:29–207.

———. *Epistles*. In Schaff, *Nicene and Post-Nicene Fathers*, 1:209–619.

———. *On Christian Doctrine*. Vol. 2 of Schaff, *Nicene and Post-Nicene Fathers*.

———. *Sermons*. Vol. 6 of Schaff, *Nicene and Post-Nicene Fathers*.

Ausonius. *Ausonius*. Translated by Hugh G. Evelyn White. 2 vols. London: William Heinemann, 1919 [4th century AD].

Austen, Jane. *Jane Austen's Letters to Her Sister Cassandra and Others*. Edited by R. W. Chapman. London: Oxford University Press, 1952.

Bacon, Francis. *The Major Works*. Edited by Brian Vickers. New York: Oxford Classics, 2002.

———. *The Promus of Formularies and Elegancies (Being Private Notes, circ. 1594, hitherto unpublished) by Francis Bacon, Illustrated and Elucidated by Passages from Shakespeare*. Edited by Mrs. Henry Pott. London: Longmans, Green, 1883.

———. *The Works of Francis Bacon*. Edited by James Spedding, Robert Leslie Ellis, and Douglas Denon Heath. 15 vols. Boston: Houghton Mifflin, 1900 [1861–79].

Bakhtin, Mikhail. *The Dialogic Imagination*. Edited by Michael Holquist. Translated by Caryl Emerson and Michael Holquist. Austin: University of Texas Press, 1981 [1975].

———. *Problems of Dostoevsky's Poetics*. Translated by Caryl Emerson. Minneapolis: University of Minnesota Press, 1984 [1929, 1963].

———. *Rabelais and His World*. Translated by Hélène Iswolsky. Cambridge MA: MIT Press, 1968 [1965].

Bakker, Paul J. J. M., and Chris Schabel. "*Sentences* Commentaries of the Later Fourteenth Century." In Evans, *Medieval Commentaries*, 425–64.

Baldwin, Barry. *The Philogelos or Laughter-Lover*. Amsterdam: J. C. Gieben, 1983.

Baldwin, Thomas Whitfield. *William Shakspere's Small Latine & Lesse Greeke*. 2 vols. Champaign: University of Illinois Press, 1944.

Ballou, Maturin Murray. *Notable Thoughts about Women: A Literary Mosaic*. Boston: Houghton Mifflin, 1882.

———. *Treasury of Thought: Forming an Encyclopedia of Quotations from Ancient and Modern Authors*. Boston: Houghton Mifflin, 1871.

Balzac, Honoré de. *Old Goriot*. Translated by Ellen Marriage. London: Everyman's Library, 1907 [1834–35].

Barnes, Julian. *A History of the World in 10½ Chapters*. New York: Alfred A. Knopf, 1989.

———. *Nothing to Be Frightened Of*. New York: Alfred A. Knopf, 2008.

Barns, John. "A New Gnomologium: With Some Remarks on Gnomic Anthologies, II." *Classical Quarterly*, n.s., 1, nos. 1–2 (1951): 1–19.

Barrett Browning, Elizabeth. *The Complete Poetical Works*. Edited by Harriet Waters Preston. Cambridge MA: Houghton Mifflin, 1900.

Bartlett, John. *Bartlett's Familiar Quotations*, 17th ed. Edited by Justin Kaplan. Boston: Little, Brown, 2002.

———. *A Collection of Familiar Quotations*. Cambridge MA: John Bartlett, 1855.

———. *A Collection of Familiar Quotations*, new ed. Cambridge MA: John Bartlett, 1856.

———. *A Collection of Familiar Quotations*, 3rd ed. Cambridge MA: John Bartlett, 1858.

———. *Familiar Quotations: Being an Attempt to Trace to Their Sources Passages and Phrases in Common Use; Chiefly from English Authors*, 4th ed. Boston: Little, Brown, 1865.

———. *Familiar Quotations: Being an Attempt to Trace to Their Sources Passages and Phrases in Common Use; Chiefly from English Authors*, 5th ed. Boston: Little, Brown, 1869.

———. *Familiar Quotations: Being an Attempt to Trace to Their Sources Passages and Phrases in Common Use; Chiefly from English Authors*, 6th ed. Boston: Little, Brown, 1874.

———. *Familiar Quotations: Being an Attempt to Trace to Their Sources Passages and Phrases in Common Use*, 7th ed. Boston: Little, Brown, 1881.

———. *Familiar Quotations: Being an Attempt to Trace to Their Sources Passages and Phrases in Common Use*, 8th ed. Boston: Little, Brown, 1882.

———. *Familiar Quotations: Being an Attempt to Trace to Their Sources Passages and Phrases in Common Use*, author's ed. London: Routledge and Sons, 1889.

———. *Familiar Quotations: A Collection of Passages, Phrases, and Proverbs Traced to Their Sources in Ancient and Modern Literature*, 9th ed. Boston: Little, Brown, 1891.

———. *Familiar Quotations: A Collection of Passages, Phrases and Proverbs Traced to Their Sources in Ancient and Modern Literature*, 10th ed. Edited by Nathan Haskell Dole. Boston: Little, Brown, 1914.

———. *Familiar Quotations: A Collection of Passages, Phrases and Proverbs Traced to Their Sources in Ancient and Modern Literature*, 11th ed. Edited by Christopher Morley and Louella D. Everett. Boston: Little, Brown, 1937.

———. *Familiar Quotations: A Collection of Passages, Phrases and Proverbs Traced to Their Sources in Ancient and Modern Literature*, 12th ed. Edited by Christopher Morley and Louella D. Everett. Boston: Little, Brown, 1948.

———. *Familiar Quotations: A Collection of Passages, Phrases and Proverbs Traced to Their Sources in Ancient and Modern Literature*, 13th ed. Edited by the staff of Little, Brown and Company. Boston: Little, Brown, 1955.

———. *Familiar Quotations: A Collection of Passages, Phrases and Proverbs Traced to Their Sources in Ancient and Modern Literature*, 14th ed. Edited by Emily Morison Beck. Boston: Little, Brown, 1968.

———. *Familiar Quotations: A Collection of Passages, Phrases and Proverbs Traced to Their Sources in Ancient and Modern Literature*, 15th ed. Edited by Emily Morison Beck. Boston: Little, Brown, 1980.

———. *Familiar Quotations: A Collection of Passages, Phrases and Proverbs Traced to Their Sources in Ancient and Modern Literature*, 16th ed. Edited by Justin Kaplan. Boston: Little, Brown, 1992.

Barzun, Jacques. *God's Country and Mine*. Boston: Atlantic Monthly Press, 1954.

Bassford, Christopher. *Clausewitz in English: The Reception of Clausewitz in Britain and America, 1815–1945*. New York: Oxford University Press, 1994.

Baudelaire, Charles. *Les fleurs du mal*. Translated by Richard Howard. Boston: David R. Godine, 1982 [1857].

Beaumont, Francis, and John Fletcher. *A King and No King*. Edited by Robert K. Turner, Jr. Lincoln: University of Nebraska Press, 1963 [1611].

Beck, Emily Morison. "The Long, Happy Life of 'Bartlett's Quotations.'" *American Heritage* 35 (August 1984): 102–7.

Beckett, Samuel. *Watt*. New York: Grove Press, 1959 [1953].

Bega [A. P. Codd]. *Last Words of Famous Men*. London: Williams and Norgate, 1930.

Benham, W. Gurney. *A Book of Quotations, Proverbs and Household Words*. London: Cassell, 1914 [1907].

———. *Putnam's Complete Book of Quotations, Proverbs and Household Words: A Collection of Quotations from British and American Authors, with many thousands of proverbs, familiar phrases and sayings, from all sources, including Hebrew, Arabic, Greek, Latin, French, German, Italian, Spanish, and other languages*. New York: G. P. Putnam's Sons, 1926.

Benjamin, Walter. *Illuminations*. Introduction by Hannah Arendt. Translated by Harry Zohn. New York: Schocken Books, 1969.

———. *Das Passagen-Werk*. Edited by Rolf Tiedemann. 2 vols. Frankfurt: Suhrkamp Verlag, 1982. Translated by Howard Eiland and Kevin McLaughlin as *The Arcades Project*. Cambridge MA: Harvard University Press, 1999.

Berkeley, Everard [pseudonym of Tryon Edwards]. *The World's Laconics; or the Best Thoughts of the Best Authors*. Introduction by William B. Sprague. New York: M. W. Dodd, 1853.

Bettmann, Otto L. *The Delights of Reading: Quotes, Notes & Anecdotes*. Boston: David R. Godine, 1987.

Bhagavad-Gītā. Translated by R. C. Zaehner. London: Oxford University Press, 1969 [between 5th and 2nd centuries BC].

Bierce, Ambrose. *The Devil's Dictionary*. New York: Dover Books, 1958 [1906].

Biggs, Mary. *Women's Words: The Columbia Book of Quotations by Women*. New York: Columbia University Press, 1996.

Blair, Sheila S. *Islamic Inscriptions*. Edinburgh: Edinburgh University Press, 1998.

Blake, William. *Complete Writings*. Edited by Geoffrey Keynes. London: Oxford University Press, 1969.

Bodenham, John. *Belvedére, or, The Garden of the Muses*. London: F. K. for Hugh Astley, 1600.

Bohn, Henry G. *A Dictionary of Quotations from the English Poets*, 5th ed. London: George Bell and Sons, 1889 [1867].

———. *A Hand-book of Proverbs*. London: H. G. Bohn, 1855.

Boller, Paul F., Jr. *George Washington & Religion*. Dallas: Southern Methodist University Press, 1963.

———. *Quotesmanship: The Use and Abuse of Quotations for Polemical and Other Purposes*. Dallas: Southern Methodist University Press, 1967.

The Book of Familiar Quotations: Being a Collection of Popular Extracts and Aphorisms selected from the Works of the Best Authors. London: Whittaker, 1852.

Book of Familiar Quotations, Containing over Three Thousand Quotations in Prose and Verse, Alphabetically Arranged. Compiled from the Works of the Great Authors, from the Earliest Ages to the Present Time. New York: American News Company, n.d.

Book of Mormon: Another Testament of Jesus Christ. Translated by Joseph Smith. Salt Lake City: Church of Jesus Christ of Latter-day Saints, 1948 [1830].

Borges, Jorge Luis. *Ficciones*. Madrid: Alianza Editorial, 1971 [1956].

———. *Labyrinths: Selected Stories and Other Writings*. Translated by Donald A. Yates et al. New York: New Directions, 1964.

———. *Nueva antología personal*. Buenos Aires: Emecé Editores, 1968.

———. *Other Inquisitions 1937–1952*. Translated by Ruth L. C. Simms. Austin: University of Texas Press, 1964.

Boswell, James. *Letters of James Boswell*. Edited by C. B. Tinker. 2 vols. Oxford: Oxford University Press, 1924.

———. *Life of Johnson*. Edited by George Birbeck Hill. Revised and enlarged by L. F. Powell. 4 vols. Oxford: Oxford University Press, 1934 [1791].

Bovee, C. N. *Intuitions and Summaries of Thought*. 2 vols. Cambridge: Riverside Press, 1862.

Bowerman, Sarah G. "John Bartlett." In *Dictionary of American Biography*. Edited by Allen Johnson, 2:6–7. New York: Charles Scribner's Sons, 1929.

Boyes, J. F. *Lacon in Council*. London: Bell and Daldy, 1865.

Brantôme, Abbé Pierre de Bourdeille. *Lives of Fair and Gallant Ladies.* Translated by A. R. Allinson. New York: Citadel Press, 1933 [1665].

Breuning, Gerhard von. *Memories of Beethoven: From the House of the Black-Robed Spaniards.* Translated by Maynard Solomon and Henry Mins. Cambridge: Cambridge University Press, 1992 [1874].

Bronchorst, Everardo. *Aphorismi politici et militares ex diversis auctoribus Graecis & Latinis per Lambertum Danaeum collecti; nuperis annis ab Everardo Bronchorst, exemplis illustrati; quibus modò in hac nova editione accessere sexcenta ferè alia, ex recentioribus historiographis Germanis, Gallis, Hispanis, Italis, Anglis, Belgis excerpta; cum syllabo auctorum & locupletissimo rerum in aphorismis & exemplis indice.* Lyon: Jacobi Marci, 1639.

Brookes, Iveson. *A Defence of Southern Slavery.* Hamburg SC: Robinson and Carlisle, 1851.

Brown, Raymond E. *The Epistles of John.* New York: Doubleday, 1982.

———. *The Gospel According to John.* New York: Doubleday, 1966.

Brown, Thomas. *Laconics: Or, New Maxims of State and Conversation Relating to the Affairs and Manners of the Present Times.* London: Thomas Hodgson, 1701.

Browne, Sir Thomas. *Religio Medici and Other Writings.* London: J. M. Dent and Sons, 1906 [1643].

Bruce, F. F. *The English Bible: A History of Translations from the Earliest English Versions to the New English Bible.* New York: Oxford University Press, 1970.

Büchmann, Georg. *Geflügelte Worte: Der Zitatenschatz des deutschen Volkes,* 32nd ed. Berlin: Haude und Spenersche Verlagsbuchhandlung, 1972 [1864].

Bühler, Winfried. *Zenobii Athoi proverbia: vulgari ceteraque memoria aucta edidit et enarravit: Volumen primum, Prolegomena complexum, in quibus codices describuntur.* Göttingen: Vandenhoeck und Ruprecht, 1987.

Bulwer, Edward, Lord Lytton. *Richelieu: Or the Conspiracy.* New York: Dodd, Mead, 1896 [1839].

Burke, Edmund. *A Philosophical Enquiry in the Origin of Our Ideas of the Sublime and Beautiful.* Edited by James T. Boulton. London: Routledge and Kegan Paul, 1958 [1757].

———. *Works.* 12 vols. London: Nimmo, 1899.

Burney, Fanny. *The Diary and Letters of Frances Burney, Madame d'Arblay.* Revised and edited by Sarah Chauncey Woolsey. 2 vols. Boston: Little, Brown, 1910 [1880].

Burrow, John. *A History of Histories: Epics, Chronicles, Romances and Inquiries from Herodotus and Thucydides to the Twentieth Century.* New York: Alfred A. Knopf, 2008.

Burton, Robert. *The Anatomy of Melancholy.* Edited by Thomas C. Faulkner, Nicholas K. Kiessling, Rhonda L. Blair, and J. B. Bamborough. 6 vols. Oxford: Oxford University Press, 1989–2000 [1621, 1624, 1628, 1632, 1638, 1651].

Butler, Samuel. *Hudibras: A New Edition, Corrected and Enlarged.* 3 vols. London: Charles and Henry Baldwyn, 1819 [1663–68].

Byrne, Robert. *The 2,548 Best Things Anybody Ever Said.* New York: Simon and Schuster, 2003.

Byron, Lord. *The Poetical Works of Lord Byron.* London: Oxford University Press, 1904.

Callimachus. *Hymns and Epigrams.* Translated by A. W. Mair, rev. ed. Cambridge MA: Harvard University Press, 1955 [3rd century BC].

Camp, Wesley D. *Camp's Unfamiliar Quotations from 2000 B.C. to the Present.* Paramus NJ: Prentice Hall, 1990.

Cappelen, Herman, and Ernie Lepore. "Quotation, Context Sensitivity, Signs and Expression." *Philosophical Issues* 16, no. 1 (2006): 43–64.

———. "Varieties of Quotation." *Mind,* July 1997, 429–50.

Carleton, G. W. *Carleton's Hand-Book of Popular Quotations.* New York: G. W. Carleton, 1877.

Carlyle, Thomas. *History of Friedrich II. of Prussia, called Frederick the Great.* 10 vols. London: Chapman and Hall, 1873 [1858–65].

Carroll, Robert P. *Wolf in the Sheepfold: The Bible as a Problem for Christianity.* London: Society for Promoting Christian Knowledge, 1991.

Casanova, Giacomo. *History of My Life.* Translated by Willard Trask. 6 vols. Baltimore: Johns Hopkins University Press, 1997 [1822–28].

Cassedy, Ben. *The Poetic Lacon, or, Aphorisms from the Poets.* New York: Lea and Blanchard, 1839.

Cassirer, Ernst. *The Renaissance Philosophy of Man.* Edited by Paul Oskar Kristeller and John Herman Randall, Jr. Chicago: University of Chicago Press, 1948.

Cassius Dio Cocceianus. *Dio's Roman History.* Translated by Earnest Cary on the basis of the version of Herbert Baldwin Foster. 9 vols. Cambridge MA: Harvard University Press, 1914–27 [AD 200–222].

Catullus. *The Poems.* Translated by F. W. Cornish. In *Catullus, Tibullus, Pervigilium Veneris,* 1–183. Cambridge MA: Harvard University Press, 1913 [1st century BC].

Cave, Terence. *The Cornucopian Text: Problems of Writing in the French Renaissance.* Oxford: Oxford University Press, 1979.

Cerquiglini, Bernard. *In Praise of the Variant: A Cultural History of Philology.* Translated by Betsy Wing. Baltimore: Johns Hopkins University Press, 1999 [1989].

Cervantes, Miguel de. *Don Quixote.* Translated by Peter Motteux. Edited by J. G. Lockhart. London: J. M. Dent, 1943 [1605, 1615].

Chadwick, Henry. *The Sentences of Sextus: A Contribution to the History of Early Christian Ethics.* Cambridge: Cambridge University Press, 1959.

Chamfort. *Products of the Perfected Civilization.* Translated by W. S. Merwin. San Francisco: North Point Press, 1984.

Chāndogya Upaniṣad. Edited by Swāmī Swāhānanda. Madras: Sri Ramakrishna Math, 1956.

Chapin, Seymour L. "A Legendary Bon Mot?: Franklin's 'What Is the Good of a Newborn Baby?'" *Proceedings of the American Philosophical Society* 129, no. 3 (1985): 278–90.

Charlesworth, James H., ed. *The Old Testament Pseudepigrapha*. 2 vols. New York: Doubleday, 1983, 1985.

Chesterfield, Philip Dormer Stanhope, 4th Earl of. "The Art of Pleasing." In *Miscellaneous Works of the Late Philip Dormer Stanhope, Earl of Chesterfield; Consisting of Letters, Political Tracts, and Poems*. 4 vols. London: n.p., 1778, 3:1–41.

———. *Letters to His Son*. 2 vols. Washington DC: M. Walter Dunne, 1901 [1774].

Christy, Robert. *Proverbs, Maxims, and Phrases of All Ages*. 2 vols. New York: G. P. Putnam's Sons, 1893.

Churchill, Winston. *A Roving Commission: The Story of My Early Life*. New York: Charles Scribner's Sons, 1944 [1930].

Cicero. *De natura deorum*. Translated by H. Rackham. Cambridge MA: Harvard University Press, 1933 [45 BC].

———. *De officiis*. Translated by Walter Miller. Cambridge MA: Harvard University Press, 1945 [44 BC].

———. *De senectute, De amicitia, De divinatione*. Cambridge MA: Harvard University Press, 1964 [1st century BC].

———. *Letters to Atticus*. Translated by D. R. Shackleton Bailey. 4 vols. Cambridge MA: Harvard University Press, 1999 [68–44 BC].

———. *Philippics*. Translated by Walter C. A. Ker. Cambridge MA: Harvard University Press, 1926 [44–43 BC].

———. *Tusculan Disputations*. Translated by J. E. King. Cambridge MA: Harvard University Press, 1945 [45 BC].

———. *Verrine Orations*. Translated by L. H. G. Greenwood. 2 vols. Cambridge MA: Harvard University Press, 1945 [70 BC].

Cioran, Emil M. *Anathemas and Admirations*. Translated by Richard Howard. London: Quartet Books, 1992 [1987].

Clark, Herbert H., and Richard R. Gerrig. "Quotations as Demonstrations." *Language* 66, no. 4 (1990): 764–805.

Cochrane, Kerry L. "'The Most Familiar Book of Its Kind': Bartlett's *Familiar Quotations*." In *Distinguished Classics of Reference Publishing*. Edited by James Rettig, 9–17. Phoenix: Oryx Press, 1993.

Cogan, Mordechai. *I Kings*. Garden City: Anchor Bible, 1988.

Cohen, I. Bernard. "Faraday and Franklin's 'Newborn Baby.'" *Proceedings of the American Philosophical Society* 131, no. 2 (1987): 177–82.

Coleridge, Hartley. *Biographia Borealis; or, Lives of Distinguished Northerns*. London: Whittaker, Treacher, 1833.

Coleridge, Samuel Taylor. *Aids to Reflection*. Edited by John Beer. Princeton: Princeton University Press, 1993 [1825; 2nd ed. 1831].

———. *Biographia Literaria, or Biographical Sketches of My Literary Life and Opinions*. Edited by James Engell and W. Jackson Bate. 2 vols. in 1. Princeton: Princeton University Press, 1983 [1817].

———. *Collected Letters*. Edited by Earl Leslie Griggs. 6 vols. Oxford: Oxford University Press, 1956–71.

———. *The Friend*. Edited by Barbara E. Rooke. 2 vols. Princeton: Princeton University Press, 1969 [1809–10, rev. 1818].

———. *Table Talk*. Edited by Carl Woodring. 2 vols. Princeton: Princeton University Press, 1990 [1835].

Colish, Marcia L. *Peter Lombard*. 2 vols. Leiden: E. J. Brill, 1994.

Colton, Charles Caleb. *Lacon: or, Many Things in Few Words; Addressed to Those Who Think*, rev. ed. New York: Charles Wells, 1836 [pt. 1, 1820; pt. 2, 1822].

Compagnon, Antoine. *La seconde main: ou le travail de la citation*. Paris: Éditions du Seuil, 1979.

Confucius. *The Analects*. Translated by David Hinton. Washington DC: Counterpoint, 1998 [5th century BC].

Connolly, Cyril. *The Unquiet Grave: A Word Cycle by Palinurus*. New York: Harper and Brothers, 1945.

Cooper, Jilly, and Tom Hartman. *Violets and Vinegar: Beyond Bartlett, Quotations by and about Women*. New York: Stein and Day, 1983.

Courcelle, Pierre. "L'Enfant et les 'Sorts Bibliques.'" *Vigiliae Christianae* 7, no. 4 (1953): 194–220.

Cozzens, Frederic Swartwout. *The Sayings of Dr. Bushwhacker, and Other Learned Men*. New York: A. Simpson, 1867.

Crane, Nathalia. *The Janitor's Boy and Other Poems*. New York: Thomas Seltzer, 1924.

Crenshaw, James L. *Prophetic Conflict: Its Effect upon Israelite Religion*. Berlin: Walter de Gruyter, 1971.

Criado, Matias Alonso. *Veinte mil pensamientos: colección de máximas y sentencias de diferentes autores de todas las épocas y países*. 2 vols. Buenos Aires: Ediciones Anaconda, 1946.

Croker, J. Wilson. *Johnsoniana: or, Supplement to Boswell, Being Anecdotes and Sayings of Dr. Johnson*. Philadelphia: Carey and Hart, 1842.

Curie, Eve. *Madame Curie*. Paris: Gallimard, 1938.

Dalbiac, Philip Hugh. *Dictionary of Quotations (English)*. London: Swan Sonnenschein, 1896.

———. *Dictionary of Quotations (German)*. London: Swan Sonnenschein, 1906.

Dalbiac, Philip Hugh, and Thomas Benfield Harbottle. *Dictionary of Quotations (French and Italian)*. London: Swan Sonnenschein, 1901.

Dante. *Purgatory.* Translated by Anthony Esolen. New York: Modern Library, 2003.

Daudet, Alphonse. *In the Land of Pain.* Translated by Julian Barnes. New York: Alfred A. Knopf, 2002.

Davidson, Donald. "Quotation." *Theory and Decision* 11, no. 1 (1979): 27–40. Reprinted in *Inquiries into Truth and Interpretation,* 2nd ed. Oxford: Clarendon Press, 2001.

Davis, Rodney O., and Douglas L. Wilson. *The Lincoln-Douglas Debates.* Urbana and Chicago: University of Illinois Press, 2008.

Day, Edward Parsons. *Day's Collacon: An Encyclopedia of Prose Quotations Consisting of Beautiful Thoughts, Choice Extracts, and Sayings, of the Most Eminent Writers of All Nations from the Earliest Ages to the Present Time.* London: Sampson Low, Marston, Searle and Rivington, 1884.

Delepierre, Octave. *Supercheries littéraires: pastiches, suppositions d'auteur, dans les lettres et dans les arts.* London: N. Trübner et Cie, 1872.

———. *Tableau de la littérature du centon chez les anciens et chez les modernes.* 2 vols. London: N. Trübner et Cie, 1875.

Delteil, Joseph. *Lafayette.* Translated by Jacques Le Clercq. New York: Minton, Balchand, 1928.

DeMallie, Raymond J., ed. *The Sixth Grandfather: Black Elk's Teachings Given to John G. Neihardt.* Lincoln: University of Nebraska Press, 1984.

Demosthenes. *Demosthenes.* Translated by J. H. Vince et al. 7 vols. Cambridge MA: Harvard University Press, 1949–78 [4th century BC].

Derrida, Jacques. *De la grammatologie.* Paris: Les Éditions de Minuit, 1967. Translated by Gayatri Chakravorty Spivak as *Of Grammatology.* Baltimore: Johns Hopkins University Press, 1976.

———. *De l'esprit.* Paris: Éditions Galilée, 1987. Translated by Geoffrey Bennington and Rachel Bowlby as *Of Spirit: Heidegger and the Question.* Chicago: University of Chicago Press, 1989 [1987].

De Vries, Simon John. *Prophet Against Prophet: The Role of the Micaiah Narrative (I Kings 22) in the Development of Early Prophetic Tradition.* Grand Rapids: William B. Eerdmans, 1978.

Dickinson, Emily. *The Complete Poems of Emily Dickinson.* Edited by Thomas H. Johnson. Boston: Little, Brown, 1960.

The Dictes and Sayings of the Philosophers. A facsimile edition of the 1477 printing by William Caxton. London: Elliot Stock, 1877.

A Dictionary of Anecdotes: Chiefly Historical, and Illustrative of Characters and Events, Ancient and Modern. Drawn from Genuine Sources, and Systematically Arranged according to the Respective Subjects. 2 vols. London: B. McMillan, 1811.

A Dictionary of Quotations from the British Poets. 3 vols. London: G. and W. B. Whittaker, 1823–25.

The Dicts and Sayings of the Philosophers. Edited by Curt F. Bühler. Translated by Stephen Scrope, William Worcester, and an anonymous translator. London: Early English Text Society, 1941.

Diels, Herrmann. *Fragmente der Vorsokratiker: Griechisch und Deutsch.* 3 vols. Dublin: Weidmann, 1972 [1903, 1907].

Dillard, Annie. *Mornings like This.* New York: HarperCollins, 1995.

Dinesen, Isak. *Seven Gothic Tales.* New York: Harrison Smith and Robert Haas, 1934.

Diogenes Laertius. *Lives of Eminent Philosophers.* Translated by R. D. Hicks. 2 vols. Cambridge MA: Harvard University Press, 1925 [ca. AD 250].

Dionysius Cato. *Disticha* and *Monosticha.* In Duff and Duff, *Minor Latin Poets,* 585–639.

Dionysius of Halicarnassus. *Roman Antiquities.* Translated by Earnest Cary. 7 vols. Cambridge MA: Harvard University Press, 1937 [ca. 7 BC].

Disraeli, Isaac. *Curiosities of Literature.* 4 vols. New York: W. J. Widdleton, 1865 [1791–1823].

Douglas, Charles Noel. *Forty Thousand Quotations, Prose and Poetical, Choice extracts on History, Science, Philosophy, Religion, Literature, etc. Selected from the standard authors of ancient and modern times, classified according to subject.* New York: George Sully, 1917 [1904].

Douglass, Frederick. *Autobiographies.* New York: Library of America, 1994.

Drayton, Michael. *The Barons' Wars, Nymphidea, and Other Poems.* London: George Routledge and Sons, 1887.

Drennan, Robert E., ed. *The Algonquin Wits.* New York: Citadel Press, 1968.

Drexler, Paul H. "On Latin Quotation." *Sewanee Review* 112, no. 3 (2004): 410–16.

Dryden, John. *Poems and Fables.* Edited by James Kinsley. London: Oxford University Press, 1962.

Duff, J. Wight, and Arnold M. Duff. *Minor Latin Poets.* Cambridge MA: Harvard University Press, 1954.

Dupré, P. *Encyclopédie des citations.* Paris: Éditions de Trévise, 1959.

The Dying Speeches and Behaviour of the Several State Prisoners that have been Executed the last 300 years. With their several Characters from the best Historians, as Cambden, Spotswood, Clarendon, Sprat, Burnet, &c. London: Printed for J. Brotherton and W. Meadows, F. Clay, C. Rivington and J. Graves, 1720.

The Dying Speeches of Several Excellent Persons, who Suffered for their Zeal against Popery, and Arbitrary Government. London: n.p., 1689.

Edgeworth, Maria. *Tales and Novels.* 10 vols. London: George Routledge, 1893.

Edinburgh Encyclopaedia of Wit; Consisting of a Choice Collection of Anecdotes, Bon Mots, Witty Sayings, &c, Being the Essence of All the Good Things Already Published; with a Number of Originals. Edinburgh: Denham and Dick, 1802.

Edwards, Tryon. *A Dictionary of Thoughts, being a Cyclopedia of Laconic Quotations from the Best Authors of the World, Both Ancient and Modern.* Detroit: F. B. Dickerson, 1902 [1891].

———. *Useful Quotations: A Cyclopedia of Quotations, Prose and Poetical, selected from the best authors of the world, both ancient and modern, alphabetically arranged by subjects.* Revised and enlarged by C. N. Catrevas and Jonathan Edwards. New York: Grosset and Dunlap, 1933.

Egbert, Walter R. *Last Words of Famous Men and Women.* Norristown PA: Herald Printing and Binding Rooms, 1898.

Ehrman, Bart D. *Misquoting Jesus: The Story Behind Who Changed the Bible and Why.* San Francisco: Harper San Francisco, 2005.

Einstein, Albert. *Essays in Humanism.* New York: Philosophical Library, 1950.

Eliot, George. *Impressions of Theophrastus Such.* Edited by Nancy Henry. Ann Arbor: University of Michigan Press, 1994 [1879].

———. *The Poetical Works of George Eliot.* New York: A. L. Burt, n.d.

Eliot, T. S. "The Waste Land." In *The Complete Poems and Plays 1909–1950,* 37–55. New York: Harcourt, Brace and World, 1962 [1922].

Ellis, Havelock. *The Dance of Life.* New York: Modern Library, 1929 [1923].

Elms, Alan C. "Apocryphal Freud: Sigmund Freud's Most Famous 'Quotations' and Their Actual Sources." *Annual of Psychoanalysis* 29 (2001): 83–104.

Emerson, Ralph Waldo. *Essays and Lectures.* Edited by Joel Porte. New York: Library of America, 1983.

———. *The Journals and Miscellaneous Notebooks, volume VI, 1824–1838.* Edited by Ralph Orth. Cambridge MA: Harvard University Press, 1966.

———. *The Journals and Miscellaneous Notebooks, volume X, 1847–1848.* Edited by Merton M. Sealts, Jr. Cambridge MA: Harvard University Press, 1973.

———. *The Journals and Miscellaneous Notebooks, volume XI, 1848–1851.* Edited by A. W. Plumstead, William H. Gilman, and Ruth H. Bennett. Cambridge MA: Harvard University Press, 1975.

———. *Lectures and Biographical Sketches.* Boston: Houghton Mifflin, 1883.

———. *Letters and Social Aims.* Boston: Houghton Mifflin, 1891.

———. *Miscellanies.* Boston: Houghton Mifflin, 1888 [1878].

———. *Society and Solitude.* Boston: Houghton Mifflin, 1892 [1870].

Epictetus. *Discourses.* Translated by W. A. Oldfather. 2 vols. Cambridge MA: Harvard University Press, 1925 [1st century AD].

Erasmus, Desiderius. *Adages: I i 1 to I v 100.* Translated by Margaret Mann Phillips. Annotated by R. A. B. Mynors. *Collected Works of Erasmus,* vol. 31. Toronto: University of Toronto Press, 1982 [1500–1536].

———. *Adages: I vi 1 to I x 100.* Translated and annotated by R. A. B. Mynors. *Collected Works of Erasmus,* vol. 32. Toronto: University of Toronto Press, 1989 [1500–1536].

————. *Adages: II i 1 to II vi 100*. Translated and annotated by R. A. B. Mynors. *Collected Works of Erasmus*, vol. 33. Toronto: University of Toronto Press, 1991 [1500–1536].

————. *Adages: II vii to III iii 100*. Translated and annotated by R. A. B. Mynors. *Collected Works of Erasmus*, vol. 34. Toronto: University of Toronto Press, 1992 [1500–1536].

————. *Adages: III iv 1 to IV ii 100*. Translated by Denis L. Drysdale. Edited by John N. Grant. *Collected Works of Erasmus*, vol. 35. Toronto: University of Toronto Press, 2005 [1500–1536].

————. *Adages IV iii 1 to V ii 51*. Translated and annotated by John N. Grant and Betty I. Knott. Edited by John N. Grant. *Collected Works of Erasmus*, vol. 36. Toronto: University of Toronto Press, 2006 [1500–1536].

————. *The Apophthegmes of Erasmus*. Translated by Nicolas Udall. Reprinted from the edition of 1564. Boston: Robert Roberts, 1877 [1531].

————. *Literary and Educational Writings 1: Antibarbari/Parabolae*. Translated by Margaret Mann Phillips and R. A. B. Mynors. Edited by Craig R. Thompson. *Collected Works of Erasmus*, vol. 23. Toronto: University of Toronto Press, 1978 [1520, 1514].

————. *Literary and Educational Writings 2: De Copia/De Ratione Studii*. Translated by Betty I. Knott and Brian McGregor. Edited by Craig R. Thompson. *Collected Works of Erasmus*, vol. 24. Toronto: University of Toronto Press, 1978 [1512, 1511].

————. *Literary and Educational Writings 5: Praise of Folly*. Translated by Betty Radice. *Collected Works of Erasmus*, vol. 27, 77–154. Toronto: University of Toronto Press, 1986 [1511].

Evans, Bergen. *Dictionary of Quotations*. New York: Delacorte Press, 1968.

Evans, G. R., ed. *Medieval Commentaries on the "Sentences" of Peter Lombard*. Leiden: E. J. Brill, 2002.

Evans, J. T., H. I. Nadjari, and S. A. Burchell. "Quotational and Reference Accuracy in Surgical Journals: A Continuing Peer Review Problem." *JAMA* 263 (1990): 242–43.

Exley, Helen. *Best of Women's Quotations*. Watford: Exley Publications, 1993.

Fehrenbacher, Don E., and Virginia Fehrenbacher. *Recollected Words of Abraham Lincoln*. Stanford: Stanford University Press, 1996.

Fenton, J. E., H. Brazier, A. De Souza, J. P. Hughes, and D. P. McShane. "The Accuracy of Citation and Quotation in Otolaryngology/Head and Neck Surgery Journals." *Clinical Otolaryngology* 25 (2000): 40–44.

Field, Eugene. *Love Affairs of a Bibliomaniac*. New York: Charles Scribner's Sons, 1907 [1896].

FitzGerald, Edward. *Polonius: A Collection of Wise Saws and Modern Instances*. Portland ME: Thomas B. Mosher, 1901 [1852].

Fitzgerald, F. Scott. *The Crack-Up*. Edited by Edmund Wilson. New York: New Directions, 1956 [1945].

Flaubert, Gustave. *Correspondance*. Edited by Jean Bruneau. 5 vols. Paris: Éditions Gallimard, 1973–2007.

Florio, John. *Florios Second Frutes: To be gathered of twelve Trees, of divers but delightsome tastes to the tongues of Italians and Englishmen. To which is annexed his Gardine of Recreation yielding six thousand Italian Proverbs*. London: Thomas Woodcock, 1591.

———. *His first Fruites: which yield familiar speech, merie Proverbes, wittie Sentences and golden sayings*. London: Thomas Woodcock, 1578.

Fortescue, John. *De Laudibus Legum Angliae*. London: Adam, for the Companie of Stationers, 1616.

Fournier, Édouard. *L'esprit dans l'histoire: recherches et curiosités sur les mots historiques*. Paris: E. Dentu, 1882.

Fowler, Henry W. *A Dictionary of Modern English Usage*. Oxford: Oxford University Press, 1926.

Foxe, John. *Actes and Monuments of Martyrs with a Generall Discourse of these latter Persecutions, horrible troubles and tumultes stirred up by Romish Prelates in the Church, with divers other things, incident especially to this Realme of Englande and Scotland*. 2 vols. London: John Daye, 1583 [1563].

France, Peter, ed. *The Oxford Guide to Literature in English Translation*. Oxford: Oxford University Press, 2000.

Franklin, Benjamin. *Writings*. New York: Library of America, 1987.

Freeman, Kathleen. *Ancilla to the Pre-Socratic Philosophers: A Complete Translation of the Fragments in Diels, "Fragmente der Vorsokratiker."* Cambridge MA: Harvard University Press, 1957.

Frege, Gottlob. *Translations from the Philosophical Writings of Gottlob Frege*. Edited by Peter Geach and Max Black. Oxford: Basil Blackwell, 1952.

Friedl, Berthold C. *Les fondements théoriques de la guerre et de la paix en U.R.S.S., suivi du cahier de Lénine sur Clausewitz*. Paris: Éditions Médicis, 1945.

Friswell, J. Hain. *Familiar Words: An Index Verborum or Quotation Handbook, with Parallel Passages, or Phrases Which Have Become Imbedded in Our English Tongue*. London: Sampson Low, Son and Marston, 1865.

Frontinus. *Stratagems* and *Aqueducts of Rome*. Translated by Charles E. Bennett. Cambridge MA: Harvard University Press, 1925 [late 1st century AD].

Frost, Robert. *The Notebooks of Robert Frost*. Edited by Robert Faggen. Cambridge MA: Harvard University Press, 2006.

Fruman, Norman. *Coleridge: The Damaged Archangel*. New York: George Braziller, 1971.

Fuller, Thomas [1608–61]. *The Holy and Profane States*. Cambridge MA: Hilliard and Brown, 1831 [1642].

Fuller, Thomas [1654–1734]. *Gnomologia: Adages and Proverbs, Wise Sentences and Witty Sayings, Ancient and Modern, Foreign and British.* London: B. Barker, A. Bettesworth and C. Hitch, 1732 [1722].

Garber, Marjorie. *Quotation Marks.* New York: Routledge, 2003.

García-Carpintero, Manuel. "Ostensive Signs: Against the Identity Theory of Quotation." *Journal of Philosophy,* May 1994, 253–64.

Gaskell, Elizabeth Cleghorn. *The Life of Charlotte Brontë.* London: J. M. Dent and Sons, 1908 [1857].

Geach, Peter T. *Logic Matters.* Berkeley: University of California Press, 1972.

Gellius, Aulus. *The Attic Nights.* Translated by John C. Rolfe, rev. ed. 3 vols. Cambridge MA: Harvard University Press, 1946–52 [ca. AD 180].

General Orders No. 100. In Schindler and Toman, *The Laws of Armed Conflicts,* 3–23.

Genette, Gérard. *Paratexts: Thresholds of Interpretation.* Translated by Jane E. Lewin. Cambridge: Cambridge University Press, 1997 [1987].

Gent, L. C. *The Book of Familiar Quotations: Being a Collection of Popular Extracts and Aphorisms from the Works of the Best Authors,* 3rd ed. London: George Routledge and Sons, 1866 [1852, 1860].

George, John, and Paul F. Boller, Jr. *They Never Said It: A Book of Fake Quotes, Misquotes, and Misleading Attributions.* New York: Oxford University Press, 1989.

Gibbon, Edward. *The Decline and Fall of the Roman Empire.* Edited by David Womersley. 3 vols. New York: Viking Penguin, 1995 [1776, 1781, 1788].

Gilbert, Josiah H. *Dictionary of Burning Words of Brilliant Writers Cyclopedia of Quotations from the Literature of All Ages.* New York: Wilbur B. Ketchum, 1895.

Ginzberg, Louis. *Legends of the Jews.* 7 vols. Baltimore: Johns Hopkins University Press, 1998 [1909–38].

Goethe, Johann Wolfgang von. *Conversations with Eckermann.* Translated by John Oxenford. San Francisco: North Point Press, 1984 [1836].

———. *Werke.* Edited by Gerhard Stenzel. 2 vols. Salzburg: Bergland-Buch, 1949.

Goldsmith, Oliver. *The Bee: Being Essays on the Most Interesting Subjects.* London: J. Wilkie, 1759.

Goldstein, Laurence. "Quotation of Types and Other Types of Quotation." *Analysis* 44, no. 1 (1984): 1–6.

———. "The Title of This Paper Is 'Quotation.'" *Analysis* 45, no. 3 (1985): 137–40.

Goodman, Nelson. "Questions Concerning Quotation." *Monist* 58, no. 2 (1974): 294–306. Reprinted in *Ways of Worldmaking,* 41–56. Indianapolis: Hackett Publishing, 1978.

Goodman, Ted. *The Forbes Book of Business Quotations: 10,000 Quotations on the Business of Life,* 90th anniversary ed. New York: Black Dog and Leventhal Publishers, 2006 [1997].

Gordan, Hanford Lennox. *Laconics*, rev. ed. New York: Shakespeare Press, 1912 [1910].

Gordis, Robert. *Koheleth — The Man and His World: A Study of Ecclesiastes*, 3rd augmented ed. New York: Schocken Books, 1968 [1951].

Gracián, Baltasar. *Oráculo manual y arte de prudencia.* In *El Héroe[,] oráculo manual y arte de prudencia.* Edited by Antonio Bernat Visratini and Abraham Madroñal. Madrid: Editorial Castilia, 2003 [1647]. Translated by Christopher Maurer as *The Art of Worldly Wisdom: A Pocket Oracle.* New York: Doubleday, 1992.

Grafton, Anthony. "Violence in Words." *Times Literary Supplement,* July 25, 2008, 3–5.

Gratzer, Walter. *Eurekas and Euphorias: The Oxford Book of Scientific Anecdotes.* New York: Oxford University Press, 2004.

Green, Jonathan. *Famous Last Words.* London: Kyle Cathie, 1997 [1979].

Green, R. P. H. "Proba's Cento: Its Date, Purpose, and Reception." *Classical Quarterly* 45, no. 2 (1995): 551–63.

Grocott, J. C. *An Index to Familiar Quotations Selected Principally from British Authors with Parallel Passages from Various Writers Ancient and Modern,* 4th ed. Liverpool: Edward Howell, 1871 [1854].

Grotius, Hugo. *De Jure Belli ac Pacis, libri tres: in quibus jus naturae & Gentium: item juris publici praecipua explicantur,* 2nd ed. Amsterdam: Guilielum Blaeuw, 1631 [1625]. Translated by John Morrice, John Spavan, and Edmund Littlehales as *The Rights of War and Peace.* Edited by Richard Tuck. 3 vols. Indianapolis: Liberty Fund, 2005 [1738].

Gsell, Paul. *Anatole France and His Circle: Being His Table-Talk Collected & Recorded.* Translated by Frederic Lees. London: John Lane, 1922.

Guelzo, Allen C. *Lincoln and Douglas: The Debates that Defined America.* New York: Simon and Schuster, 2008.

Guicciardini, Francesco. *Maxims and Reflections of a Renaissance Statesman.* Translated by Mario Domandi. New York: Harper and Row, 1965.

Guillaume, Alfred. *The Traditions of Islam: An Introduction to the Study of Hadith Literature.* Oxford: Oxford University Press, 1924.

Gutas, Dimitri. "Classical Arabic Wisdom Literature: Nature and Scope." *Journal of the American Oriental Society* 101, no. 1 (1981): 49–86.

———. *Greek Wisdom Literature in Arabic Translation: A Study of the Graeco-Arabic Gnomologia.* New Haven: American Oriental Society, 1975.

Guthke, Karl S. *Last Words: Variations on a Theme in Cultural History.* Princeton: Princeton University Press, 1992 [1990].

Gutjahr, Paul C. *An American Bible: A History of the Good Book in the United States, 1777–1880.* Stanford: Stanford University Press, 1999.

Haines, Jennie Day. *Christmasse Tyde; Being a Collection of Seasonable Quotations.* San Francisco: Paul Elder, 1907.

————. *Sovereign Woman versus Mere Man: A Medley of Quotations.* San Francisco: Paul Elder, 1905.

————. *Weather Opinions: A Book of Quotations with Interleaves on Weather Subjects.* San Francisco: Paul Elder, 1907.

————. *Ye Gardeyne Boke: A Collection of Quotations Instructive and Sentimental.* San Francisco: Paul Elder, 1906.

Hale, Sarah Josepha. *A Complete Dictionary of Poetical Quotations: comprising the most excellent and appropriate passages in the old British poets; with choice and copious selections from the best modern British and American poets.* Philadelphia: E. Claxton, 1854 [1849].

Hamilton, Alexander. *Writings.* New York: Library of America, 2001.

Handbook of Familiar Quotations: Chiefly from English Authors, 3rd ed. London: John Murray, 1859 [1853].

Hardy, Thomas. *Under the Greenwood Tree: or, the Mellstock Quire: A Rural Painting of the Dutch School.* New York: Holt and Williams, 1873 [1872].

Harnack, Adolf von. "The 'Sic et Non' of Stephanus Gobarus." *Harvard Theological Review* 16, no. 3 (1923): 205–34.

Harrill, J. Albert. "The Use of the New Testament in the American Slave Controversy: A Case History in the Hermeneutical Tension between Biblical Criticism and Christian Moral Debate." *Religion and American Culture* 10, no. 2 (2000): 149–86.

Haskins, Charles Homer. *The Renaissance of the 12th Century.* Cleveland: World Publishing, 1957 [1927].

Havens, Earle. *Commonplace Books: A History of Manuscripts and Printed Books from Antiquity to the Twentieth Century.* New Haven: Beinecke Rare Book and Manuscript Library, 2001.

Hayward, Thomas. *The British Muse, or, a Collection of Thoughts Moral, Natural, and Sublime, of our English Poets: who flourished in the Sixteenth and Seventeenth Centuries.* 3 vols. London: F. Cogan and J. Nourse, 1738.

Hazlitt, William. *Characteristics: In the Manner of Rochefoucault's Maxims,* 2nd ed. London: J. Templeman, 1837 [1823].

————. *Table Talk.* London: J. M. Dent and Sons, 1908 [1822].

Hemingway, Ernest. *A Movable Feast.* Edited by Séan Hemingway. New York: Scribner's, 2009 [1964].

Henderson, C. G. *Shakespeare Laconics: A Selection of Pithy Sentences from Shakespeare, Designed as a Manual of Reference for the Student and General Reader.* Philadelphia: C. G. Henderson, 1853.

Herbert, George. *The Works of George Herbert.* Edited by F. E. Hutchinson. Oxford: Oxford University Press, 1941.

Herodotus. *Histories.* Translated by A. D. Godley. 4 vols. Cambridge MA: Harvard University Press, 1920–25 [5th century BC].

Hesiod. *Works and Days*. In *Hesiod*, 2–65. Translated by H. G. Evelyn-White. Cambridge MA: Harvard University Press, 1914 [8th century BC?].

Heywood, John. *Iohn Heywoodes Woorkes. A Dialogue Conteynyng the number of the effectuall proverbes in the Englishe tounge, compact in a matter concernynge two maner of maryages. With one hundred of epigrammes: and thrée hundred of epigrammes upon thrée hundred proverbes: and a fifth hundred of epigrams. Wherunto are now newly added a syxt hundred of epigrams by the sayde Iohn Heywood*. London: Thomas Powell, 1562 [1549].

———. *The Proverbs and Epigrams of John Heywood, reprinted from the original (1562) edition, and collated with the second (1566) edition*. Manchester: Spenser Society, 1867.

———. *A Woman Killed with Kindness*. Edited by R. W. Van Fossen. Cambridge MA: Harvard University Press, 1961 [1603].

Higginson, Thomas W. *Carlyle's Laugh, and Other Surprises*. Boston: Houghton Mifflin, 1909.

Hijiya, James A. "The *Gita* of J. Robert Oppenheimer." *Proceedings of the American Philosophical Society* 144, no. 2 (2000): 123–67.

Hilton, Conrad. *Be My Guest*. New York: Simon and Schuster, 1994 [1957].

Hobbes, Thomas. *Leviathan: On the Matter, Forme and Power of a Commonwealth Ecclesiasticall and Civil*. Edited by Michael Oakeshott. New York: Collier, 1962 [1651].

Holmes, Oliver Wendell. *The Autocrat of the Breakfast-Table*. Boston: Houghton Mifflin, 1890 [1858].

———. *The Poet at the Breakfast-Table*. Boston: Houghton Mifflin, 1883 [1859].

———. *The Professor at the Breakfast-Table*. Boston: Houghton Mifflin, 1883 [1859].

Homer. *The Iliad*. Translated by A. T. Murray. Revised by William F. Wyatt. 2 vols. Cambridge MA: Harvard University Press, 1999 [8th century BC].

———. *The Iliad of Homer*. Translated by Walter Leaf et al. London: Macmillan, 1883.

———. *The Odyssey*. Translated by Robert Fagles. New York: Viking Penguin, 1996 [8th century BC].

Homes, Richard. *Coleridge: Darker Reflections, 1804–1834*. New York: Pantheon, 1999 [1998].

Horace. *Odes and Epodes*. Translated by Niall Rudd. Cambridge MA: Harvard University Press, 2004 [1st century BC].

———. *Satires, Epistles, and Ars Poetica*. Translated by H. R. Fairclough. Cambridge MA: Harvard University Press, 1926 [1st century BC].

Howard, V. A. "On Musical Quotation." *Monist* 58, no. 2 (1974): 307–18.

Howell, James. Παροιμιογραφια: *Proverbs, or, Old sayed sawes & adages in English (or the Saxon Toung), Italian, French, and Spanish, whereunto the British for their great Antiquity and weight are added.* London: Printed by J. G., 1659.

Hoyt, Jehiel Keeler. *The Cyclopedia of Practical Quotations*, rev. ed. New York: Funk and Wagnalls, 1896 [1882].

———. *The New Cyclopedia of Practical Quotations.* Edited by Kate Louise Roberts. New York: Funk and Wagnalls, 1922.

Hoyt, J[ehiel] K[eeler], and Anna L. Ward. *The Cyclopedia of Practical Quotations, English and Latin, with an Appendix containing Proverbs from the Latin and Modern Foreign Languages, Law and Ecclesiastical Terms and Significations; Names, Dates and Nationality of Quoted Authors, etc., with Copious Indexes.* New York: I. K. Funk, 1882.

Huizinga, Johan. *Erasmus and the Age of Reformation.* Translated by F. Hopman. New York: Charles Scribner's Sons, 1924.

Hume, David. *The History of England under the House of Tudor.* London: A. Millar, 1759.

Hunt, Leigh. *Table-Talk, to which are added Imaginary Conversations of Pope and Swift.* London: Smith, Elder, 1902 [1851].

Huxley, Aldous. *Crome Yellow.* New York: George H. Doran, 1922.

———. *Ends and Means.* New York: Harper and Brothers, 1937.

Hvidt, Niels Christian. *Christian Prophecy: The Post-Biblical Tradition.* Oxford: Oxford University Press, 2007.

Ibn 'Aṭā'illāh. *Ṣūfī Aphorisms (Kitāb al-Ḥikam).* Translated by Victor Danner. Leiden: E. J. Brill, 1973 [ca. 1280].

Ibn Khaldûn. *The Muqaddimah: An Introduction to History.* Translated by Franz Rosenthal. 3 vols. Princeton: Princeton University Press, 1958 [1384].

Ingleby, Leonard Cresswell. *Oscar Wilde: Some Reminiscences.* London: T. Werner Laurie, 1912.

Isocrates. *Isocrates.* Translated by George Norlin. 3 vols. Cambridge MA: Harvard University Press, 1928–45 [436–338 BC].

Jackson, Holbrook. *The Anatomy of Bibliomania.* Urbana and Chicago: University of Illinois Press, 1999 [1950].

Jacobs, Joseph. *History of the Aesopic Fable.* New York: Burt Franklin, 1970 [1889].

Jacobus de Voragine. *The Golden Legend: Readings on the Saints.* Translated by William Granger Ryan. 2 vols. Princeton: Princeton University Press, 1993 [ca. 1260].

Janouch, Gustav. *Conversations with Kafka.* Translated by Goronwy Rees, 2nd ed. New York: New Directions, 1971 [1968].

Jardine, Lisa. *Erasmus, Man of Letters.* Princeton: Princeton University Press, 1993.

Jeffares, A. Norman, and Martin Gray. *Collins Dictionary of Quotations*. New York: HarperCollins, 1995.

Jeffery, Arthur. *The Qur'ān as Scripture*. New York: Russell F. Moore, 1952.

Jerrold, Walter. *A Book of Famous Wits*. New York: McBride, Nast, 1912.

John of Damascus. *Exposition of the Orthodox Faith*. Translated by S. D. F. Salmond. In Schaff and Wace, *Nicene and Post-Nicene Fathers*, 9:9–101 [early 8th century AD].

Johnson, Samuel. *Lives of the English Poets*. Edited by Robert Lonsdale. 4 vols. Oxford: Oxford University Press, 2006 [1779–81].

———. *Notes on Shakespeare's Plays. Johnson on Shakespeare*. Edited by Arthur Sherbo, 1:117–2:1048. 2 vols. New Haven: Yale University Press, 1968.

———. *The Rambler*. Vols. 3, 4, and 5 of *The Yale Edition of the Works of Samuel Johnson*. Edited by Walter Jackson Bate and Albrecht B. Strauss. New Haven: Yale University Press, 1969 [1750–52].

Jones, Hugh Percy. *Dictionary of Foreign Phrases and Classical Quotations Comprising 14,000 Idioms, Proverbs, Maxims, Mottoes, Technical Words and Terms, and Press Allusions from the Works of the Great Writers in Latin, French, Italian, Greek, German, Spanish, Portuguese, alphabetically arranged with English translations and equivalents*. Edinburgh: John Grant, 1958 [1900].

Jones, John Richter. *Slavery Sanctioned by the Bible*. Philadelphia: J. B. Lippincott, 1861.

Jonson, Ben. *Timber, or Discoveries*. London: J. M. Dent, 1951 [1641].

Josephus. *Against Apion*. Translated by H. St. J. Thackeray. In *Josephus*, 1:161–411. 10 vols. Cambridge MA: Harvard University Press, 1926–65 [ca. AD 100].

Joyce, James. *Ulysses*. London: Bodley Head, 1993 [1922].

Junius. *The Letters of Junius*. Edinburgh: Cameron and Murdoch, 1798 [1769–72].

Kant, Immanuel. "What Is Enlightenment?" In *On History*. Edited and translated by Lewis White Beck, 3–10. Indianapolis: Bobbs-Merrill Educational Publishing, 1963 [1784].

Kaplan, Justin. "The Booklist Interview." *Booklist*, February 1, 1991, 1152–53.

Keats, John. *You Might As Well Live: The Life and Times of Dorothy Parker*. New York: Simon and Schuster, 1970.

Keith, Arthur Berriedale. *A History of Sanskrit Literature*. Delhi: Oxford University Press, 1973 [1928].

Keller, Helen. *The Story of My Life*. Garden City: Doubleday, Doran, 1931 [1904].

Kelly, James. *A Complete Collection of Scottish Proverbs Explained and Made Intelligible to the English Reader*. London: William and John Innys, 1721.

Keyes, Cheryl L. *Rap Music and Street Consciousness*. Urbana and Chicago: University of Illinois Press, 2002.

Keyes, Ralph. *"Nice Guys Finish Seventh": False Phrases, Spurious Sayings, and Familiar Misquotations*. New York: HarperCollins, 1992.

———. *The Quote Verifier: Who Said What, Where, and When*. New York: St. Martin's Press, 2006.

Kierkegaard, Søren. *Papers and Journals, a Selection*. Translated by Alastair Hannay. London: Penguin Books, 1996.

———. *Repetition: An Essay in Experimental Psychology*. Translated by Walter Lowrie. Princeton: Princeton University Press, 1941 [1843].

Klopsch, Louis. *Many Thoughts of Many Minds: A Treasury of Quotations from the Literature of Every Land and Every Age*. New York: Christian Herald, 1896.

Knowles, Elizabeth. *What They Didn't Say: A Book of Misquotations*. Oxford: Oxford University Press, 2006.

Knox, A[lfred] D[illwyn]. *The First Greek Anthologist: With Notes on Some Choliambic Fragments*. Cambridge: Cambridge University Press, 1923.

Knox, Vicesimus. *Winter Evenings: Or, Lucubrations on Life and Letters*. 3 vols. London: Charles Dilly, 1788.

Koestler, Arthur. *The Ghost in the Machine*. New York: Macmillan, 1967.

Koran. Translated by N. J. Dawood. London: Penguin Books, 1956.

Kraus, Karl. *Half-Truths & One-and-a-Half Truths: Selected Aphorisms*. Translated by Harry Zohn. Chicago: University of Chicago Press, 1990.

Krystal, Arthur. "Age of Reason." *New Yorker*, October 22, 2007, 94, 96, 98–100, 102–3.

La Bruyère, Jean de. *Les caractères ou les Moeurs de ce siècle*. Paris: Éditions Garnier Frères, 1962 [1688]. Translated by Henri van Laun as *The Characters, or The Manners of the Age*. London: George Routledge and Sons, 1929.

La Fontaine, Jean de. *Oeuvres complètes*. Edited by Pierre Clarac. 2 vols. Paris: Gallimard, 1958.

Landor, Walter Savage. *Imaginary Conversations*. 6 vols. London: J. M. Dent, 1891 [1824, 1826, 1846].

Lao Tzu. *Tao te Ching*. Translated by D. C. Lau. Harmondsworth: Penguin Books, 1963 [4th century BC].

La Rochefoucauld, François de. *Maximes*. Edited by Jacques Truchet. Paris: Éditions Garnier Frères, 1967 [1665]. Translated by Louis Kronenberger as *Maxims*. New York: Random House, 1959.

Latham, Edward. *Famous Sayings and Their Authors: A Collection of Historical Sayings from English, French, German, Greek, Italian and Latin*, 2nd ed. London: Swan Sonnenschein, 1906 [1904].

Lavater, Johann Caspar. *Aphorisms on Man*. London: J. Johnson, 1788.

Lec, Stanislaw. *More Unkempt Thoughts*. Translated by Jacek Galazka. New York: Funk and Wagnalls, 1968 [1963].

———. *Unkempt Thoughts*. Translated by Jacek Galazka. New York: St. Martin's Press, 1962 [1957].

Le Compte, Edward S. *Dictionary of Last Words*. New York: Philosophical Library, 1955.

Lelli, Emanuele. *I proverbi greci: le raccolte di Zenobio e Diogeniano*. Soveria Mannelli: Rubbettino, 2006.

Le Sage, Alain-René. *The Adventures of Gil Blas of Santillane*. Translated by Tobias Smollett. New York: A. L. Burt Publishers, n.d. [1715–35].

Levy, Ernst. *Pauli Sententiae: A Palingenesia of the Opening Titles of a Specimen of Research in West Roman Vulgar Law*. Ithaca NY: Cornell University Press, 1945.

Lewis, Russell. *Margaret Thatcher: A Personal and Political Biography*. London: Routledge and Kegan Paul, 1984.

Lichtenberg, Georg Christoph. *Aphorisms*. Translated by R. J. Hollingdale. London: Penguin Books, 1990.

Lichtheim, Miriam. *Ancient Egyptian Literature, Volume 1: The Old and Middle Kingdoms*. Berkeley: University of California Press, 1973.

Lincoln, Abraham. *Collected Works of Abraham Lincoln*. Edited by Roy P. Basler. 9 vols. New Brunswick NJ: Rutgers University Press, 1953.

———. *Speeches and Writings 1832–1858*. Edited by Don E. Fehrenbacher. 2 vols. New York: Library of America, 1989.

Lindey, Alexander. *Plagiarism and Originality*. New York: Harper, 1952.

Ling, Nicholas. *Politeuphuia: Wits Commonwealth*, 9th ed. London: W. S. for I. Smethwicke, 1615 [1598].

Linkletter, Art. *Kids Say the Darndest Things*. Englewood Cliffs: Prentice Hall, 1957.

Linn, S. P. *Golden Gleams of Thought from the Words of Leading Orators, Divines, Philosophers, Statesmen and Poets*, 10th ed. Chicago: A. C. McClurg, 1909 [1881].

Little, Charles Eugene. *Historical Lights: Six Thousand Quotations from Standard Histories and Biographies*. New York: Funk and Wagnalls, 1886.

Livy. *History of Rome*. Translated by B. O. Foster et al. 14 vols. Cambridge MA: Harvard University Press, 1919–59 [ca. 27 BC].

Locke, John. *An Essay Concerning Human Understanding*. 2 vols. London: J. M. Dent and Sons, 1961 [1690; the Dent ed. reproduces the 5th ed. of 1706].

Lombard, Peter. *Sententiae in IV libris distinctae*, 3rd ed. 2 vols. Rome: Collegii S. Bonaventurae ad Claras Aquas, 1971 [1155–57].

Longinus. *On the Sublime*. Translated by W. Hamilton Fyfe. In *Aristotle*, Loeb Library, vol. 23. Cambridge MA: Harvard University Press, 1927 [3rd century AD].

Lowell, James Russell. *Literary Essays*. 3 vols. Cambridge MA: Riverside Press, 1890.

———. *The Poetical Works*, family ed. Boston: Houghton Mifflin, 1890.

Lowell, Robert. *Imitations*. New York: Farrar, Straus and Giroux, 1961.

Lucan. *The Civil War*. Translated by J. D. Duff. Cambridge MA: Harvard University Press, 1928 [ca. AD 65].

Lucian. *Hermotimus, or, Concerning the Sects. Lucian*, 6.259–415. Translated by K. Kilbrun. Cambridge MA: Harvard University Press, 1959 [2nd century AD].

———. *Lucian*. Translated by A. M. Harmon, K. Kilburn, and M. D. MacLeod. 8 vols. Cambridge MA: Harvard University Press, 1913–67 [late 2nd century AD].

Lucretius. *De rerum natura*. Edited and translated by Cyril Bailey. 3 vols. Oxford: Oxford University Press, 1947 [1st century BC].

Luther, Martin. *Table Talk*. Edited and translated by Theodore G. Tappert. Philadelphia: Fortress Press, 1967 [1566].

———. *The Table Talk or Familiar Discourse of Martin Luther*. Translated by William Hazlitt. London: David Bogue, 1848.

Macdonnel, D[avid] E[vans]. *A Dictionary of Quotations in Most Frequent Use, taken chiefly from the Latin and French, but Comprising Many from the Greek, Spanish and Italian Languages, Translated into English; with Illustrations Historical and Idiomatic*. London: G. G. and J. Robinson, 1797.

———. *A Dictionary of Quotations in Most Frequent Use, taken chiefly from the Latin and French, but Comprising Many from the Greek, Spanish and Italian Languages, Translated into English; with Illustrations Historical and Idiomatic*, 2nd ed. London: G. G. and J. Robinson, 1798.

———. *A Dictionary of Quotations in Most Frequent Use, taken chiefly from the Latin and French, but Comprising Many from the Greek, Spanish and Italian Languages, Translated into English; with Illustrations Historical and Idiomatic*, 3rd ed. London: G. G. and J. Robinson, 1799.

———. *A Dictionary of Quotations in Most Frequent Use, taken chiefly from the Latin and French, but Comprising Many from the Greek, Spanish and Italian Languages, Translated into English; with Illustrations Historical and Idiomatic*, 4th ed. London: G. Wilkie and J. Robinson, 1803.

———. *A Dictionary of Quotations in Most Frequent Use, taken chiefly from the Latin and French, but Comprising Many from the Greek, Spanish and Italian Languages, Translated into English; with Illustrations Historical and Idiomatic*, 5th ed. London: G. Wilkie and J. Robinson, 1809.

———. *A Dictionary of Quotations in Most Frequent Use, taken chiefly from the Latin and French, but Comprising Many from the Greek, Spanish and Italian Languages, Translated into English; with Illustrations Historical and Idiomatic*, 6th ed. London: G. Wilkie and J. Robinson, 1811.

———. *A Dictionary of Quotations in Most Frequent Use, taken chiefly from the Latin and French, but Comprising Many from the Greek, Spanish and Italian Languages, Translated into English; with Illustrations Historical and Idiomatic*, 7th ed. London: G. Wilkie, 1817.

———. *A Dictionary of Quotations in Most Frequent Use, taken chiefly from the Latin and French, but Comprising Many from the Greek, Spanish and Italian Languages, Translated into English; with Illustrations Historical and Idiomatic*, 8th ed. London: G. and W. B. Whittaker, 1822.

———. *A Dictionary of Quotations in Most Frequent Use, taken chiefly from the Latin and French, but Comprising Many from the Greek, Spanish and Italian Languages, Translated into English; with Illustrations Historical and Idiomatic*, 9th ed. London: George B. Whittaker, 1826.

Machiavelli, Niccolò. *The Chief Works and Others*. Translated by Allan Gilbert. 3 vols. Durham NC: Duke University Press, 1989.

Macrobius. *The Saturnalia*. Translated by Percival Vaughan Davies. New York: Columbia University Press, 1969 [early 5th century AD].

Madigan, Daniel A. *The Qur'ān's Self-Image: Writing and Authority in Islam's Scripture*. Princeton: Princeton University Press, 2001.

Maggio, Rosalie. *The New Beacon Press Book of Quotations by Women*. Boston: Beacon Press, 1996.

Mahābhārata. Book 5. *Preparations for War*. Translated by Kathleen Garbutt. 2 vols. New York: New York University Press, 2008.

Maimonides [Moses ben Maimon]. *The Guide of the Perplexed*. Translated by Shlomo Pines. 2 vols. Chicago: University of Chicago Press, 1963.

Main, Alexander. *Wise, Witty and Tender Sayings in Prose & Verse Selected from the Works of George Eliot*. Edinburgh: William Blackwood and Sons, 1875.

Marcus Aurelius. *Meditations*. Translated by Maxwell Staniforth. Harmondsworth: Penguin Books, 1964 [ca. 180].

Marshall, John David. "John Bartlett and His Quotation Book." *Wilson Library Bulletin* 30 (November 1955): 250–52.

Marvin, Frederic Rowland. *The Last Words (Real and Traditional) of Distinguished Men and Women*. New York: Fleming H. Revell, 1901.

Mather, Cotton. *A Token, for the Children of New-England. Or, Some Examples of Children, in whom the Fear of God was Remarkably Budding, before they Dyed; in Several parts of New-England. Preserved and published, for the encouragement of piety in other children. And, added as supplement, unto the excellent Janewayes Token for children: upon the re-printing of it, in this countrey*. Boston: Printed by Timothy Green, for Benjamin Eliot, 1700.

[Mathias, Thomas James.] *Pursuits of Literature. A Satirical Poem in Four Dialogues, with Notes*. Philadelphia: H. Maxwell, 1800 [1794–97].

McFarland, Thomas. "Coleridge's Plagiarisms Once More: A Review Essay." *Yale Review* 63, no. 2 (1974): 252–86.

McIntyre, Helen Lucile. "A Study of Selected American Dictionaries of Quotations." Master's thesis, University of Illinois, Urbana, 1941.

McKinley, Mary B. *Words in a Corner: Studies in Montaigne's Latin Quotations.* Lexington KY: French Forum, 1981.

McLeod, Kembrew. *Freedom of Expression®: Overzealous Copyright Bozos and Other Enemies of Creativity.* New York: Doubleday, 2005.

McMurtrie, Douglas C. "Concerning Quotation Marks." *Gazette of the Grolier Club,* April 1926, 177–81.

McNeill, John T. "Folk-Paganism in the Penitentials." *Journal of Religion* 13, no. 4 (1933): 50–66.

McPhee, Carol, and Ann Fitzgerald. *Feminist Quotations: Voices of Rebels, Reformers, and Visionaries, 200 Years of Acute, Profound, Witty, Cerebral and Salty Comments on the Status of Women by American and British Feminists.* New York: Thomas Y. Crowell, 1979.

Melville, Herman. *Moby Dick: or, The Whale.* Edited by Harrison Hayford, Hershel Parker, and G. Thomas Tanselle. Evanston IL: Northwestern University Press, 1988 [1851].

Menander. *Menander.* Edited and translated by W. G. Arnott. 3 vols. Cambridge MA: Harvard University Press, 1979, 1996, 2000 [3rd century BC].

———. *Testimonia et fragmenta. Poetae comici Graeci.* Edited by R. Kassel and C. Austin, vol. 6.2. Berlin: Walter de Gruyter, 1998.

Mencken, H. L. *A New Dictionary of Quotations on Historical Principles from Ancient & Modern Sources.* New York: Alfred A. Knopf, 1942.

Merton, Robert K. *On the Shoulders of Giants: A Shandean Postscript.* New York: Free Press, 1965.

Metschies, Michael. *Zitat und Zitierkunst in Montaignes Essais.* Geneva: Droz, 1966.

Meyer, Herman. *Das Zitat in der Erzählkunst,* 2nd ed. Stuttgart: J. B. Metzlersche Verlagsbuchhandlung, 1967. Translated by Theodore and Yetta Ziolkowski as *The Poetics of Quotation in the European Novel.* Princeton: Princeton University Press, 1968.

Michelsen, E. H. *A Manual of Quotations, from the Ancient, Modern, and Oriental Languages, Including Law Phrases, Maxims, Proverbs, and Family Mottoes.* London: John Crockford, 1856.

Mieder, Wolfgang. *"A House Divided": From Biblical Proverb to Lincoln and Beyond.* Burlington: University of Vermont, 1998.

Miller, Joaquin. *In Classic Shades.* Chicago: Belford-Clarke, 1890.

Mishnah. Translated by Herbert Danby. Oxford: Oxford University Press, 1933.

Moberly, R. W. L. "Does God Lie to His Prophets?: The Story of Micaiah ben Imlah as a Test Case." *Harvard Theological Review* 96, no. 1 (2003): 1–23.

Moers, Ellen. *Literary Women: The Great Writers.* Garden City: Doubleday, 1976.

Monkshood, G. F. *Woman and Her Wits: Epigrams on Woman, Love, and Beauty.* New York: H. M. Caldwell, 1899.

Montagu, Elizabeth. *The Letters of Mrs. Elizabeth Montagu, with Some of the Letters of Her Correspondents*. 3 vols. Boston: Wells and Lilly, 1825.

Montaigne, Michel de. *The Complete Essays*. Translated by M. A. Screech. London: Penguin Press, 1991 [1580, 1588, 1595].

———. *Oeuvres complètes*. Edited by Albert Thibaudet and Maurice Rat. Paris: Bibliothèque de la Pléiade, 1962.

Moore, Hugh. *A Dictionary of Quotations from Various Authors in Ancient and Modern Languages with English Translations and Illustrated by Remarks and Explanations*. London: Whittaker, Treacher, 1831.

Morawski, Stefan. "The Basic Functions of Quotation." In *Sign, Language, Culture*. Edited by A. J. Greimas et al., 690–705. The Hague: Mouton, 1970.

Morson, Gary Saul. "Bakhtin, the Genres of Quotation, and the Aphoristic Consciousness." *Slavic and East European Journal* 50, no. 1 (2006): 213–27.

Morton, Agnes H. *Quotations*. Philadelphia: Penn Publishing, 1895.

Napier, Robina. *Johnsoniana: Anecdotes of the Late Samuel Johnson, LL.D.* London: George Bell and Sons, 1884.

Neihardt, John G. *Black Elk Speaks, as told through John G. Neihardt (Flaming Rainbow) by Nicholas Black Elk*, twenty-first-century ed. Lincoln: University of Nebraska Press, 2000 [1932].

New Dictionary of Quotations from the Greek, Latin, and Modern Languages. London: John F. Shaw, 1859.

Newhall, S. M. "The Indication of Quotations." *Science*, October 29, 1926, 427.

Nietzsche, Friedrich. *Basic Writings of Nietzsche*. Translated by Walter Kaufmann. New York: Modern Library, 1968.

———. *Human, All Too Human*. Translated by Marion Faber and Stephen Lehmann. Lincoln: University of Nebraska Press, 1984 [1878].

———. *The Portable Nietzsche*. Translated by Walter Kaufmann. New York: Viking Press, 1954.

———. *Sämtliche Werke*. Edited by Giorgio Colli and Mazzino Montinari. 15 vols. Berlin: Walter de Gruyter, 1980.

Nissinen, Martti. *Prophets and Prophecy in the Ancient Near East*, with contributions by C. L. Seow and Robert K. Ritner. Leiden: E. J. Brill/Society of Biblical Literature, 2003.

Norden, Eduard. *Die antike Kunstprosa*. 2 vols. Leipzig: Teubner, 1898.

Northend, Charles. *Gems of Thought; Being a Collection of More than a Thousand Choice Selections, or Aphorisms from nearly Four Hundred and Fifty Different Authors, and on One Hundred and Forty Different Subjects*. New York: D. Appleton, 1888.

Norton, L. Wesley. "The Bible in the Slavery Dispute after 1830." Master's thesis, Department of History, University of Illinois, 1956.

Nostradamus. *The Complete Prophecies of Nostradamus*. Translated by Henry C. Roberts, rev. ed. Oyster Bay NY: Nostradamus, 1982 [1555].

Otts, John M. P. *Laconisms: The Wisdom of Many in the Words of One*. Philadelphia: J. B. Lippincott, 1888.

Ouida [Marie Louise de la Ramée]. *Wanda*. London: Chatto and Windus, 1884 [1883].

Owen, Rev. Dr. Henry. *The Modes of Quotation Used by the Evangelical Writers Explained and Vindicated*. London: J. Nichols, 1789.

Oxford Classical Dictionary, 3rd ed. Edited by Simon Hornblower and Antony Spawforth. Oxford: Oxford University Press, 1996.

Oxford Dictionary of Quotations. Oxford: Oxford University Press, 1941.

Oxford Dictionary of Quotations, 2nd ed. Oxford: Oxford University Press, 1953.

Oxford Dictionary of Quotations, 3rd ed. Oxford: Oxford University Press, 1979.

Oxford Dictionary of Quotations, 4th ed. Edited by Angela Partington. Oxford: Oxford University Press, 1992.

Oxford Dictionary of Quotations, 5th ed. Edited by Elizabeth Knowles. Oxford: Oxford University Press, 1999.

Oxford Dictionary of Quotations, 6th ed. Edited by Elizabeth Knowles. New York: Oxford University Press, 2004.

Oxford Dictionary of Quotations, 7th ed. Edited by Elizabeth Knowles. New York: Oxford University Press, 2009.

Paine, Thomas. *Collected Writings*. New York: Library of America, 1994.

Parkes, M. B. *Pause and Effect: An Introduction to the History of Punctuation in the West*. Berkeley: University of California Press, 1993.

Partee, Barbara Hall. "The Syntax and Semantics of Quotations." In *A Festschrift for Morris Halle*. Edited by Stephen R. Anderson and Paul Kiparksy, 410–18. New York: Holt, Rinehart and Winston, 1973.

Partnow, Elaine. *The Quotable Woman*. New York: Facts on File, 2010.

———. *The Quotable Woman: The First 5,000 Years*. New York: Facts on File, 2001.

Pascal, Blaise. *Oeuvres complètes*. Edited by Louis Lafuma. Paris: Éditions du Seuil, 1963.

———. *Pensées: Thoughts on Religion and Other Subjects*. Translated by William Finlayson Trotter. New York: Washington Square Press, 1965.

Pearson, Hesketh. *Common Misquotations*. London: H. Hamilton, 1934.

———. *The Whispering Gallery*. London: Phoenix Press, 2000 [1926].

Penfield, Joyce. *Communicating with Quotes: The Igbo Case*. Westport CT: Greenwood Press, 1983.

Pepper, Charles M. *Life-Work of Louis Klopsch: Romance of a Modern Knight of Mercy*. New York: Christian Herald, 1910.

Perry, Gen Edwin. *Aesopica: A Series of Texts Relating to Aesop or Ascribed to Him or Closely Connected with the Literary Tradition that Hears His Name*. Urbana and Chicago: University of Illinois Press, 2007 [1952].

Pertile, Lino. "Paper and Ink: The Structure of Unpredictability." In *O un amy!: Essays on Montaigne in Honor of Donald M. Frame*. Edited by Raymond La Charité, 190–218. Lexington KY: French Forum, 1977.

Petrarch, Francesco. "The Ascent of Mont Ventoux." Translated by Hans Nachod. In Cassirer, *Renaissance Philosophy of Man*, 36–46.

———. "On His Own Ignorance and That of Many Others." Translated by Hans Nachod. In Cassirer, *Renaissance Philosophy of Man*, 47–133.

———. *Rerum familiarum libri, I–VIII*. Translated by Aldo S. Bernardo. Albany: State University of New York Press, 1975.

———. *Rerum memorandarum libri*. Edited by Giuseppe Billanovich. Florence: G. C. Sansoni, 1943.

Pettit, James Andrews. *The History of Great Britain, Connected with the Chronology of Europe*. 2 vols. London: T. Cadell, 1794.

Pfeiffer, Rudolf. *History of Classical Scholarship from 1300 to 1850*. Oxford: Oxford University Press, 1976.

Phaedrus. *Fabularum Aesopiarum*. In *Babrius and Phaedrus*. Edited and translated by Ben Edwin Perry, 189–371. Cambridge MA: Harvard University Press, 1965.

Phillips, Margaret Mann. *The "Adages" of Erasmus: A Study with Translations*. Cambridge: Cambridge University Press, 1964.

Piozzi, Hester Lynch. *Anecdotes of the Late Samuel Johnson, LL.D. during the Last Twenty Years of his Life*, 3rd ed. London: T. Cadell, 1786.

Plato. *The Collected Dialogues*. Edited by Edith Hamilton and Huntington Cairns. Princeton: Princeton University Press, 1961 [4th century BC].

———. *Cratylus, Parmenides, Greater Hippias, Lesser Hippias*. Translated by H. N. Fowler. Cambridge MA: Harvard University Press, 1926.

———. *Laws*. Translated by R. G. Bury. 2 vols. Cambridge MA: Harvard University Press, 1952.

Pliny. *Natural History*. Translated by H. Rackham and D. E. Eichholz. 10 vols. Cambridge MA: Harvard University Press, 1938–62 [AD 77].

Plutarch. "Apophthegmata Laconica." In *Moralia*, 3:240–421. Translated by Frank Cole Babbitt. Cambridge MA: Harvard University Press, 1931 [ca. AD 110].

———. "The Education of Children." In *Moralia*, 1:1–69. Translated by Frank Cole Babbitt. Cambridge MA: Harvard University Press, 1927 [ca. AD 110].

———. "The Obsolescence of Oracles." In *Moralia*, 5:348–501. Translated by Frank Cole Babbitt. Cambridge MA: Harvard University Press, 1936 [ca. AD 110].

———. "On Listening to Lectures." In *Moralia*, 1:199–259. Translated by Frank Cole Babbitt. Cambridge MA: Harvard University Press, 1941 [ca. AD 110].

———. *Table Talk (Symposiakon biblia)*. Vols. 8 and 9 of *Moralia*, vol. 8 translated by P. A. Clement and H. B. Hoffleit, vol. 9 translated by E. L. Minar, Jr., F. H. Sandbach, and W. C. Helmbold. Cambridge MA: Harvard University Press, 1961, 1969 [ca. AD 110].

Polybius. *The Histories*. Translated by W. R. Paton. 6 vols. Cambridge MA: Harvard University Press, 1922 [1st century BC].

Poole, Josua. *The English Parnassus, or, A Helpe to English Poesie, containing a Collection of all rhyming monosyllables, the choicest epithets, and phrases: with some general forms upon all occasions, subjects, and theams, alphabeticaly digested: together with a short institution to English poesie*. London: Thomas Johnson, 1657.

Pope, Alexander. *The Poems of Alexander Pope*. Edited by John Butt. New Haven: Yale University Press, 1963.

Powers, George W. *Handy Dictionary of Poetical and Prose Quotations*. 2 vols. New York: Thomas Y. Crowell, 1901.

Powers, Richard. *The Gold Bug Variations*. New York: William Morrow, 1991.

———. *Prisoner's Dilemma*. New York: Birch Tree Books/William Morrow, 1988.

Price, Steven D. *1001 Dumbest Things Ever Said*. Guilford CT: Lyons Press, 2004.

Priest, Josiah. *Bible Defence of Slavery; or the Origin, History, and Fortunes of the Negro Race as Deduced from History, both Sacred and Profane, Their Natural Relations — Moral, Mental, and Physical — to the Other Races of Mankind, Compared and Illustrated — Their Future Destiny Predicted, Etc.* Louisville KY: Willis A. Bush, 1851.

Prior, Matthew. *Poems on Several Occasions*. Edited by A. R. Waller. Cambridge: Cambridge University Press, 1905 [1707].

Ptahhotep. "The Instruction of Ptahhotep." In *Ancient Egyptian Literature, Volume 1: The Old and Middle Kingdoms*. Edited by Miriam Lichtheim, 61–80. Berkeley: University of California Press, 1973.

Publilius Syrus. *Sententiae*. In Duff and Duff, *Minor Latin Poets*, 3–111.

Quine, Willard Van Orman. *Mathematical Logic*. Cambridge MA: Harvard University Press, 1940.

———. *Word and Object*. Cambridge MA: MIT Press, 1960.

Quintilian. *Institutio oratoria*. Translated by H. E. Butler. 4 vols. Cambridge MA: Harvard University Press, 1920–22 [ca. AD 80].

Quotable Quotes. Pleasantville NY: Reader's Digest Association, 1997.

Rabelais, François. *Oeuvres complètes*. Edited by Pierre Jourda. 2 vols. Paris: Éditions Garnier Frères, 1962.

Randall, Marilyn. *Pragmatic Plagiarism: Authorship, Profit, and Power*. Toronto: University of Toronto Press, 2001.

Ray, John. *A Collection of English Proverbs Digested into a convenient Method for the speedy finding any one upon occasion*. Cambridge: John Hayes, 1670; 2nd ed. 1678.

———. *A Compleat Collection of English Proverbs; also the Most Celebrated Proverbs of the Scotch, Italian, French, Spanish and Other Languages*, 3rd ed. London: H. Slater et al., 1742.

Recanati, François. "Open Quotation." *Mind,* July 2001, 637–87.

Rees, Nigel. *Brewer's Quotations: A Phrase and Fable Dictionary.* London: Cassell, 1994.

———. *Cassell Companion to Quotations.* London: Cassell, 1997.

———. *"Quote . . . Unquote."* New York: St. Martin's Press, 1979.

———. *Sayings of the Century.* London: George Allen and Unwin, 1984.

———. *Why Do We Quote?* London: Blandford Press, 1989.

———. *Word of Mouth.* London: George Allen and Unwin, 1983.

Reimer, Marga. "Quotation Marks: Demonstratives or Demonstrations?" *Analysis,* July 1996, 131–41.

Reynolds, David. *In Command of History: Churchill Fighting and Writing the Second World War.* New York: Random House, 2005.

Reynolds, Myra. *The Learned Lady in England 1650–1760.* Boston: Houghton Mifflin, 1920.

Rhetorica ad herennium. Translated by H. Caplan. Cambridge MA: Harvard University Press, 1954 [ca. 80 BC].

Rice, Rev. William. *Moral and Religious Quotations from the Poets: Comprising Choice Selections from 600 Authors.* New York: Carlton Porter, 1866.

Riddell, Peter G., and Tony Street, eds. *Islam: Essays on Scripture, Thought and Society: A Festschrift in Honour of Anthony H. Johns.* Leiden: E. J. Brill, 1997.

Rig Veda: A Metrically Restored Text. Edited by Barend A. van Nooten and Gary B. Holland. Cambridge MA: Harvard University Press, 1994.

Robinson, Ray. *Famous Last Words, Fond Farewells, Deathbed Diatribes, and Exclamations upon Expiration.* New York: Workman Publishing, 2003.

Rogers, Samuel. *Recollections of the Table Talk of Samuel Rogers.* New York: D. Appleton, 1856.

Ronell, Avital. *Finitude's Score: Essays for the End of the Millennium.* Lincoln: University of Nebraska Press, 1989.

———. *Stupidity.* Urbana and Chicago: University of Illinois Press, 2002.

———. *The Telephone Book: Technology, Schizophrenia, Electric Speech.* Lincoln: University of Nebraska Press, 1989.

Rosenthal, Franz. *Humor in Early Islam.* Leiden: E. J. Brill, 1956.

Ross, Rev. Fred A. *Slavery Ordained of God.* Philadelphia: J. B. Lippincott, 1859.

Rouse, Richard H., and Mary A. Rouse. *Preachers, Florilegia and Sermons: Studies on the* Manipulus florum *of Thomas of Ireland.* Toronto: Pontifical Institute of Mediaeval Studies, 1979.

Saka, Paul. "Quotation and the Use-Mention Distinction." *Mind,* January 1998, 113–35.

Sand, George. *The George Sand–Gustave Flaubert Letters.* Translated by Aimee L. McKenzie. New York: Boni and Liveright, 1921.

Sandburg, Carl. *Abraham Lincoln: The War Years.* 4 vols. New York: Harcourt, Brace and World, 1939.

Sanford, Eva Matthews. "The Use of Classical Latin Authors in the *Libri Manuales.*" *Transactions and Proceedings of the American Philological Association* 55 (1924): 190–248.

Santa Cruz de Dueñas, Melchior de. *Floresta española.* Edited by Maria Pilar Cuartero and Maxime Chevalier. Barcelona: Crítica, 1997 [1574].

Savran, George W. *Telling and Retelling: Quotation in Biblical Narrative.* Bloomington: Indiana University Press, 1988.

Sayings of the Desert Fathers: The Alphabetical Collection. Translated by Benedicta Ward, SLG. London: A. R. Mowbray, 1975.

Schaff, Philip, ed. *The Nicene and Post-Nicene Fathers of the Christian Church,* 1st series. 14 vols. Grand Rapids MI: W. R. Eerdmans, 1956 [1888].

Schaff, Philip, and Henry Wace. *Nicene and Post-Nicene Fathers of the Christian Church,* 2nd series. 14 vols. Peabody MA: Hendrickson Publishers, 1995 [1899].

Schindler, Dietrich, and Jiří Toman, eds. *The Laws of Armed Conflicts: A Collection of Covenants, Resolutions and Other Documents.* Leiden: A. W. Sijthoff, 1973.

Schopenhauer, Arthur. "On Authorship and Style." In *Parerga and Paralipomena.* Translated by E. F. J. Payne, 2:501–53. 2 vols. Oxford: Oxford University Press, 1974 [1851].

Schultz, Richard L. *The Search for Quotation: Verbal Parallels in the Prophets.* Journal for the Study of the Old Testament Supplement Series, 180. Sheffield: Sheffield Academic Press, 1999.

Scriptores historiae augustae. Translated by David Magie. 3 vols. Cambridge MA: Harvard University Press, 1921–32.

Sei Shōnagon. *The Pillow Book of Sei Shōnagon.* Translated by Ivan Morris. London: Folio Society, 1979 [10th century AD].

Selden, John. *Table Talk of John Selden.* Edited by Sir Frederick Pollock. London: Quaritch, 1927 [1689].

Seldes, George. *Encyclopedia of the Great Quotations.* Introduction by J. Donald Adams. New York: Lyle Stuart, 1960.

Seneca, Lucius Annaeus [Seneca the Elder]. *Declamations.* Translated by Michael Winterbottom. 2 vols. Cambridge MA: Harvard University Press, 1992 [ca. 40 BC].

Seneca, Lucius Annaeus [Seneca the Younger]. *Epistles.* Translated by Richard M. Gummere. 2 vols. Cambridge MA: Harvard University Press, 1917–25 [AD 63–65].

Sergeant, Elizabeth Shepley. *Robert Frost: The Trial by Existence.* New York: Holt, Rinehart and Winston, 1960.

Shakespeare, William. *The Complete Works.* Edited by Alfred Harbage. New York: Viking, 1969.

———. *Hamlet.* Edited by Ann Thompson and Neil Taylor. London: Arden Shakespeare, 3rd series, 2006 [1604].

Shapiro, Fred R. *The Yale Book of Quotations.* New Haven: Yale University Press, 2006.

Shaw, Henry W. *The Complete Works of Josh Billings.* New York: G. W. Dillingham, 1899.

Shenstone, William. *Essays on Men and Manners.* Stourport: George Nicholson, 1812 [1764].

Sherrin, Ned. *Oxford Dictionary of Humorous Quotations,* 3rd ed. Oxford: Oxford University Press, 2005 [1995].

Shestov, Lev. *Dostoevsky and Nietzsche: The Philosophy of Tragedy.* Translated by Spencer Roberts. In *Dostoevsky, Tolstoy and Nietzsche,* 141–322. Athens: Ohio University Press, 1969 [1903].

Shipps, Anthony W. *The Quote Sleuth: A Manual for the Tracer of Lost Quotations.* Urbana and Chicago: University of Illinois Press, 1990.

Ṣiddīqī, Muhammad Zubayr. *Ḥadīth Literature: Its Origin, Development and Special Features.* Cambridge: Islamic Texts Society, 1993.

Simmons, Charles. *A Laconic Manual and Brief Remarker, Containing over a Thousand Subjects, Alphabetically and Systematically Arranged.* Toronto: Robert Dick, 1852.

Sinclair, Catherine. *The Kaleidoscope of Aphorisms and Anecdotes.* London: Richard Bentley, 1851.

Singer, Samuel. *Thesaurus proverbiorum medii aevi: Lexikon der Sprichwörter des romanisch-germanischen Mittelalters.* 14 vols. Berlin: Walter de Gruyter, 1995–2002.

Sites, Maud Kay, ed. *Quotations and Inscriptions in the Federal and Public Buildings on Capitol Hill.* Baltimore: Norman T. A. Munder, 1934.

Smiles, Samuel. *The Autobiography of Samuel Smiles, LL.D.* Edited by Thomas Mackay. London: John Murray, 1905.

———. *Character.* Chicago: Belford, Clarke, 1881 [1871].

Smith, Alexander. *Dreamthorp: A Book of Essays Written in the Country.* Edinburgh: W. P. Nimmo, Hay and Mitchell, 1863.

Smollett, Tobias. *The Expedition of Humphrey Clinker.* Vols. 11 and 12 of *The Works of Tobias Smollett.* 12 vols. London: Navarre Society, 1902 [1771].

Smyth, Ethel. *Streaks of Life.* London: Longmans, Green, 1921.

Sontag, Susan. *On Photography.* New York: Farrar, Straus and Giroux, 1978 [1977].

Southgate, Henry. *Many Thoughts of Many Minds: Being a Treasury of Reference: Selections from the Writings of the Most Celebrated Authors from the Earliest to the Present Time.* London: Charles Griffin and Company, 1870 [1858].

————. *What Men Have Said about Women. A Collection of Choice Sentences.* London: George Routledge and Sons, 1866.

Speake, Jennifer. *Oxford Dictionary of Proverbs*, 4th ed. Oxford: Oxford University Press, 2003.

Spectator. 8 vols. London: J. and R. Tonson, 1744.

Spence, Joseph. *Anecdotes, Observations and Characters of Books and Men Collected from the Conversations of Mr. Pope and other Eminent Persons of His Time.* Carbondale: Southern Illinois University Press, 1964 [1820].

Ssu-ma Ch'ien. *The Grand Scribe's Records.* Translated by Weiguo Cao, Scott W. Galer, William H. Nienhauser, Jr., and David W. Pankenier. 8 vols. Bloomington: Indiana University Press, 1994–2008 [1st century BC].

Stanley, Christopher D. *Arguing with Scripture: The Rhetoric of Quotations in the Letters of Paul.* New York: T&T Clark International, 2004.

Starrett, Vincent. *Books Alive.* New York: Random House, 1940.

Sternbach, Leo, ed. *Gnomologium Vaticanum e Codice Vaticano Graeco 743.* Berlin: Walter de Gruyter, 1963 [1887–89].

Stevens, Wallace. *Opus Posthumous.* New York: Alfred A. Knopf, 1957.

Stevenson, Burton. *The Home Book of Quotations, Classical and Modern*, 10th ed. New York: Dodd, Mead, 1967 [1934].

Stibbs, Ann. *Like a Fish Needs a Bicycle: Over 3,000 Quotations by and about Women.* London: Bloomsbury Publishing, 1992.

————. *A Woman's Place: Quotations about Women.* New York: William Morrow, 1993.

Stobaeus, Johannes. *Florilegium.* Edited by Augustus Meineke. 4 vols. Leipzig: B. G. Teubner, 1855.

————. *Florilegium.* Edited by Thomas Gaisford. 4 vols. Leipzig: Bibliopolio Kuehniano, 1823.

Stoddard, William O. *The Table Talk of Abraham Lincoln.* New York: Frederick A. Stokes, 1894.

Sturm, Harlan. *The Libro de los buenos proverbios: A Critical Edition.* Lexington: University Press of Kentucky, 1970.

Suetonius, Gaius. *Lives of the Caesars.* Translated by J. C. Rolfe. 2 vols. Cambridge MA: Harvard University Press [ca. AD 120].

Sun Tzu. *The Art of War.* Translated by Samuel B. Griffith. London: Oxford University Press, 1963 [4th century BC].

Swift, Jonathan. *Prose Works.* Edited by Herbert Davis. 14 vols. Oxford: Basil Blackwell, 1957–68.

Tacitus. *Agricola, Germanicus, Dialogus.* Translated by M. Hutton and W. Peterson. Revised by R. M. Ovilgie, E. H. Warmington, and M. Winterbottom. Cambridge MA: Harvard University Press, 1985.

———. *Annals.* Translated by John Jackson. 2 vols. Cambridge MA: Harvard University Press, 1969 [AD 116].

Talleyrand, Charles-Maurice de [prince de Bénévent]. *Memoirs.* Edited by the duc de Broglie. Translated by Mrs. Agnus Hall. 5 vols. New York: G. P. Putnam's Sons, 1892.

Tan, Amy. *The Opposite of Fate.* New York: G. P. Putnam's Sons, 2003.

Tarski, Alfred. *Logic, Semantics, Metamathematics: Papers from 1923 to 1938.* Translated by J. H. Woodger. Oxford: Oxford University Press, 1956.

Taylor, Archer. *The Proverb.* Hatboro PA: Folklore Associates, 1962 [1931].

Taylor, John. *The Pocket Lacon, comprising nearly One Thousand Extracts from the Best Authors.* London: John Thomas Cox, 1837.

Taylor, Theodore. *The Golden Treasury of Thought: A Gathering of Quotations from the Best Ancient and Modern Authors.* London: Chatto and Windus, 1874.

Tegg, William. *Laconics; or, Good Words of the Best Authors.* London: William Tegg, 1876 [1875].

Tertullian. *Against the Valentinians.* Translated by Dr. Roberts. In *The Anti-Nicene Fathers,* 3:503–20. New York: Christian Literature Company, 1890 [early 3rd century AD].

———. *De carne Christi.* Edited and translated by Ernest Evans. London: Society for Promoting Christian Knowledge, 1956 [early 3rd century AD].

A Texan. *The Yankee Slave-Dealer; or, An Abolitionist Down South.* Nashville: Published for the author, 1860.

Thierfelder, Andreas, ed. *Philogelos der Lachfreund.* Munich: Heimeran Verlag, 1968.

Thucydides. *The Landmark Thucydides.* Translated by Richard Crawley. Edited by Robert B. Strassler. New York: Free Press, 1996 [ca. 431–400 BC].

Thuesen, Peter J. *In Discordance with the Scriptures: American Protestant Battles over Translating the Bible.* New York: Oxford University Press, 1999.

Tibbles, Thomas Henry. *Buckskin and Blanket Days: Memoirs of a Friend of the Indians.* Lincoln: University of Nebraska Press, 1969 [1957; written in 1905].

———. *The Ponca Chiefs: An Account of the Trial of Standing Bear.* Edited by Kay Graber. Lincoln: University of Nebraska Press, 1972 [1880].

Tiedemann, Rolf. "Dialectics at a Standstill: Approaches to the *Passagen-Werk.*" In *On Walter Benjamin: Critical Essays and Recollections.* Edited by Gary Smith, 260–91. Cambridge MA: MIT Press, 1988.

Timbs, John. *English Eccentrics and Eccentricities.* London: Chatto and Windus, 1877.

———. *Laconics: Or the Best Words of the Best Authors.* 3 vols. Philadelphia: Carey, 1829 [1827].

Todd, Janet. *Mary Wollstonecraft: A Revolutionary Life.* New York: Columbia University Press, 2000.

Tolstoy, Leo. *Anna Karenina.* Translated by Louise and Alymer Maude. New York: W. W. Norton, 1970 [1875–77].

Tomkins, John, and John Field. *Piety Promoted, Being a Collection of the Dying Sayings of Many of the People called Quakers.* Dublin: Samuel Fairbrother, 1721.

Treffry, Elford. *Stokes's Encyclopedia of Familiar Quotations.* New York: Frederick A. Stokes, 1900.

Tsohatzidis, Savas L. "The Hybrid Theory of Mixed Quotation." *Mind,* July 1998, 661–64.

Tsouras, Peter G. *The Greenhill Dictionary of Military Quotations.* Mechanicsburg PA: Stackpole Books, 2000.

Tyson, Bryan. *The Institution of Slavery in the Southern States, Religiously and Morally Considered.* Washington DC: H. Polkinhorn, 1863.

Unamuno, Miguel de. *Del sentimiento trágico de la vida.* Madrid: Alianza Editorial, 1986 [1912]. Translated by Anthony Kerrigan as *The Tragic Sense of Life in Men and Nations.* Princeton: Princeton University Press, 1972.

Upanishads. Translated and edited by Swami Nikhilananda. New York: Harper and Row, 1964.

Usher, M. D. *Homeric Stitchings: The Homeric Centos of the Empress Eudocia.* New York: Rowman and Littlefield, 1998.

———. "Prolegomenon to the Homeric Centos." *American Journal of Philology* 118, no. 2 (1997): 305–21.

Valerius Maximus. *Memorable Doings and Sayings.* Translated by D. R. Shackleton Bailet. 2 vols. Cambridge MA: Harvard University Press, 2000 [ca. AD 30].

Valéry, Paul. *Masters and Friends.* Translated by M. Turnell. Princeton: Princeton University Press, 1968.

———. *Oeuvres.* Edited by Jean Hytier. 2 vols. Paris: Gallimard, 1957–60.

Vicinus, Martha. *Intimate Friends: Women Who Loved Women, 1778–1928.* Chicago: University of Chicago Press, 2004.

Villey, Pierre. *Sources & l'évolution des essais de Montaigne.* 2 vols. Paris: Hachette, 1908.

Virgil. *Virgil.* Translated by H. Rushton Gairclough. Revised by G. P. Goold. 2 vols. Cambridge MA: Harvard University Press, 1999 [1st century BC].

Voltaire. *Romans et contes.* Edited by René Groos. Paris: Gallimard, 1954.

Wallis, Charles L. *The Treasure Chest: A Heritage Album Containing 1064 Familiar and Inspirational Quotations, Poems, Sentiments, and Prayers from Great Minds of 2500 Years.* New York: Harper and Row, 1965.

Walpole, Horace. *Walpoliana.* Compiled by John Pinkerton, 2nd ed. 2 vols. London: R. Phillips, 1804 [1799].

Walsh, William S. *The International Encyclopedia of Prose and Poetical Quotations from the Literature of the World,* new ed. Chicago: John C. Winston, 1931 [1908].

Walton, Isaak. *Life of Mr. George Herbert.* In *Lives,* 251–321. London: Oxford University Press, 1927 [1670].

Ward, Anna L. *A Dictionary of Poetical Quotations.* New York: Thomas Y. Crowell, 1883.

———. *A Dictionary of Quotations in Prose from American and Foreign Authors, Including Translations from Ancient Sources.* New York: Thomas Y. Crowell, 1889.

Ward, Mrs. Humphrey. *Robert Elsmere.* Lincoln: University of Nebraska Press, 1967 [1888].

Washington, Corey. "The Identity Theory of Quotation." *Journal of Philosophy,* November 1992, 582–605.

Watson, John T. *Poetical Quotations; or, Elegant Extracts on Every Subject.* Philadelphia: Lindsay and Blakiston, 1865 [1847].

Webster's Dictionary of Quotations: A Book of Ready Reference, for All Familiar Words and Phrases in the English Language. London: Ward, Lock and Tyler, ca. 1880.

Webster's New World Dictionary of Quotations. Hoboken NJ: Wiley, 2005.

Welles, Gideon. *Diary of Gideon Welles.* 3 vols. Boston: Houghton Mifflin, 1911.

Wells, H. G. *The Outline of History.* London: Waverly Book, 1920.

Werner, Jakob. *Lateinische Sprichwörter und Sinnsprüche des Mittelalters aus Handschriften gesammelt,* 2nd rev. ed. by Peter Fleury. Heidelberg: Carl Winter, 1966 [1912].

White, Harold Ogden. *Plagiarism and Imitation during the English Renaissance: A Study in Critical Distinctions.* Cambridge MA: Harvard University Press, 1935.

Wilde, Oscar. *The Picture of Dorian Gray.* New York: Modern Library, 1926 [1891].

Williams, Henry Llewellyn, ed. *Lincolnics: Familiar Sayings of Abraham Lincoln.* New York: G. P. Putnam's Sons, 1906.

Williams, Valentine. *World of Action.* Boston: Houghton Mifflin, 1938.

Wilson, Woodrow. *George Washington.* New York: Frederick Ungar, 1963 [1896].

Wimsatt, W. K., Jr., and Margaret H. Wimsatt. "Self-Quotations and Anonymous Quotations in Johnson's Dictionary." *English Literary History* 15, no. 1 (1948): 60–68.

Wittgenstein, Ludwig. *Philosophical Remarks.* Edited by Rush Rhees. Translated by Raymond Hargreaves and Roger White. Oxford: Basil Blackwell, 1975.

Woetzel, Robert K. *The Nuremberg Trials in International Law with a Postlude on the Eichmann Case.* New York: Frederick A. Praeger, 1962.

Wollstonecraft, Mary. *A Vindication of the Rights of Woman.* Edited by Carol H. Poston. New York: W. W. Norton, 1975 [1792].

Wood, Rev. James. *Dictionary of Quotations from Ancient and Modern, English and Foreign Sources.* London: Frederick Warne, 1893.

Woolcott, Alexander. *While Rome Burns.* New York: Grosset and Dunlap, 1934.

Wooléver, Adam. *Encyclopedia of Quotations: A Treasury of Wisdom, Wit and Humor, Odd Comparisons and Proverbs*, 6th ed. Philadelphia: David McKay, 1893 [1876].

Woolf, Virginia. *A Room of One's Own*. Annotated by Susan Gubar. Orlando FL: Harcourt, 2005 [1929].

Wordsworth, William. *Poetical Works*. Edited by Thomas Hutchinson. Revised by Ernest de Selincourt. Oxford: Oxford University Press, 1965.

Xenophon. *Memorabilia, Oeconomicus, Symposium, Apology*. Translated by F. C. Marchant and O. J. Todd. Cambridge MA: Harvard University Press, 1923 [4th century BC].

———. *Symposium*. In *Xenophon*. Translated by O. J. Todd, 4:527–635. Cambridge MA: Harvard University Library, 1923 [early 4th century BC].

Yaeger, Patricia. "Editor's Column: The Polyphony Issue." *PMLA* 122, no. 2 (2007): 433–48.

Yeames, H. H. "On Teaching Virgil." *School Review* 20, no. 1 (1912): 1–26.

Yessne, Peter, ed. *Quotations from Mayor Daley*. New York: G. P. Putnam's Sons, 1969.

Young, Edward. *The Poetical Works of Edward Young*. London: Gall and Inglis, 1870.

Zahn, Theodor. *Tatian's Diatessaron*. Forschungen zur Geschichte des neutestamentlichen Kanons und altkirchen Literatur, vol. 1. Erlangen: Andreas Deichert, 1881.

Zahniser, Jill Diane. *And Then She Said: Quotations by Women for Every Occasion*. St. Paul: Caillech Press, 1990.

Zaleski, Carol. *Otherworld Journeys: Accounts of Near-Death Experience in Medieval and Modern Times*. New York: Oxford University Press, 1987.

INDEX

In the Stages Series

To order or obtain more information
on these or other University of
Nebraska Press titles, visit
www.nebraskapress.unl.edu.